THE
LEGAL ASPECTS
OF
BUSINESS
TRANSACTIONS

A COMPLETE GUIDE TO THE LAW GOVERNING

BUSINESS ORGANIZATION, FINANCING, TRANSACTIONS, AND GOVERNANCE

THE
LEGAL ASPECTS
OF
BUSINESS
TRANSACTIONS

A COMPLETE GUIDE TO THE LAW GOVERNING
BUSINESS ORGANIZATION, FINANCING, TRANSACTIONS, AND GOVERNANCE

2019 EDITION

THOMAS WILLIAM BAKER, M.B.A, J.D.

Legal Aspects of Business Transactions:
A Complete Guide to the Law Governing Business Organization,
Financing, Transactions, and Governance
2019 Edition

For information about this title or to order other books and/or electronic media, contact the publisher:

Thomas William Baker, Esq.
Coronat Services, LLC
(404) 276-1337 (Telephone)
www.coronatservices.com
tom.baker@coronatservices.com

ISBNs:
978-1-7326694-2-0 (print)
978-1-7326694-3-7 (eBook)

Printed in the United States of America

Cover and Interior design: 1106 Design

TABLE OF CONTENTS

INTRODUCTION: UNDERSTANDING APPLICATION OF THE LAW TO
BUSINESS TRANSACTIONS 1

    I. What is the Law? 1

CHAPTER 1: UNDERSTANDING FUNDAMENTAL CONTRACT LAW: CONTRACTS 101 . . 5

    I. Understanding Contractual Relationships 1–5

    II. What Law is Applied to Contractual Arrangements? 1–5

    III. What is a Contract? 1–7

    IV. Mutual Assent 1–7

    V. What Kinds of Consideration or Substitutes for Consideration Make
        a Promise Enforceable? 1–9

    VI. What Kinds of Contracts are Enforceable? 1–10

    VII. What Contracts Must be in Writing to be Enforceable? 1–10

    VIII. What Kinds of Contracts are Unenforceable? 1–10

    IX. What if There is a Mistake? 1–12

    X. Once Created, How is a Contract Interpreted? 1–13

    XI. What Terms and Conditions are Typically Found in Contracts? 1–14

    XII. What Remedies are Available for a Breach of Contract? 1–22

    XIII. What Defenses are Typically Raised in Breach of Contract Cases? 1–23

    XIV. Contract Drafting 1–24

    XV. Contract Negotiation 1–25

CHAPTER 2: EMPLOYMENT AND INDEPENDENT CONTRACTOR AGREEMENTS . . **27**

    I. What are the Essential Elements of an Employment Relationship? **2–27**

    II. What are the Essential Elements of Any Employment Agreement? **2–28**

    III. What are the Key Negotiation Points for an Executive
Employment Agreement? **2–32**

    IV. What is an Independent Contractor Agreement? **2–38**

CHAPTER 3: FUNDAMENTALS OF BUSINESS ORGANIZATIONS **41**

    I. Evolution of Business Organizations **3–41**

    II. Sole Proprietorship **3–41**

    III. General Partnerships **3–42**

    IV. Corporations **3–44**

    V. Limited Liability Companies **3–49**

    VI. Limited Partnerships **3–52**

    VII. Limited Liability Partnerships **3–53**

    VIII. How are Business Organizations Used in Asset Protection Strategies? . . . **3–54**

CHAPTER 4: FUNDAMENTALS OF EQUITY FINANCING **55**

    I. How are Business Ventures Capitalized? **4–55**

    II. What are the Typical Equity Capital Sources? **4–57**

    III. What are the Fundamentals of Equity Capital Investment? **4–58**

    IV. What Rules Govern Private Placement of Securities? **4–61**

    V. How are Private Equity Fund and Venture Capital Transactions Negotiated? . . **4–68**

CHAPTER 5 FUNDAMENTALS OF DEBT FINANCING **73**

    I. What Laws Govern Debt Financing Transactions? **5–73**

    II. What are the Types of Debt Transactions? **5–73**

III.   What are the Fundamental Terms of Loan Agreements? 5-76

IV.   What is a Promissory Note? 5-78

V.   What is a "Secured Transaction" and What is the Importance of a Security Agreement? 5-80

VI.   What is a Guaranty Agreement? 5-84

VII.   What Other Forms of Security May be Required by a Lender? 5-85

VIII.   Lender Remedies When a Loan is in Default. 5-85

IX.   Overview of Bankruptcy Law 5-86

CHAPTER 6: FUNDAMENTALS OF MERGERS AND ACQUISITIONS 89

I.   Baker's Rules of Business Transactions 6-89

II.   What are the Typical Acquisition Forms? 6-89

III.   How Does the Acquisition Process Usually Flow? 6-94

IV.   What are the Typical Terms and Conditions of Definitive Acquisition Agreements? 6-97

V.   What Happens After the Definitive Agreement is Executed? 6-102

VI.   How is a Business Valued for Mergers and Acquisitions? 6-103

VII.   What Other Structuring Issues Must be Considered? 6-104

CHAPTER 7: UNDERSTANDING FUNDAMENTAL ANTITRUST LAW 107

I.   What is "Antitrust Law"? 7-107

II   What are the Essential Concepts for Understanding and Applying Antitrust Law? 7-109

III.   What are the Essential Characteristics of the Sherman Act? 7-111

IV.   What are the Essential Characteristics of the Clayton Act? 7-117

V.   What are the Essential Characteristics of the Federal Trade Commission Act? 7-118

VI.   What Conduct is Exempt from Application of the Federal Antitrust Laws? 7-119

VII. What are the Penalties for Violating Antitrust Law? 7-120

VIII. How can You Mitigate Antitrust Risk? 7-121

CHAPTER 8: UNDERSTANDING FUNDAMENTAL INTELLECTUAL PROPERTY LAW . . . 127

I. What is "Intellectual Property"? 8-127

II. What are the Fundamentals of Trade Secret Law? 8-129

III. What are the Fundamentals of Patent Law? 8-131

IV. What are the Fundamentals of Copyright Law? 8-136

V. What are the Fundamentals of Trademark Law? 8-141

CHAPTER 9: CORPORATE GOVERNANCE AND FIDUCIARY DUTY 151

I. Fundamentals of Corporate Governance 9-151

II. Duties of Officers and Directors to Shareholders 9-152

III. Directors' and Officers' Fiduciary Duties to Creditors 9-156

IV. Does a Shareholder Ever Have Fiduciary Duty to the Corporation? . . . 9-158

V. Fiduciary Duties in Partnerships and Joint Ventures 9-158

VI. Individual Responsibility for Corporate or Organizational Acts 9-159

VII. Federal Sentencing Guidelines: The Birthplace of Corporate Compliance . . . 9-165

VIII. Characteristics of Corporate Compliance Plans 9-166

IX. Starting the Compliance Process: The Regulatory Assessment 9-167

X. Required Elements of a Corporate Compliance Plan 9-167

XI. Implementation of a Corporate Compliance Program 9-169

XII. Federal Agency Compliance Plan Implementation Guidance 9-170

XIII. The Role of Business Ethics in Regulatory Compliance 9-183

About the Author 187

INTRODUCTION

UNDERSTANDING APPLICATION OF THE LAW
TO BUSINESS TRANSACTIONS

I. WHAT IS THE LAW?

A. **United States Constitution.** The United States Constitution defines federal and state powers and generally incorporates English common law as the law of the land. Everything not defined in the Constitution as a federal power is left to the states. The Constitution also divides power among the legislative, judicial, and executive branches of government. In addition, the "Commerce Clause" in the Constitution permits the Congress of the United States to pass laws that regulate commerce between the states, and federal courts have broadly construed and interpreted what constitutes "interstate commerce" for purposes of federal legislation.

B. **Federal Statutes and Regulations.** The United States Congress passes federal laws, which apply equally to all of the United States.

  1. **Federal Regulations.** Federal laws are implemented by federal regulations. Regulations are substantially more detailed than the statutes they implement.

  2. **Administrative Procedures Act.** Federal regulations are implemented in accordance with the Administrative Procedures Act, which generally requires publication of proposed regulations in the Federal Register and opportunity for public comment. Once federal regulations pass through the notice and comment period, they are published in the Federal Register as "final rules" and have the full force and effect of law. Sometimes, however, federal laws are passed but never become effective because federal regulations in accordance with the Administrative Procedures Act are never implemented.

C. **Federal Courts.** The federal courts have jurisdiction over all cases regarding the United States Constitution and federal laws. The Supreme Court of the United States is the final arbiter for issues arising under the United States Constitution. The federal courts can also have jurisdiction over claims between citizens of different states (called "diversity of citizenship"), and, in "diversity" cases, the federal courts are required to make their rulings in accordance with the governing state law.

D. **Federal Manuals.** Federal agencies such as the Department of Defense and the Department of Health and Human Services, through its agency, the Centers for Medicare and Medicaid Services ("CMS"), have the power to publish manuals that interpret the federal regulations. Although the manuals do not have the force and effect of law, they are given "great deference" by the courts, and their provisions are sometimes treated like laws and regulations for other purposes (such as application of the federal False Claims Act).

E. **The Common Law.** The "common law" generally governs relationships between private parties (property, torts, and contracts). Each state's law is generally based on common law principles. There is some federal common law, but its application is very limited.

F. **State Statutes and Regulations.** The states similarly pass laws and implement state laws through state rules and regulations, some of which either codify or modify common law principles. Most business regulation is accomplished through state laws. When the states have a common interest in uniform laws, each state can separately enact a law that is virtually identical in all states. Examples of uniform laws include the Uniform Commercial Code and the Uniform Trade Secrets Act.

G. **State Courts.** The state courts interpret the common law and state legislation. For example, most contract disputes claims are resolved by state courts.

H. **Federal Law Preemption of State Law.** Some federal laws completely "preempt" or supersede state laws, but some bodies of federal law address the same areas as state laws. For example, prior to 1976, there were two bodies of copyright law: federal and state. However, under the power of the United States Constitution "commerce clause," the United States Congress passed the Copyright Act of 1976, which preempts all state law. Consequently, copyright law is now uniformly applied in all of the United States. Similarly, federal patent law preempts state law. By contrast, there continue to be two bodies of trademark law: the United States trademark law does not preempt state trademark laws. Examples of other bodies of law covered in this textbook that affect business transactions and are enforced under both federal and state law are securities law involving issuance of investment instruments and antitrust law.

I. **How Has the Law Evolved?** In modern times, a substantial portion of the law involves the relationship of citizens with government and its agencies, not other citizens. Virtually every business enterprise is required to comply with some body of federal law that imposes potential civil or criminal sanctions, and sometimes both. Notable examples include federal securities law, government contracts law, tax law, participation in the Medicare and Medicaid programs, and environmental law. There are also less obvious bodies of law, such as intentional violation of copyright law and Racketeer Influenced Corrupt Organization ("RICO") claims arising from conducting a "criminal enterprise." Also, tax exempt organizations are potentially exposed to allegations of violation of Internal Revenue Code provisions governing charitable organizations.

CHAPTER 1

UNDERSTANDING FUNDAMENTAL CONTRACT LAW: CONTRACTS 101

I. UNDERSTANDING CONTRACTUAL RELATIONSHIPS

A. **Life Is a Series of Contractual Arrangements.** Understanding contract law is important because life is a series of contractual arrangements. Contractual terms and conditions are omnipresent and permeate every aspect of our existence. For example, businesses depend on agreements to borrow funds from banks and other lenders; employment and independent contractor agreements to obtain human resources as well as retirement and benefit plans for their personnel; contracts with sources that supply goods and services that are essential for business operations; licensing of intellectual property such as software and copyrightable works; contracts that govern mergers and acquisitions; and many other contractual arrangements. Individuals also have many contractual relationships, such as agreements to purchase a new car, to obtain a credit card, and to obtain a home mortgage. Therefore, although every person can benefit from an understanding of the general law of contracts, it is absolutely essential for business managers and entrepreneurs.

B. **Contracts Create Rights and Obligations.** In essence, contracts create rights, which may or may not be assignable, and obligations or duties, which may or may not be delegable.

II. WHAT LAW IS APPLIED TO CONTRACTUAL ARRANGEMENTS?

A. **Federal Contract Law.** The Congress of the United States has enacted legislation, and the executive branch has adopted implementing regulations, for defense contracts, government contracts, and other contractual arrangements that involve the federal government, such as contracts involving health care providers that participate in the Medicare program. These bodies of law are very specific and beyond the scope of a discussion of general contract law. However, Congress has also enacted other legislation that has more universal application, such as the Magnuson-Moss Warranty Act, which is discussed in more detail below.

B. **State Statutes and Regulations.** Most aspects of contractual relationships are governed by state law.

1. **General Law of Contracts.** In all states, the common law principles of contract law are "codified" into laws enacted by the state legislature. The general law of contracts applies to all contractual arrangements except for specific kinds of contracts that are governed by the Uniform Commercial Code ("UCC").

2. **Uniform Commercial Code ("UCC").** Because state law governs most contractual arrangements, and because the states want to facilitate interstate commerce, a model act called the "Uniform Commercial Code" (referred to as the "UCC") was developed. Article 2 of the UCC, which will be discussed in detail in this chapter, governs the purchase and sale of goods. "Goods" means all things (including specially manufactured goods) that are movable at the time of identification. Each state, except Louisiana, whose state law is not based on the English common law, has enacted a version of the UCC. Louisiana has enacted all parts of the UCC except Article 2, so contracts for the purchase and sale of goods in Louisiana are governed by Louisiana civil laws. In general, UCC Article 2 does not cover contracts for the purchase and sale of services, intangible property rights (such as copyrights, patents, and trademarks), or real property. The UCC also sets forth the primary law regarding negotiable instruments (such as promissory notes) and security interests (which, for example, lenders use to secure payment on money loaned to a person or business), which are described in other chapters.

3. **Two Bodies of Contract Law Exist in Each State.** Therefore, in each state there are two separate and mutually exclusive bodies of contract law: (1) the UCC, which governs the purchase and sale of goods (in each state except Louisiana), the creation and conveyance of negotiable instruments (in all states), and the enforcement of security interests (in all states); and (2) the general law of contracts, which is a code that is usually founded on the principles of the English common law of contracts and governs all other contractual relationships. When the UCC sets forth specific provisions for contracts, the UCC applies. When it does not, the common law of contracts applies. In other words, when the UCC applies, it supersedes the common law of contracts. There is never a situation in which both bodies of law apply: it is either one or the other. Therefore, in any contract analysis, you first must ask: does the UCC apply?

C. **State Courts.** The state courts interpret the general law of contracts and state legislation such as the UCC. Since contracts and contract disputes generally arise under state law, most contract disputes are resolved by state courts, and federal courts are required to apply applicable state law when the federal court has jurisdiction in a diversity of citizenship case.

D. **Contracts Create Private Law.** Within the context of state and applicable federal law, contracts, in essence, create a private "law" that governs a specific transaction or arrangement. The key question to ask when a contract dispute arises is: What was the intent of the parties? Consequently, if a contract dispute arises, the first place to look is within the four corners of the agreement (if it is in writing) or other evidence of the intent of the parties.

III. WHAT IS A CONTRACT?

A. **Enforceable Promise and Risk Allocation Mechanism.** People make promises every day. A contract is an enforceable promise. In other words, one party to a contract can, by getting an order from a court, force the other party to do what they promised. Contracts are also risk allocation mechanisms. There are risks inherent in every contractual arrangement. For example, if a business purchases a piece of equipment, there is a risk that it will malfunction. To mitigate that risk, the purchaser will negotiate a warranty. Therefore, every contract involves a series of "if this happens, then what are the consequences?" questions and answers. However, no matter how experienced the parties are, they may never be able to identify all of the possible risks, and, at the heart of each contractual arrangement, each party must trust the other party.

B. **What Are the Elements of an Enforceable Promise?** In, general, there are three fundamental elements to each contractual arrangement.

    1. **Offer.** Each contract requires an offer, which is an expression of willingness to enter into a bargain.

    2. **Acceptance.** To form a contract, there must be acceptance of an offer. Acceptance is a manifestation of assent to the terms and conditions of the offer. Therefore, an enforceable contract requires mutual assent to an ascertainable set of terms and conditions.

    3. **Consideration.** "Consideration" generally means something of value given in exchange for a promise. Many offers are made, and many are accepted, but, for contracts in the normal course of business, "consideration" distinguishes enforceable promises from unenforceable promises.

IV. MUTUAL ASSENT

A. **Two Components of Mutual Assent.** The two components of mutual assent are offer and acceptance. The "reasonable person" common law standard is applied: would a reasonable and prudent person believe that an offer was made or accepted? The common law term for mutual assent is the "meeting of the minds."

B.   **Offer.** An offer occurs when one person confers upon another the power to create contractual relations between them. The offeror creates power of acceptance in the offeree.

   1.   **Offeror Controls the Offer.** The offeror is the master of offer and can decide what conditions apply.

   2.   **How Is the Offer Nullified?** The offer will be null, void, and of no further effect upon occurrence of any of the following:

      a.   revocation by the offeror at any time prior to acceptance;

      b.   an unreasonable lapse of time for acceptance;

      c.   the death or incapacity of either party;

      d.   rejection by the offeree; or

      e.   a counteroffer by the offeree. Since most negotiations involve a series of counteroffers, this is the most common way in which an offer is nullified.

   3.   **What If the Offer is Ambiguous?** Any ambiguity should be construed against the offeror.

C.   **Acceptance.** Acceptance is a manifestation of assent in a manner invited or required by the offer. Once appropriately accepted, an enforceable contract is formed and both parties are bound. Therefore, each offer and counteroffer must be carefully weighed to determine whether there is sufficient mutual gain to make the arrangement acceptable to both parties. Acceptance can be manifested in any manner reasonable under the circumstances.

   1.   **How Is the Power of Acceptance Terminated?** The power of acceptance may be terminated upon occurrence of any of the following:

      a.   rejection or counteroffer by the offeree;

      b.   an unreasonable lapse of time;

      c.   revocation by the offeror;

    d.   death or incapacity of either party; or

    e.   non-occurrence of a condition of acceptance under the terms of the offer.

2.   **Who Can Accept an Offer?** Only the person who is invited by the offeror to accept may accept an offer.

3.   **What Happens If an "Acceptance" Includes Additional Terms?** If an acceptance adds additional terms that the offeror must accept, then it is not an acceptance, but a counteroffer. This was known in common law as the "mirror image rule."

V. WHAT KINDS OF CONSIDERATION OR SUBSTITUTES FOR CONSIDERATION MAKE A PROMISE ENFORCEABLE?

A.   **What Is "Consideration"?** Consideration is a bargained for exchange that has elements of mutual inducement. In general, each party to the contract must promise to provide something of value to the other party.

    1.   **What Happens If the Consideration is Nominal?** If the consideration is nominal, the courts may find that no consideration was exchanged and the contract is unenforceable. Under the English common law, some parties tried to make agreements enforceable by stating that the consideration for the contractual agreement was an "acorn." However, this would likely be deemed inadequate consideration for an enforceable contractual obligation.

    2.   **Are Promises to Make Gifts or Charitable Contributions Enforceable?** Generally, oral promises to make gifts or charitable contributions are "gratuitous promises" that lack the essential element of a bargained for exchange and are not enforceable. However, if the pledge is in writing, and the charitable organization proceeds in detrimental reliance on the pledge, the promise may be enforceable.

B.   **When Can a Contract Be Enforceable Without Consideration?**

    1.   **Quasi-Contract or Unjust Enrichment.** Sometimes, a promise plus subsequent benefit can be enforceable. If a party provides a benefit that the other party accepts knowing that the supplying party expects payment, the agreement could be enforceable to prevent "unjust enrichment."

    2.   **Option Contracts.** A contract providing a party with an option that can be exercised in the future does not require consideration.

3. **Guaranties.** The guaranty of another party's debts or obligations does not require consideration to the guarantor. However, if the underlying contract is unenforceable, there is nothing to guaranty.

VI. WHAT KINDS OF CONTRACTS ARE ENFORCEABLE?

A. **Freedom of Contract.** There is a long line of cases in virtually every jurisdiction that provides that persons who are able to enter into contracts are free to enter into any agreement that is not illegal or otherwise void as against public policy, even if the contract terms seem unfair or onerous.

B. **Folly Is Not Fraud.** Some parties to seemingly unfair or onerous contracts have asserted that the unfairness constitutes "fraud." However, most courts will hold that "folly is not fraud." In other words, even if one could question the complete lack of judgment of one party to a contract, that party's "folly" is not "fraud."

VII. WHAT CONTRACTS MUST BE IN WRITING TO BE ENFORCEABLE?

A. **Are Oral Contracts Enforceable?** Unless the law requires otherwise, oral contracts are enforceable. However, it is more difficult to prove the terms and conditions of an oral contract. In the business context, there is a presumption that the parties intend their oral agreements to be enforceable.

B. **What Contracts Must Be in Writing?** The Statute of Frauds, which traces its roots to a law enacted in England in 1677 and is part of the statutory or common law of virtually all jurisdictions, requires certain contracts to be in writing to be enforceable. Examples include the following:

1. **Real Property.** Contracts for the purchase or sale of real estate.

2. **The "One Year" Rule.** Contracts that cannot be performed within one year.

3. **Surety.** Any contract under which a party agrees to be responsible for the debts or obligations of another party, such as a guaranty of a loan.

4. **UCC Statute of Frauds.** The UCC has its own Statute of Frauds, which, in most jurisdictions, provides that all contracts for the purchase of goods in excess of $500 must be in writing.

VIII. WHAT KINDS OF CONTRACTS ARE UNENFORCEABLE?

A. **Doctrine of Unconscionability.** The doctrine of unconscionability applies when an agreement is unfair on its face. Determination of whether a contract is "unconscionable" is independent of the consideration doctrine.

1. **Substantive Unconscionability.** Substantive unconscionability could apply when there is a disparity in value. Is there a significant difference between the cost of the good or service in the community and the cost in the contract?

2. **Procedural Unconscionability.** Procedural unconscionability arises from an unfair advantage in or abuse of the bargaining process. This is sometimes called "adhesion contracts," meaning that, because of the substantial bargaining power of one party, the other party has no choice but to sign the contract.

3. **Reconciliation with Other Doctrines.** Note that the doctrine of "unconscionability" seems to directly contradict the doctrine of "freedom of contract" and its related maxim in equity that "folly is not fraud." This leads to an important learning point: in contract disputes, there is almost always "another side to the story."

B. **Pre-Existing Duty Rule.** Under the common law, the performance of, or the promise to perform, a pre-existing duty is not consideration. In other words, if there is a pre-existing duty, there can be no "inducement" to enter into a promise.

C. **Illegal Contracts.** Contracts that are contrary to law are illegal and unenforceable. Examples are as follows:

1. **Contract to Perform an Illegal Act.** A contract to perform an illegal act cannot be enforced, even if the act is performed.

2. **Contracts in General Restraint of Trade.** Contracts that generally restrain trade, such as contracts to create a monopoly, are illegal and unenforceable. However, as explained below, contracts in partial restraint of trade may be enforceable if the restraint is "reasonable."

D. **Capacity.** A contract with a person who does not have "capacity" to understand what they are doing is unenforceable. For example, contracts with minors or persons with diminished mental capacity (called "*non compos mentis*") are unenforceable. Contracts entered into during a spell of temporary incapacity, such as intoxication, may be enforceable.

E. **Authority.** To enforce the contractual obligations of an entity such as a corporation, the person who executes the agreement must have the "authority" to enter into the agreement on behalf of the entity. "Actual authority" is authority that is expressly conferred on a person to act on behalf of an entity. "Apparent authority" arises when a person "apparently" has authority to bind an entity to a contractual obligation, even though the person may not have "actual authority." Some persons who have managerial titles such as "President" or "Chief Executive Officer" have apparent authority to bind a corporation to a contractual arrangement, even if the corporation's bylaws prohibit it. For example, the President of a corporation may enter into an agreement to acquire capital equipment for a purchase price of $250,000 without approval of the Board of Directors, but the corporation's bylaws may provide that any capital expenditure in excess of $100,000 requires approval of the Board of Directors. The corporation cannot avoid the contractual obligation on the grounds that the President did not have "actual authority" because the equipment supplier reasonably and detrimentally relied on the President's apparent authority to bind the corporation to the contract.

F.   **Agreements to Agree.** Any agreement, even if signed by the parties, that states that it is subject to a more definitive agreement or is otherwise conditioned on a future agreement is generally unenforceable. A common commercial example of an "agreement to agree" is a "Letter of Intent" executed in connection with a proposed merger or acquisition as described in Chapter 7. While the Letter of Intent typically describes the expected financial terms and conditions of the transaction, it also typically states that enforceability of the arrangement is contingent upon execution of a "definitive agreement" for the transaction. This is a clear example of an "agreement to agree," so the terms and conditions of the transaction described in the Letter of Intent are enforceable.

G.   **Conditions Precedent and Conditions Subsequent.** Some contracts require the fulfillment of some condition prior to commencement of a contractual obligation (a "condition precedent"). Also, the occurrence of some condition after a contract is executed but before it is completely performed (a "condition subsequent") may frustrate the purpose of the agreement and render it unenforceable. For example, an employment agreement between a medical practice and a physician may provide that commencement of the agreement is conditioned on the physician obtaining a license in the state where the medical practice is located. This is a "condition precedent." Using the same example, the physician may obtain the license, but the medical practice may be acquired before the employment agreement commences. Since the medical practice no longer exists, the contract is "frustrated" and cannot be enforced. This is a "condition subsequent."

IX. WHAT IF THERE IS A MISTAKE?

A.   **What If the Mistake is Mutual?** There is no mutual assent if both parties know that they have attached different meanings to their promises, and the contract can be voided.

B.   **What Is a "Mutual Mistake"?** The essential elements of a "mutual mistake" are as follows:

   1.   **Basic Assumption**. The mistake must relate to a basic assumption on which the contract was made.

   2.   **Material Effect.** The mistake must have a material effect on the agreed upon exchange.

3. **Risk.** The adversely affected party must not have imposed the risk.

C. **What Is Not a Mutual Mistake?** Assumptions of future events that do not take place are not mutual mistakes. For example, a change in market conditions that makes a contract disadvantageous does not constitute a mutual mistake.

D. **What If the Mistake is Unilateral?** When only one party is mistaken, it is more difficult to avoid the contract. The aggrieved party must also show that the other party had reason to know about the mistake, that the other party somehow caused the mistake, or that forcing the mistaken party to proceed with the contract would be "unconscionable."

E. **What If the Party Was Mistaken Because of a Failure to Read the Contract Carefully?** This is not a mistake that will lead to relief. The courts will generally enforce contracts, even if they appear unbalanced, if they are entered into by competent parties. This is an example of the "freedom of contract" principle.

X. ONCE CREATED, HOW IS A CONTRACT INTERPRETED?

A. **All Contract Interpretation Focuses on the Intent of the Parties.** Since a contract, in essence, creates "private law" for a specific transaction or arrangement, the key purpose to all contract interpretation is ascertaining the intent of the parties.

B. **General Rule: The Contract Speaks for Itself.** In general, if a contract is clear and unambiguous within "the four corners of the agreement," then the agreement is deemed to be "fully integrated," and no other evidence regarding the meaning of the contract is admissible.

C. **What Happens When the Contract Language is Incomplete?**

1. **Parol Evidence Rule.** If the contract is not fully integrated, then the "parol evidence rule" applies, and parties can introduce oral evidence of the missing or incomplete terms.

2. **Strict Construction.** There are some contract provisions that are subject to "strict construction." The contract terms must be clear on the face of the document, and oral testimony regarding intent of the parties will not be admitted. Examples of such clauses are "restrictive covenants" that are in partial restraint of trade and "surety" contracts that require a party to be responsible for a third-party's obligations, including a personal guaranty of a corporate obligation such as a lease or a promissory note.

D. **What Happens When the Contract Language Is Ambiguous?** Generally, courts will construe contracts against the party who drafted the agreement. To mitigate this, some contracts include clauses that state that the parties had equal opportunity to review the contract and, therefore, the contract should not be construed against the drafting party. Also, courts almost always allow outside evidence to clarify ambiguous terms.

E.   **Are There Other Ways That Outside Evidence Can Be Introduced to Interpret the Intent of the Parties?** Most courts allow outside testimony or evidence related to the following:

   1.   **Course of Performance.** Evidence describing how the parties have actually performed under the agreement is admissible.

   2.   **Course of Dealing.** If the parties have engaged in a series of transactions, then evidence of their course of dealing with each other is admissible.

   3.   **Custom and Usage in the Industry.** Evidence of custom and usage in the industry is also admissible. For example, "custom and usage" evidence can be entered to define terms commonly used or business practices typically followed in a specific industry.

XI. WHAT TERMS AND CONDITIONS ARE TYPICALLY FOUND IN CONTRACTS?

A.   **Substantive Terms and Conditions.** Most contract negotiations are focused on the substantive terms and conditions of the transaction or arrangement. Substantive terms and conditions may include: (1) a description of the goods, services, or other property being provided or conveyed; (2) financial and payment terms; and (3) term and termination of the agreement. For example, a business may enter into an agreement for consulting or management services. If so, the parties are inclined to focus on describing the scope of the services, payment terms, the term of the agreement, and how it may be terminated, and, perhaps, intellectual property rights during the negotiation process.

B.   **Special Terms and Conditions.** Many agreements include special terms and conditions. Examples include, without limitation, indemnification, warranty, limitation of liability, liquidated damages, and restraint of trade clauses, each of which merits specific attention.

C.   **Indemnification Clauses.**

   1.   **What Is an Indemnification Clause?** Indemnification clauses are perplexing and among the most difficult provisions to understand and negotiate. In general, "indemnify" means to compensate another party for damages, losses, or expenses they incur. For example, in a construction contract, the owner may require the construction contractor to indemnify the owner for any claims made against the owner by third parties arising from the contractor's negligence. As another example, a hospital that engages the services of a management

company may require the manager to indemnify the hospital for claims made against the hospital arising out of a failure by the management company to perform its services in a manner that complies with the statutes and regulations governing the health industry. As a final example, an entity that enters into a license agreement that permits the use of computer software or other work that may be governed by copyright or patent law may require an indemnification clause that requires the licensor to indemnify the licensee for claims of infringement by third parties arising from use of the computer software. These seem like simple concepts. However, the language used in indemnification clauses is often confusing.

2. **Example of an Indemnification Clause.** This is a sample indemnification clause:

> **Indemnification.** Each party hereby agrees to indemnify, defend, and hold harmless the other party and its officers, partners, employees, and agents from and against any and all claims, losses, damages, costs, expenses, liabilities, assessments, judgments, or deficiencies of any nature whatsoever, including, without limitation, reasonable attorneys' fees and other costs and expenses incident to any suit, action, or proceeding, which may arise out of, result from, or constitute any breach of any representation, warranty, or covenant contained in this Agreement.

3. **Negotiation of Indemnification Clauses.** As a general rule, parties want to avoid indemnification obligations. Therefore, when confronted with an indemnification clause, the first position to take is to request deletion of all indemnification obligations. If the other party insists on indemnification, then the usual response is to make the indemnification obligations mutual when this makes sense. The clause set forth above is an example of a simple mutual indemnification clause.

4. **Limitations on Indemnification Obligations.** Under the law of most jurisdictions, an indemnification clause cannot apply if the indemnified party is responsible for the costs or damages. In other words, you cannot be indemnified for your own negligent acts or contract breaches. Also, the parties can negotiate limitations on indemnification obligations. For example, in mergers and acquisition contracts, it is typical for the parties to negotiate a threshold "basket" amount that must be reached before there are any indemnification obligations that arise as well as time limitations for asserting indemnification claims.

D. **Warranties.** A "warranty" is, in general, an assurance of some particular matter that is an essential element of the contractual arrangement. Warranties can be express (stated in clear terms in the contract) or implied (not expressly stated but understood by custom and usage in the industry, a course of dealing between the parties, or the nature of the transaction to be an essential part of the contractual arrangement). In general, breach of a warranty will result in damages to the other party.

1. **Warranties in General Contracts.** In many contracts, representations and warranties are expressly made and form the core of the agreement. For example, in contracts for mergers and acquisitions or for capital financing, the seller or borrower is required to make extensive representations and warranties, and a breach would lead to indemnification obligations as described above. For example, a seller or borrower is typically required to represent and warrant that the seller or borrower is not involved in any litigation that might decrease the value of its business or threaten its ability to repay a loan.

2. **Warranties Related to the Purchase and Sale of Goods.** Warranties related to the purchase and sale of goods are governed by the UCC. In addition to any warranties expressly provided in the contract, the UCC also provides implied warranties of merchantability, implied warranties arising from a course of dealing or custom and usage in a trade, and implied warranties of fitness for a specific purpose unless the contract expressly excludes those warranties. Therefore, most contracts for the purchase and sale of goods (to which the UCC applies), and many contracts for the purchase of items to which the UCC may not apply (such as computer software), contain warranty disclaimer provisions.

3. **Warranty Disclaimer Provisions.** One way to exclude warranties is to include an "as is" clause in the contract. Under this provision, the seller agrees to provide the property or services under the contract "as is, where is, and with no further warranties." The UCC also has specific requirements for warranty disclaimers, and clauses that comply with the UCC requirements are sometimes used in contracts to which the UCC does not apply. A typical warranty disclaimer clause is as follows:

EXCEPT AS PROVIDED IN THE SPECIFIC WARRANTIES SET OUT HEREIN, ALL SERVICES AND PRODUCTS PROVIDED UNDER THIS AGREEMENT ARE PROVIDED ON AN "AS IS" BASIS. NEITHER SELLER NOR ANY OF ITS AFFILIATES, EMPLOYEES, OFFICERS, DIRECTORS, AGENTS, OR LICENSORS WARRANTS THAT THE SERVICES OR PRODUCTS PROVIDED PURSUANT TO THIS AGREEMENT WILL BE DEFECT FREE, NOR DO THEY WARRANT THAT CERTAIN RESULTS MAY BE OBTAINED BY PURCHASER IN CONNECTION WITH SELLER'S RENDERING OF SERVICES OR PROVISION OF PRODUCTS HEREUNDER. SELLER AND ITS AFFILIATES, EMPLOYEES, OFFICERS, DIRECTORS, AGENTS, AND LICENSORS MAKE NO WARRANTY, GUARANTEE, OR REPRESENTATION, EITHER EXPRESS OR IMPLIED, REGARDING THE MERCHANTABILITY, TITLE, OR FITNESS FOR A PARTICULAR PURPOSE OF ANY SERVICES OR PRODUCTS PROVIDED UNDER THIS AGREEMENT.

4. **Magnuson-Moss Warranty Act.** The Magnuson-Moss Warranty Act is a federal consumer protection law that applies to the purchase and sale of consumer products that come with an express written warranty. The Act distinguishes between "full" and "limited" warranties, requires warranties to be presented conspicuously, and provides consumers with remedies for a breach of warranty. The Act does not preempt state law. Therefore, all state laws, including the UCC, also apply to transactions that are regulated by the Magnuson-Moss Warranty Act. Any entity that offers consumer products for sale must obtain a complete understanding of the Magnuson-Moss Warranty Act.

E. **Limitation of Liability.** Contractual provisions that limit liability of the parties are another way to limit the risk of a breach of a warranty. Limitation of liability clauses are found in all types of agreements, but are frequently based on the specific contractual arrangement. There are several ways in which liability may be limited, including limitation on the amount of damages that may be recovered, limitation of the types of damages that may be asserted, and limitation on the time for asserting a claim of breach of contract. For example, a contract between a consultant and business may provide that any damages under the arrangement are limited to the amount that the business paid the consultant for its services and that the claim must be made within a year of the date when services were terminated. Also, the UCC has specific requirements for limitation of liability clauses. A typical limitation of liability clause that complies with the UCC is as follows:

> **NOTWITHSTANDING ANY TERM OR PROVISION CONTAINED IN THIS AGREEMENT, IN NO EVENT SHALL SELLER BE LIABLE TO PURCHASER OR TO ANY OTHER PERSON OR ENTITY, FOR ANY INDIRECT, INCIDENTAL, SPECIAL, CONSEQUENTIAL, EXEMPLARY, OR PUNITIVE DAMAGES, OR OTHER SIMILAR TYPE OF DAMAGES, ARISING OUT OF OR IN ANY WAY RELATED TO THIS AGREEMENT, THE PERFORMANCE THEREOF, THE USE OF THE PRODUCTS PROMISED OR SERVICES DELIVERED PURSUANT TO THIS AGREEMENT OR SELLER'S ALLEGED BREACH OF THIS AGREEMENT, REGARDLESS OF WHETHER SELLER KNEW OR SHOULD HAVE KNOWN OF THE POSSIBILITY OF SUCH DAMAGES IN ADVANCE.**

> **UNDER NO CIRCUMSTANCES WHATSOEVER SHALL SELLER BE LIABLE TO PURCHASER OR TO ANY OTHER PERSON OR ENTITY FOR DAMAGES OF ANY KIND ARISING OUT OF OR IN ANY WAY RELATED TO THIS AGREEMENT, THE PERFORMANCE THEREOF, THE PRODUCTS OR SERVICES DELIVERED PURSUANT TO THIS AGREEMENT, OR SELLER'S ALLEGED BREACH OF THIS AGREEMENT, IN ANY AMOUNT OF MONEY WHICH SHALL EXCEED THE AMOUNT OF THE FEE PAID BY PURCHASER TO SELLER WITH RESPECT TO THE PRODUCTS OR SERVICES PROVIDED UNDER THIS AGREEMENT.**

THE LIMITATIONS ON LIABILITY SET FORTH IN THIS SECTION SHALL APPLY TO ALL CAUSES OF ACTION, INCLUDING, WITHOUT LIMITATION, BREACH OF CONTRACT, BREACH OF WARRANTY, STRICT LIABILITY, NEGLIGENT MISREPRESENTATION AND OTHER TORTS, AND LIABILITY BASED UPON THE PROVISIONS OF ANY PART OF THIS AGREEMENT AND ANY FEDERAL, STATE, OR LOCAL LAW/OR ORDINANCE. THE LIMITATIONS ON LIABILITY REPRESENT A FUNDAMENTAL TERM OF THIS AGREEMENT, AND SELLER WOULD NOT HAVE ENTERED INTO THIS AGREEMENT WITHOUT THEIR INCLUSION.

NO ACTION, REGARDLESS OF FORM, ARISING OUT OF THIS AGREEMENT, MAY BE BROUGHT BY PURCHASER AGAINST SELLER MORE THAN ONE YEAR AFTER THE CAUSE OF ACTION HAS ARISEN.

F.   **Liquidated Damages.** Sometimes the parties agree in advance to the amount of damages that might arise from a breach and put that specific amount in the contract. This is referred to as a "liquidated damages" clause. A "liquidated damages" clause is appropriate when actual damages will be difficult or impossible to ascertain and the parties agree in advance upon a reasonable amount of damages arising from a breach of contract. For example, a contract may have a restrictive covenant that restrains competition, and the parties may agree that, in the event of a breach, the breaching party will pay the non-breaching party $150,000. Liquidated damages clauses are very common in construction contracts as a means to measure damages arising from construction delays. However, the amount of the liquidated damages cannot be either a penalty or forfeiture, which would be unenforceable. Therefore, there is always some risk that a liquidated damages clause could be challenged as being an illegal penalty.

G.   **Agreements in Restraint of Trade.** Agreements in general restraint of trade (such as agreements to create a monopoly) have long been illegal and unenforceable under the common law and general contract law. However, agreements in partial restraint of trade are enforceable if they are "reasonable." Such provisions, also called "restrictive covenants," are commonly found in employment agreements and in mergers and acquisitions agreements. For example, if a business purchases another business, the purchaser does not want the seller to turn around and start a competing business. In general, such clauses are enforceable if they are reasonable as to time, territory, and activity restrained and are also reasonable as to each party and the general public. The law governing agreements in restraint of trade has peculiarities in each state, and such clauses must be closely scrutinized.

H.   **"Boilerplate" Contract Terms are Important.** Regardless of the substantive terms and conditions of a contract, virtually all contracts include terms and conditions at the end of the contract that are referred to as "boilerplate" provisions. The term "boilerplate" may lead you to believe that the terms and conditions that are commonly found in virtually all contracts are unimportant. This is a misconception. "Boilerplate" terms and conditions are extremely important for allocating contractual risk, and careful attention to boilerplate clauses can lead to litigation avoidance. Also, there are several different ways in which the "boilerplate" terms may be expressed. A comprehensive, but by no means exhaustive, list of boilerplate contract terms is as follows:

1. **Entire Agreement.** This clause is generally buried at the end of a contract but it may be the most important boilerplate clause. In general, this clause will provide that (a) the agreement constitutes the entire agreement between the parties and (b) all prior representations of the parties, whether written or oral, are merged into the agreement. In other words, if something is not expressed in the agreement, even if the parties discussed it, it is not enforceable. In my experience, I have seen this clause help to avoid many lawsuits. Parties will frequently take the position that, regardless of the terms and conditions of the agreement, the parties had a side deal or separate understanding. This clause can kill those arguments. Every contract should include an "entire agreement" clause.

2. **Amendments.** If the agreement constitutes the entire agreement of the parties, the parties must agree on how the agreement can be amended. In most agreements, amendments must be in writing and signed by the parties. However, there may be items that can be changed without formal amendment of the agreement. Therefore, you may need to consider how to amend the contract.

3. **Waiver of Breach.** Sometimes, one party may be in technical breach of the precise terms and conditions of the agreement, but, if the only remedy available is termination of the agreement, the non-breaching party may want to give the breaching party a second chance and not terminate the agreement. However, the non-breaching party will not want this isolated instance to constitute a waiver of the breaching party's obligations if it happens again. Therefore, you will frequently see a clause that provides that the waiver by either party of a breach or violation of any provision of the agreement shall not operate as or be construed to be a waiver of any subsequent breach of the same or other provisions of the agreement. For example, this clause is very important in construction contracts.

4. **Assignment.** When parties enter into an agreement, they generally intend to do business with each other. Therefore, a typical clause provides that no assignment of the agreement or the rights and obligations under the agreement will be valid without the specific written consent of both parties. However, there are frequently exceptions that need to be considered. For example, one party may be looking forward to a liquidation event in which either all of the party's assets are sold or the party is merged into an acquiring entity, and it is not uncommon to see a clause that permits assignment to an entity that purchases all or substantially all of an entity's assets or an entity into which a party is merged.

5.   **Force Majeure.** Sometimes, parties will want to avoid performance if there is an unforeseen event. For example, the events of September 11, 2001 made it impossible for performance of some contracts. Therefore, some agreements provide that neither party shall be liable nor deemed to be in default for any delay or failure in performance under the agreement or other interruption of service resulting directly or indirectly from acts of "force majeure," including acts of God; acts of civil or military authorities; acts of public enemies or war; accidents; fires; explosions; earthquakes; floods; failure of transportation; pandemic disease; strikes or other work interruptions by either party's employees; or any cause beyond the reasonable control of either party.

6.   **Governing Law.** When parties are in different states, they may want the agreement to be governed by the law of their own state. If there is not a governing law clause, the governing law will be decided by the principles of "conflicts of laws." Therefore, it is important to include a governing law clause in a contract. However, unless the choice of law is California, New York, or another state that has a complicated statutory and regulatory system, negotiation of the governing law clause should rarely be a deal killer.

7.   **Attorneys' Fees.** Under the English legal system, the party that loses in litigation pays the winner's court costs and attorneys' fees. In the United States, however, the general rule is that each party pays its own costs and attorneys' fees, regardless of the outcome. Therefore, to dissuade frivolous litigation, agreements sometimes include a clause providing that, in the event that either party resorts to legal action to enforce the terms and provisions of the agreement, the successful party shall be entitled to recover the costs of such action so incurred including, without limitation, reasonable attorneys' fees.

8.   **Third-Party Beneficiaries.** Some agreements intend to provide a specific third party with rights under the agreement, even when the third parties are not direct parties to the agreement. This is known as an "intended third-party beneficiary." Conversely, an "incidental beneficiary" has no rights under the contract. Therefore, it is a good practice to include a clause that identifies intended third-party beneficiaries.

9.   **Notices.** Many contracts will provide that the parties are required to provide each other with "notice" to assert certain rights under the agreement. For example, if there is a breach of the agreement, the non-breaching party will need to provide "notice" of the breach to the allegedly breaching party before proceeding with termination or other contractual rights. Therefore, each agreement must have a "notice" clause. It was formerly common practice to allow notice to be given by "certified mail, return receipt requested." However, this is a slow and antiquated method of providing notice. Modern contracts allow notice to be delivered by a reliable overnight delivery service that provides evidence of receipt or, in

some instances, by facsimile or electronic mail. Therefore, careful attention must be given to the notice provision.

10.   **Counterparts.** Frequently, the parties are not in the same place when the contract is executed. Also, most states now allow contracts to be executed by electronic signature. In fact, today there are rarely face-to-face closings of agreements, even large merger and acquisition agreements. Therefore, many agreements need a clause providing that the agreement and any amendments thereto may be signed in multiple counterparts and that each counterpart shall be deemed an original, but all counterparts together shall constitute one and the same instrument.

11.   **Additional Assurances.** To avoid arguments that the agreement is found in the four corners of the document, it is helpful to include a clause stating the terms and conditions of the agreement are self-operative and shall not require further agreement by the parties except as specifically provided to the contrary.

12.   **Severability.** It is common practice to include a clause providing that the terms and conditions of the agreement are severable. A typical clause will provide that, in the event any provision of the agreement is held to be unenforceable for any reason, the unenforceability thereof shall not affect the remainder of the agreement, which shall remain in full force and effect and enforceable in accordance with its terms, unless such would frustrate the original purposes thereof.

13.   **Headings.** It is common practice to put headings on sections of the agreement, but they should not be used in interpreting the meaning of the precise terms and conditions of the agreement. A typical clause provides that the articles and other headings contained in the agreement are for reference purposes only and shall not affect in any way the meaning or interpretation of the agreement.

I.   **Other Special Terms and Conditions.**

1.   **Examples of Other Special Terms and Conditions.** Contracts may include special clauses, such as dispute resolution clauses requiring arbitration or mediation of contract disputes instead of judicial proceedings; representations and warranties that the parties have certain qualifications, certifications, or licenses; clauses requiring compliance with specific laws and regulations; clauses addressing intellectual property rights, including patent, copyright, trademark, and trade secret rights; and clauses that are intended to protect the relationship of the parties, such as exclusive dealing agreements.

2.   **"Best Efforts" Clauses.** In general, the common law implies a duty on both parties to use their "best efforts" to fulfill the terms and conditions of the contract. In addition, when a

party perceives it may be difficult to accomplish a contractual obligation, the party may want to modify the duty but requiring only that it use its "best efforts" to accomplish the duty. For example, a hospital may enter into a contract with a management company that requires the management company to obtain certain insurance coverage. However, the manager cannot control the insurance markets, and it may be difficult to procure insurance precisely as described. Therefore, the manager will negotiate a clause that provides that the manager will use its "best efforts" to procure the insurance. Some parties try to modify "best efforts" by asking for either a "reasonable best efforts" or "commercially reasonable best efforts" clause under the fear that a court will interpret "best efforts" to mean every possible effort, regardless of cost or consequences, but most courts will imply a "reasonableness" standard to a best efforts clause, and "commercially reasonable" is generally construed to be the same as "reasonable" best efforts.

XII. WHAT REMEDIES ARE AVAILABLE FOR A BREACH OF CONTRACT?

A.   **What Is the General Rule for Breach of Contract Remedies?** The general rule is that the damaged party will be "made whole." In other words, the damaged party will be able to either receive the benefit of the bargain or be put into a position where the damaged party does not suffer any loss.

B.   **What Are the General Kinds of Remedies Available?** Two kinds of remedies are generally available: remedies available at law, such as monetary damages; and equitable remedies.

C.   **What Remedies Are Available at Law?** Examples of how an aggrieved party can be "made whole" as a matter of law follows:

   1.   **Compensatory Damages.** A party can recover "compensatory" damages, which means actual monetary damages. Note: compensatory or monetary damages should not be confused with liquidated damages, which are reasonable estimates of damages agreed to in advance.

   2.   **Liquidated Damages.** As stated above, the parties can agree in advance in the contract to a specific amount of damages for a breach of contract, provided that, when the contract was executed, actual damages would be difficult or impossible to ascertain and the amount of the liquidated damages is a reasonable estimate of the amount of damages that the party would suffer. The courts will not enforce a liquidated damages clause that is, in essence, a penalty.

D.   **What Are "Equitable Remedies"?** Equitable remedies are generally applied to prevent something unfair or unjust from happening when there is no adequate remedy at law (in other words, monetary damages alone will not be the appropriate remedy). Some examples are as follows:

1. **Specific Performance.** This requires the breaching party to complete the transaction. It is seen most frequently in contracts for the sale of unique property (such as real property).

2. **Rescission.** Rescission is an equitable remedy, and it means that the contract is nullified and the parties are restored to the positions they had before entering into the contract.

3. **Reformation.** Reformation is an equitable remedy that requests the court to rewrite or correct a contract to make it conform to the original agreement of the parties. Reformation can be used when the parties have reached an agreement but the written contract inaccurately reflects that agreement.

4. **Injunctions and Restraining Orders.** Courts will issue injunctions and restraining orders when there is no adequate remedy at law, there is a likelihood of success of the merits of the case, and the party seeking the relief would otherwise suffer irreparable harm.

E. **What Remedies Are Not Generally Available for Breach of Contract?**

1. **Punitive Damages.** "Punitive damages" are generally assessable only when there is an intentional tort (such as, in the context of contractual arrangements, fraud), and are intended to "punish" the culpable party. Since "punishment" is not a part of contract law, punitive damages are generally not awarded in contract cases.

2. **Costs and Attorneys' Fees.** Costs and attorneys' fees related to breach of contract litigation are generally not recoverable unless the parties agree otherwise in the contract or, in some states, there is an award based on the "stubbornly litigious" conduct of the breaching party.

F. **Mitigation of Damages.** When a contract is breached, the non-breaching party generally has a duty to "mitigate" the potential damages (in other words, to act in a manner that minimizes the damages). For example, if a business contracts with a supplier of widgets and the supplier breaches the contract, the business must try to find another source of widgets to "mitigate" its damages.

XIII. WHAT DEFENSES ARE TYPICALLY RAISED IN BREACH OF CONTRACT CASES?

A. **Illegality.** As stated above, illegal contracts are unenforceable. One ground that may arise in the business context is performance of services without a required license or permit.

B. **Duress.** A contract will not be enforced if a party can show that it was unfairly coerced into entering the contract (for example, threats of violence or imprisonment or the illegal taking of property).

C.   **Unconscionability.** As described above, a party may allege that the contract was procedurally or substantively unconscionable. However, whether the agreement is "unconscionable" needs to be balanced against the doctrine of "freedom of contract" and its related maxim in equity, "folly is not fraud."

D.   **Impossibility.** The doctrine of impossibility applies if there is either a change in circumstances or the discovery of unknown preexisting circumstances that makes performance of the contract impossible. "Impossibility" has its roots in ancient common law.

E.   **Impracticability.** Sometimes intervening events occur that may not make it impossible for the parties to perform but may make it impracticable for a party to perform because of excessive or unreasonable cost. Impracticability is a more difficult defense than impossibility because it is more difficult to prove and also needs to be assessed in the context of "freedom of contract" and "folly is not fraud."

F.   **Capacity or Authority.** In a business context, the person who signed the agreement had no actual or apparent authority to bind the party to a contract.

G.   **Fraud.** Sometimes a party may allege that it was fraudulently induced into entering into a contractual arrangement. "Fraud" is a tort that is based upon a misrepresentation or concealment of a material fact that induced a party to act in a certain way. Therefore, a tort claim for "fraud" is sometimes alleged in the same complaint that alleges a breach of contract, which opens up the possibility of recovery of punitive damages as well as costs and attorneys' fees, which may be awarded in a tort lawsuit. In a lawsuit alleging "fraud," the plaintiff must specifically and particularly describe the facts upon which the fraud claim is based in the complaint. Also, as stated above, "folly is not fraud."

XIV. CONTRACT DRAFTING

A.   **Each Contract Is Unique.** With the possible exception of standardized purchase orders and adhesion contracts, business contracts are like snowflakes. Even when the parties have substantial contract drafting experience, business contracts are rarely identical for many reasons. For example, contracts will reflect the bargaining power of the parties; economic shifts; changes in management, advisors, accountants, and legal counsel; changing laws and regulations; and experience of the parties in identifying potential risks. While it is common practice to begin drafting with an existing contract, most business contracts will evolve over time.

B.   **Use Clear, Precise Language.** Contract drafting requires clear, precise, descriptive, and grammatically correct language. While it may be commonly held that attorneys intentionally draft ambiguous contracts, the opposite is true. Each contract must expressly state the intent of the parties. The goal is to produce a fully integrated contract that is easily understood within the "four corners" of the document.

1. **Delete Unnecessary Words.** When drafting a contract, review it carefully. If unnecessary words appear, delete them. Economy of language will be rewarded with certainty of contractual rights and obligations.

2. **Define Terms.** If a contractual phrase or provision will be used throughout the document, create a definition. This will eliminate ambiguity and create a shorter document. This can be done either by defining terms when the contractual phase first appears in the document or creating a definition section that sets forth all of the defined terms in the agreement.

C. **The Danger of Do-It-Yourself Contracting.** Although this may seem like a self-serving statement for the engagement of legal counsel, businesses should avoid trying to prepare their own material contracts. Since contracts are unique, modifying them yourself or combining provisions from multiple documents is fraught with drafting danger. For example, the defined terms in two combined contracts may be different, and the combined language can easily create ambiguities.

XV. CONTRACT NEGOTIATION

A. **Negotiation of Contracts.** Some contracts, known as "adhesion" contracts, must be accepted without negotiation. For example, when you apply for a credit card, you are compelled to accept the terms offered by the credit card company without negotiation, and the credit card company reserves the right to amend the contract without the cardholder's consent. Also, when you purchase a new car, the form includes many provisions on a printed form, and the dealer generally will not deviate from the terms and conditions on the printed form. Many business contracts, however, are negotiable.

B. **Contracts Require Mutual Gain.** The key to concluding contractual negotiations is to find the point where each party receives the benefit of the bargain. Some negotiation experts refer to this as the "mutual gain line," which is the point where each party essentially gets what it wants.

C. **Finding the Mutual Gain Line.** The best way to find the mutual gain line is to discover what the other party wants and then, to the extent possible without compromising the benefit of the bargain for you, giving it to them. This is accomplished by getting information from the other party. When you enter into any contract negotiation, you should prepare a series of questions beginning with the word "what" that are designed to discover what the other party wants. Some experts say that, when negotiating a contract, it is better to get more information than you give.

D. **Discredited Negotiation Strategies.** Although others may debate what might be the most effective negotiation strategy, some strategies are not recommended. For example, in labor law, there was formally a negotiation technique called "Boulwarism," which, in effect, was a "take it or leave it strategy" and refusal to negotiate any terms and conditions. This usually does not work. Similarly, the techniques of "win through intimidation" or "zero sum game" are not terribly effective.

E. **Smart Is Dumb and Dumb Is Smart.** Since the key to negotiation is to get more information than you give, trying to show how knowledgeable or intelligent you are may not be an effective negotiation strategy. When you are confronted with a party that makes a bold or definitive statement with which you may disagree, instead of refuting it, you should say that you do not fully understand and ask the other party to rephrase the question. For some reason, the rephrased statement is never as forceful as the first, and this frequently leads to balanced negotiations.

F. **Keep Your Emotions Under Control.** The party that loses his or her temper is always at a negotiating disadvantage. Keep your emotions under control. When the other party becomes temperamental, you can defuse it by saying: "This seems to make you angry. Tell me why it upsets you."

G. **Playing the "Deal Breaker" Card.** At least once in every negotiation you are likely to reach an impasse on a critical deal point. If it is truly a deal breaker, it is permissible to say so and advise the other party that, if they do not concede, then you will walk away from the table. However, there are two conditions to playing this card. First, you can only play it one time. Second, you have to mean it.

H. **Be Guided by Reasonableness.** Even if you are entirely confident that your contract is inherently fair and clearly articulated, reasonable people may review your work and find ambiguities or place a different meaning on a contractual provision than you intended. It is best to keep an open mind and not get trapped by "pride of authorship."

I. **Read and Understand the Contract.** Last, you need to actually read what you are being asked to sign and clearly understand your rights and obligations. If you do not understand something, ask questions. If there are blanks in the contract, be sure they are filled in before you execute the contract. If a dispute ever arises, the terms and conditions of what you signed govern, and it is up to you to know what you have agreed to do or not to do.

CHAPTER 2

EMPLOYMENT AND INDEPENDENT CONTRACTOR AGREEMENTS

I. WHAT ARE THE ESSENTIAL ELEMENTS OF AN EMPLOYMENT RELATIONSHIP?

A. **Employment Under the Common Law.** Modern employment law is founded on "master-servant" common law principles.

B. **Duties of Loyalty and Confidentiality.** Some duties arise under the common law, even in the absence of a written contract, including the duties of loyalty and confidentiality. In general, the duty of loyalty means that the employee must not engage in conduct that constitutes a "conflict of interest" with the employer. Also, employees are generally required to maintain confidentiality of an employer's trade secrets for all time, regardless of whether the parties have entered into a written employment agreement.

C. **Oral Versus Written Employment Agreements.**

    1. **Oral Agreements.** Most employment agreements are oral and are terminable at will by either party.

    2. **Written Agreements.** Written employment agreements give both parties more rights and obligations than general law provides.

D. **What Bodies of Law Govern Employment and Independent Contractor Agreements?**

    1. **State Law.** Most aspects of employment and independent contractor agreements are governed by state laws and judicial decisions.

2.　**Federal Law.** There is no true federal contracts law, but certain aspects of employment and independent contractor agreements are governed by federal law. For example, some federal laws govern all employment relationships (for example, the Equal Employment Opportunity Act and the Family and Medical Leave Act). However, those laws are beyond the scope of this book.

II. WHAT ARE THE ESSENTIAL ELEMENTS OF ANY EMPLOYMENT AGREEMENT?

A.　**Duties**. The employment duties should be described.

　　1.　**Full Time Employment.** The agreement usually requires full time services.

　　2.　**Permitted Activities**. If there are any permitted outside activities, they should be clearly described.

B.　**Compensation and Benefits.** Physician compensation can take many forms, including the following:

　　1.　**Fixed Salary.** A fixed amount for performance of all services.

　　2.　**Bonus or Productivity Based Compensation.** Many businesses have incentive compensation programs that tie earnings to accomplishing objective goals for productivity, overall profitability, innovation, and many other ways.

　　3.　**Fringe Benefits.** Typical fringe benefits include health insurance, retirement plan benefits, an automobile allowance, and a cellular phone and personal device with related cellular service. Some enterprises give special fringe benefits, such as incentive stock options.

　　4.　**Relocation and Moving Expenses.** Relocation and moving expense reimbursement is sometimes provided, but it is typically tied to continued employment and possible repayment obligations.

　　5.　**Time Away from Employment; Vacation.** It is generally preferable to lump vacation, sick leave, and other paid time off together. From an employer's perspective, it is important to provide that time away from employment will not accrue from year to year, and, upon termination of the employee's employment for any reason, the employee shall not be entitled to payment for any unused time away from employment.

　　6.　**Deferred Compensation and Internal Revenue Code Section 409A Compliance.** In 2004, Congress enacted Internal Revenue Code Section 409A to provide rules regarding the taxation of deferred compensation, including severance pay arrangements. To comply with Section 409A, the time, form, and triggering event for deferred compensation arrangements must be established when the agreement is entered into. Once established, subsequent changes in the form, time of payment, or payment itself are heavily restricted. The stakes are high because non-compliant deferred compensation must be included in the recipient's gross income immediately, even if not paid. All agreements that provide for deferred compensation or severance benefits need to be scrutinized for compliance with Internal Revenue Code Section 409A.

H.   Term and Termination.

1.   Term. The actual term of the contract is not as important as the right to terminate. Most agreements have "evergreen" clauses, which automatically renew from year to year, but some have fixed terms with an expiration date.

2.   Termination.

a.   Probation Period. Some agreements have a probationary period, during which the agreement can be terminated at any time and for any reason.

b.   Without Cause. This can be a fixed period at any time (such as 30, 60, or 90 days) or fixed in relation to the term (for example, if notice is given 90 days before expiration of the term).

c.   Employer's Termination for Cause. Employers want to be able to terminate for "cause," and "cause" is frequently defined in the agreement. Some examples are as follows: (i) the discovery of conduct by the employee that is harmful to the business of the employer; (ii) the employee's failure to maintain any professional license; (iii) the employee's indictment for, conviction of, or pleading no contest to any other criminal offense involving moral turpitude; or (iv) any breach of any material term or condition of the agreement by the employee that is not cured within a reasonable period of time after written notice from the employer specifying the breach and requesting that it be cured.

d.   Employee's Termination for Cause. The employee may sometimes terminate the employee's employment under the agreement for cause, but these rights are usually very limited. For example, (i) the employer's filing (whether voluntarily or involuntarily) any petition for bankruptcy or (ii) the employer's material breach of the agreement that is not cured within a reasonable period of time after written notice from the employee specifying the breach and requesting that it be cured.

e.   **Disability.** Employment agreements may be terminated (subject to federal law) if the employee becomes "disabled," but the definition of "disability" is sometimes heavily negotiated.

D.   Covenants in Partial Restraint of Trade.

1.   **Restrictive Covenant or Noncompetition Agreement.** A traditional "restrictive covenant" or "noncompetition agreement" restrains an employee from competing with the employer for a certain period time in a specific geographic territory.

2.   **The "Reasonableness" Test.** To be enforceable, the covenant generally must be reasonable to the employee, the employer, and the public; must protect only an employer's legitimate business interests; and must be reasonable as to time, territory, and activity restrained. Each element of the reasonableness test must be separately analyzed.

3.   **Strict Construction.** Agreements in partial restraint of trade are "strictly construed." The restrictions must be precisely clear: oral testimony regarding the intent of the parties is not admissible evidence. An "overly broad" restrictive covenant is "void as against public policy" and therefore unenforceable.

4.   **The "Blue Penciling" Rule.** Some states follow a rule that, if an "overly broad" covenant can be made reasonable by striking out a word or phrase (referred to as "blue penciling"), the restrictive covenant is enforceable as modified.

5.   **Non-Solicitation of Customers.** To protect its customer base, an employer may also require an employee to agree that the employee will not divert, solicit, or contact, or attempt to divert, solicit, or contact, any customer for the purpose of having the customer provided with services or products offered by the employer from a competitor. This is an alternative "restrictive covenant" that must pass a "reasonableness" test. Usually, enforcement of a non-solicitation clause requires only a reasonable time restraint.

6.   **Non-Solicitation of Employees.** To protect its valuable human resources, an employer may also require an employee to agree that the employee will not hire, solicit, recruit, or induce any employee, consultant, or independent contractor employed or otherwise engaged by the employer to sever his or her relationship with the employer or to be employed or otherwise engaged by any competitor. This type of covenant also generally requires a reasonable time restraint.

7. **Covenant Not to Disclose or Confidentiality Agreement.** There are two types of information that may be subject to a non-disclosure or confidentiality obligation:

    a. **Trade Secrets.** Under the Uniform Trade Secrets Act and the common law, trade secrets as defined under applicable state law are protectable for all time and for so long as they are maintained by the employer as trade secrets, even in the absence of a written contract. A standard definition of trade secrets includes lists of actual or potential customers and referral sources, lists of actual or potential suppliers, technical and non-technical data, formulae, patterns, compilations, programs, devices, methods, techniques, drawings, processes, financial data, financial plans, and product plans, which are known only to the employer and those of its employees in whom the information must be confided for business purposes.

    b. **Other Confidential Information.** Otherwise confidential information that does not rise to the level of a "trade secret" may also be subject to a non-disclosure obligation, but some jurisdictions require a written confidentiality agreement with a time limit on the non-disclosure or confidentiality obligation.

8. **Non-Disparagement.** Although not technically a covenant in partial restraint of trade, some employers may ask an employee not to engage in public or private disparagement of the employer or its business methods, operations, programs, or employees, or prepare articles or other written material for publication that specifically negatively refer to, or are critical of, the employer or its business methods, operations, programs, employees, agents, officers, directors, or other representatives after termination of the agreement. However, such provisions are difficult to enforce.

9. **Remedies.** If a restrictive covenant is breached, the typical remedy is a temporary or permanent injunction against the employee prohibiting any further violation of any such covenant. The employer can also seek monetary damages.

E. **Intellectual Property.** Three forms of intellectual property may be relevant to an employment relationship: trade secret; patent; and copyright. Each requires a different contract provision. As stated above, an employer's trade secrets are protected even in the absence of a written contract. Because patent rights arise with the individual and not the employer, patent rights need to be individually assigned by the employee in writing. However, the employer owns the copyright in all copyrightable works produced by the employee within the scope of employment under the "works made for hire" doctrine, and a separate contract clause is unnecessary.

F.   **Assignment.** Typically, because the contract is for an employee's personal services, the employee may not assign, transfer, or subcontract the employee's rights and obligations under the agreement to any other person or entity. However, the employer usually wants the right to assign its rights and obligations under the agreement to any legal entity or individual that acquires or otherwise continues the business currently conducted by the employer.

G.   **Indemnification.** Under an indemnification obligation, a party is required to defend and hold harmless the other party from and against any and all claims, losses, damages, costs, or expenses, arising out of any breach of any representation, warranty, or covenant contained in the agreement or any claims for damages or injury against the other party that are caused by or result from negligent acts or omissions by the other party in the performance of their respective duties and obligations. Employees frequently object to indemnification clauses in employment agreements. Indemnification may be appropriate in a professional services agreement.

H.   **Waiver.** The waiver by either party of a breach or violation of any provision of the agreement shall not operate as or be construed to be a waiver of any subsequent breach hereof.

I.   **Notices.** Most contracts provide that the parties must give the other party notice in certain situations. For example, most agreements require notice of termination. Therefore, most contracts describe how to give effective notice to the other party. If a notices clause is added, the procedure must be followed.

J.   **Governing Law.** Typically, the agreement is governed according to the substantive laws of the state of employment without regard to principles of conflicts of law.

K.   **Entire Agreement.** It is very important, in any contract, to include a clause stating that the agreement constitutes the entire agreement of the parties regarding the subject matter thereof, that all prior representations of the parties, whether written or oral, are merged therein, and that the agreement may be modified or amended only by a writing executed by both parties.

III. WHAT ARE THE KEY NEGOTIATION POINTS FOR AN EXECUTIVE EMPLOYMENT AGREEMENT?

A.   **Executive Employment Agreement Negotiation.** In general, many of the issues related to all employment agreements also apply to executive employment agreements. However, executive employment agreements have many unique issues. Since this book is intended for individuals, we will focus on contract negotiation for an individual Executive.

B. **Essential Elements of Executive Employment Negotiation from the Executive's Perspective.** From the Executive's perspective, the essential elements are as follows:

1. **Formal Written Contract.** The Executive's employment terms should be set forth in a formal written contract.

2. **Scope of Responsibilities.** The Executive's responsibilities must be delineated clearly. This is important because a description of responsibilities typically inter-relates with restrictive covenants and "for cause" termination provisions. The Executive should report only to the Board of Directors and should be given reasonable latitude to exercise executive discretion. The Executive may also want to ensure that the Executive has a place on the company's Board of Directors.

3. **Full Time and Efforts Clause.** Employment agreements often require that the Executive devote all of the Executive's productive business time and efforts to the Executive's employment related responsibilities. If the Executive employment agreement includes such a provision, then exceptions must be made for the Executive's outside "permitted activities" such as serving on the Board of Directors of non-competing companies and, perhaps, involvement with civic, charitable, or professional organizations.

4. **Location of Employment.** This needs to be fixed in the contract. Any variation needs the Executive's prior written approval. Reasonably required travel (up to a certain number of weeks per year) can be accepted.

5. **Term of Employment.** Ideally, the term should be indefinite or as long as possible. Avoid short (two to five year) terms. Early termination by the company should only occur (a) if the Executive is terminated "for cause", provided that "cause" is precisely defined, or (b) upon the mutual agreement of the Executive and the company.

6. **Early Termination by the Company.**

    a. **General.** The agreement should clearly specify those circumstances under which the Executive's employment term can be cut short by the company. Ideally, it should occur only if the Executive has been "really bad" or if the parties mutually agree that the Executive's employment should end. The company should not be able to terminate the Executive employment at its whim or discretion (and, in the event that it does, either in accordance with or in breach of the agreement, the Executive should have a very attractive "parachute" package of benefits). In some situations, when the Executive is giving up an established secure position and taking one with a fair amount of associated risk, the Executive might want to negotiate a "free walk" that allows him, after a relatively short period of time (for example, three months), to walk away from the position with no strings attached on either side.

b. **For "Cause".** The company may want the right to terminate the Executive "for cause." The agreement should clearly delineate an exclusive list of items that will constitute grounds for termination "for cause." The Executive should strongly resist inclusion of the following items as grounds for "cause" termination: (i) fuzzy, unspecific grounds (for example "the company's failure to perform as well as projected") or (ii) performance based grounds (for example "Executive's failure to perform the Executive's duties as required"). The following grounds are generally acceptable: (x) conviction of a felony; (y) material breach by the Executive of certain provisions in the Executive's employment contract (such as a restrictive covenant provision) and failure of the Executive to cure the breach within a reasonable time period; and (z) embezzlement or fraud of the Executive in performing services for the company.

c. **Death or Total Disability.** Certain termination benefits should flow from such an occurrence. It is important to define "total disability" carefully.

7. **Early Termination by Executive.** The Executive should be able to terminate employment early for "good reason" including the following: (a) the Executive loses the title or managerial position or the Executive's authority is materially undercut (perhaps even if the Executive loses his or her seat on the Board of Directors); (b) the company's executive offices are relocated more than a certain distance from the current location; (c) the company commits a material breach of the employment contract and does not cure the breach within a certain period of time after being provided notice of the breach; and (d) a "change of control" occurs in the company or if a substantial portion of the company's assets or equity is sold to a third party. Certain severance benefits should flow to the Executive if the Executive terminates for good reason.

8. **Compensation and Benefits.**

a. **Base Salary.** Consider setting this as a minimum figure (for example, "The Company shall pay Executive an annual cash salary that is no less than $_____"). Also provide that the salary will increase each year in accordance with a cost of living index (CPI).

b. **Annual Bonus.** "C level" Executives should be entitled to some form of annual incentive cash bonus, regardless of whether other executives are entitled to one. The standards should be as objective as possible, although the Board of Directors should be entitled to pay the Executive an additional bonus based on subjective criteria. Sometimes annual bonuses are paid in the form of stock options, although it is common for executives to get a bonus of both stock and cash.

c. **Benefit Plans.** The Executive should be given the opportunity to participate in a variety of employee benefit plans such as 401K plans, retirement savings plans, supplemental benefit plans, qualified and non-qualified stock option plans, phantom stock plans, long term incentive plans, disability plans, and life, dental, and disability insurance plans. Most companies have plans such as these already set up for members of senior management. The company should not be able later to cut the Executive out of these plans, and, if it does scale back on any plan, then the Executive should be given the economic equivalent in cash so the Executive is in no worse financial position when compared to the benefits provided when the agreement was executed.

d. **Stock Ownership.** It is generally advantageous for an Executive to own shares in his or her company. In fact, private equity and venture capital funds usually require Executives to be incentivized by stock ownership. The advantages usually far outweigh the disadvantages, particularly if the Executive can obtain shares on a favorable basis (for example, through stock options, bonus grants, or stock appreciation rights). The first advantage is the power that share ownership brings. An Executive is subject ultimately to the whim of the controlling shareholders; they have the power to elect the Executive to or remove the Executive from the Board of Directors and in some cases to remove the Executive as an officer of the company. Another advantage of share ownership is the ability of the shareholders to profit if the value of the company increases. Ascertaining a value in a small privately-owned company is not as obvious, so the upside for appreciation is not usually discernible until a major corporate opportunity presents itself to the company such as a sale of the company or an opportunity for the company to "go public." There is little downside to owning shares since a shareholder's personal liability for corporate liabilities is generally limited to the amount of the shareholder's investment. Most well run (and well-advised) privately owned companies require their shareholders to enter into shareholder agreements.

e. **Automobile Allowance.** Executives typically receive an automobile allowance.

f. **Expense Reimbursement.** The company should reimburse the Executive for any employment related expenses incurred by the Executive, including reasonable recreational expenses (for example, dinner with clients and prospects). Reasonable entertainment expenses should be reimbursable as well (notwithstanding the decrease in tax benefits that are allowable to companies under recent changes in the Internal Revenue Code).

g. **Vacation.** Four weeks paid vacation is typical. Vacation time should accrue.

h. **Travel Perks.** First class air travel is often negotiated for top line executives.

i. **Club Memberships.** Companies often agree to reimburse executives for executives' private and business club expenses and dues.

j. **Financial Consulting.** Companies often reimburse executives (subject to a cap) for expenses incurred by the executives in connection with financial and tax counseling and tax return preparation.

9. **Deferred Compensation.** As stated above but bears repeating, compensation arrangements that include any deferred compensation or deferred benefits arrangements must be written to comply with strict requirements under Internal Revenue Code Section 409A. Deferred compensation is a legally binding right arising during a taxable year to compensation that, pursuant to the terms of the arrangement, is or may be payable after the end of the taxable year. Failure to conform such arrangements to these strict requirements will result in the executive employee (or independent contractor) immediately paying income tax on the deferred compensation as well as an additional 20% penalty and interest. Some examples of deferred compensation that are typically negotiated in Executive employment agreements include: salary deferral arrangements (but not 401(k) and similar plans); termination or severance payments; and equity compensation arrangements such as discounted stock options and stock appreciation rights, and stock buy-back features at other than fair market value.

10. **Severance Compensation.** The agreement should carefully identify any compensation or benefits that are to be paid to the Executive upon the termination of the Executive's employment, which also must comply with Internal Revenue Code Section 409A. The degree of benefits typically will range from virtually none (other than accrued salary and bonuses) to quite lavish (in the case of a termination by employee for good reason or an arbitrary termination by the company). The following is an example of how severance compensation can be handled:

a. **"Parachute" Type Payment in the Event of Termination by Executive for Good Reason or by the Company in Breach of the Employment Contract.** The Executive should be entitled to receive the monetary equivalent of his or her salary and benefits (including the minimum amount of any guaranteed bonuses) for a certain period of time after the effective date of termination (two to three years is not uncommon). The vesting for all stock options should accelerate. Office space and executive placement services should be provided by the company. The company has a right to ask for restrictive covenants (for example, no compete covenants) during any period that the Executive is getting parachute type payments. Though it may not be good for tax reasons, getting all projected benefits and continued salary in a single lump sum payment up front would prevent the company from being able to cease paying benefits later.

b. **Severance in the Event of Executive's Death or Total Disability.** In the event of physical or mental incapacity, death, or permanent disability, the company should continue at least the salary portion of the Executive's compensation package for a certain period of time (for example, two to three years) following the Executive's incapacity, death, or disability. This package is usually less "sweet" than the parachute package.

11. **Restrictive Covenants.** It is commonplace for a company to ask its senior executives to enter into restrictive covenants. The elements for enforceability of an Executive employment agreement restrictive covenant are the same as the elements described previously: the covenant must be reasonable as to time, territory, and activity restrained. The "reasonableness" test must take into account the size of the enterprise (is the company a national enterprise like Microsoft or is it a uniquely regional enterprise?) and the nature of the company's competitor enterprises. In that regard, a covenant that might be considered "overly broad" for a salesman might be reasonable when applied to a "C-suite" Executive. While the Executive should resist onerous post-termination restrictive covenants, it is not reasonable for the Executive to expect to be provided post-termination severance benefits and not to be bound by restrictive covenants, at least during the period of time the Executive receives these severance benefits. That is why accelerating and paying in lump sum severance benefits may be desirable: there is not the same rationale supporting long post-termination restrictive covenants. In the rare event that the company does not offer the Executive any (or only modest) severance benefits, the Executive should resist being required to sign anything more than minimal restrictive covenants.

12. **Indemnification.** The company should give the Executive maximum indemnification allowed under the laws. The indemnity should cover, for example, losses and liabilities sustained by the Executive in carrying out his express duties at the direction of the Board of Directors. The company's governance documents (for example, by-laws, articles of incorporation or organization, and shareholder agreements) should be scrutinized closely to ensure that the Executive gets maximum protection.

13. **"Most Favored Executive Status".** Any benefits or perks given to any other senior member of management during the Executive's period of employment should also be offered to the Executive on similar terms.

14. **Excessive Compensation Taxes.** Although it is tempting for an Executive to negotiate the highest compensation package possible, the Tax Cuts and Jobs Act of 2018 imposes new taxes on "excessive compensation" for both "for profit" and tax exempt organizations. A publicly held corporation generally may not take a tax deduction for C level employee remuneration in excess of $1 million annually. Tax exempt organizations that compensate C level employees in an amount in excess of $1 million annually are exposed to payment of an excise tax.

IV. WHAT IS AN INDEPENDENT CONTRACTOR AGREEMENT?

A. **What Distinguishes an Independent Contractor Agreement from an Employment Agreement?**

1. **Common Law Test.** For many years, the IRS and the common law used a twenty point test to determine whether a relationship is properly characterized as an "employment" or "independent contractor" relationship.

2. **New Eleven Factor Test.** In 2006, in response to complaints that the twenty factor test was too difficult to interpret and apply, the IRS promulgated a new eleven factor test that consolidates the original twenty factors and organizes the factors into three groups: behavioral control; financial control; and the relationship between the parties. The elements of the eleven point test are set forth on **Attachment 2-A**.

   a. **Behavioral Control.** Behavioral control factors test whether the business has the right to direct and control how the worker performs the task for which the worker was hired, usually through instruction and training.

   b. **Financial Control.** Financial control factors test whether the business has a right to control the business aspects related to tasks performed by the worker. The factors consider whether the worker has unreimbursed business expenses, the extent of the worker's investment, the extent to which the worker provides services to others, how the business compensates the worker, and whether the worker can realize a gain or loss.

   c. **Relationship Between the Parties.** Factors regarding the relationship between the parties include whether there is a written contract that describes the intentions of the parties, whether the business provides benefits to the worker, whether the relationship is intended to be permanent, and the extent to which the worker's services are a key element of the company's business.

3. **Duties of Loyalty and Confidentiality.** The duty of loyalty arises in employment relationships by law. Therefore, such duties must be expressly addressed in an independent contractor relationship.

4. **Tax Law Issues.** Characterization of the relationship has a direct impact on tax collection. It is easier for the IRS to collect taxes from an employer, which directly pays Social Security and Medicare taxes and is subject to income tax withholding oversight. An independent contractor must file quarterly "estimated tax" returns and pay self-employment tax. An employee gets a W-2 with taxes removed. An independent contractor gets a 1099 with no tax withholding.

B. **What Terms and Conditions are in Independent Contractor Agreements That are Not in Employment Agreements?** Most terms and conditions are the same. However, duties of loyalty and confidentiality need to be specifically addressed because they arise automatically under a *bona fide* employment relationship but must be specifically contracted in an independent contractor relationship. Also, intellectual property laws need to be addressed. Like employment agreements, patent rights need to be assigned. Copyright ownership in works created by the independent contractor must be transferred because the "works made for hire" doctrine does not apply.

ATTACHMENT 2-A

INTERNAL REVENUE SERVICE EMPLOYMENT TEST

1. Compliance with instructions—independent contractors cannot be told when, where, or how to do the job.

2. Training—independent contractors do not go through any type of instructional training period with a more experienced employee to learn how to do the job. Independent contractors specialize in the field in which you have employed them and do not need to be trained.

3. Payment of business or travel expense—an independent contractor is generally responsible for his/her own business or travel expense. If paid by an employer, the employer must include in the independent contractor's 1099, unless the assets are verifiable under the accountable plan rules.

4. Investment in facilities—if the independent contractor maintains an office on the employer's premises, the independent contractor pays a rent or lease payment for the office space as well as overhead.

5. Worker's availability to the general public—an independent contractor makes services available to the public on a regular and consistent basis.

6. Payment by the hour, week, or month—an independent contractor is paid in a lump sum fee basis when the job is done.

7. Risk of profit or loss—independent contractors realize a profit or sustain a loss based on their success in performing the work or service.

8. Written contracts—describe the relationship the parties intend to create.

9. Benefits—an independent contractor is not provided with company benefits.

10. Permanency of the relationship—an independent contractor's relationship does not continue indefinitely with the company.

11. Key services—independent contractors do not provide services that are a key aspect of the company's regular business activity.

CHAPTER 3

FUNDAMENTALS OF BUSINESS ORGANIZATIONS

I. EVOLUTION OF BUSINESS ORGANIZATIONS

A.   **History of Business Organizations.** Since the dawn of commerce, business organizations have evolved. The first businesses were financed entirely by their owners. Now it is possible for businesses to be owned by the public. Consequently, as capitalization models evolved, the law of business organizations has evolved with it.

B.   **Choice of Entity.** Today businesses have a wide variety of organizational choices. Considerable thought is required to insure the right "choice of entity."

II. SOLE PROPRIETORSHIP

A.   **Origin of Business Enterprises.** At the dawn of the common law, the merchants and vendors were individual "sole proprietors," such as the village blacksmith or baker. Consequently, "sole proprietorship" is the oldest and simplest form of doing business. In a sole proprietorship, no organizational or other documents are required to commence and conduct business (with the exception of required permits, licenses, etc.). An individual simply holds himself or herself out to the public as being in business.

B.   **Disadvantages of a Sole Proprietorship.** There are two material disadvantages to a sole proprietorship. First, because the sole proprietorship's identity is the same as its owner's, it affords the owner no protection against personal liability. If the customer has a claim against the business, it is the same as having a claim against the individual person, and all of the individual person's assets can be taken if a court enters a judgment arising from operation of the business. In a litigious society, it is virtually never advisable to do business as a sole proprietor because it puts all of the sole proprietor's individual assets at risk. While engaging in a hobby-like business might be suitable for a sole proprietor, if there is any risk of litigation, such as providing professional medical services, a sole proprietorship is not a viable choice of organization. Second, a sole proprietorship can be capitalized only by the individual sole proprietor.

C.　**Tax Reporting.** The sole proprietor reports the activities of the business on his or her individual tax return. Under the Tax Cuts and Jobs Act of 2017, sole proprietorships are eligible to receive a 20% deduction on taxable income up to certain income limits, which could stimulate "cottage industry" growth.

III. GENERAL PARTNERSHIPS

A.　**Common Law Definition.** A general partnership is formed when two or more persons associate themselves to carry on, as co-owners, a business "for profit". The partnership, therefore, is the second oldest form of doing business and the oldest form of "business organization."

B.　**Who Can Form a Partnership?** A general partnership can be formed by individuals, corporations, estates, trusts, or any combination thereof.

C.　**How Is a Partnership Formed?** No written documents are required to form a general partnership and, at times, courts have found that a general partnership exists even when the parties did not expressly intend to form one. However, general partnerships are usually governed by either an oral or written partnership agreement, but, since oral agreements are difficult to prove, it is always advisable to enter into a written partnership agreement.

D.　**What Terms Are in a Typical Partnership Agreement?**

　　1.　**Purpose.** The purpose is usually clearly stated.

　　2.　**Capital.** The amount of initial capital requirements and how additional capital will be raised.

　　3.　**Distributions.** The manner and method of distributing profits and losses, including the percentage interests held by each partner, should be described.

　　4.　**Governance.** How the partnership will be managed and any limitations on the general rule that any partner can bind the partnership should be described. In general, each partner has an equal vote unless the partnership agreement provides otherwise.

　　5.　**Limitations on Transfer of Partnership Interest.** In general, partnership interests are not conveyable assets. Permitted transfers are specifically described.

6. **Dissolution.** Provisions regarding dissolution and winding up of the partnership's affairs are advisable. Under the common law and partnership laws in most states, a partnership dissolves if one partner dissociates from the partnership unless the partnership agreement provides otherwise. Consequently, a written partnership agreement can, and typically does, provide otherwise.

7. **Confidentiality Agreements and Restrictive Covenants.** These provisions may be included in the partnership agreement to protect the core value of the enterprise. Just like restrictive covenants in employment agreements, to be enforceable, restrictive covenants in partnership agreements must be reasonable as to time, territory, and activity restrained. However, the rules governing enforceability of a restrictive covenant regarding a business ownership interest are more relaxed than the rules governing enforcement of restrictive covenants in employment agreements.

E.   What Are the Advantages of a Partnership?

1. **"Pass Through" for Taxation.** The greatest advantage of a partnership is that it allows for "flow through" taxation of gains and losses. Flow through taxation means that there is no tax payable at the entity level, only at the partner level. Also, entities taxed as partnerships provide great flexibility with respect to allocation and distribution of profits and losses. Like a sole proprietorship, a partnership also qualifies for a 20% deduction on taxable income under the Tax Cuts and Jobs Act of 2017.

2. **Simplicity.** Another advantage of a general partnership is that it is simpler and less costly to organize and operate than other forms of business entities. Specifically, a general partnership is purely a creation of private parties and is not created by registering the entity with a state's Secretary of State like other forms of business organizations.

F.   What Are the Disadvantages of a Partnership?

1. **General Liability.** The main disadvantage of a general partnership is that each partner is personally liable for both the debts of the general partnership and the acts of other partners acting as agents of the general partnership. Consequently, in a litigious society, doing business as a general partnership is rarely (if ever) recommended because it puts the partners' personal assets at risk like a sole proprietorship. In fact, any business that actively engages in commerce should not be organized as a general partnership. For example, if a medical device company is organized as a general partnership, and the organization is sued on the grounds that the product is defective, each general partner is exposed to joint and several

liability for any costs and damages arising from the litigation. In other words, a plaintiff can recover all of the damages from one general partner if, for example, one partner has attachable assets and one partner does not.

2. **Transferring and Valuing Partnership Interests.** Other disadvantages of the general partnership form are that transferring partnership interests requires more legal and tax analysis than transferring corporate stock or limited liability company membership interests.

3. **Raising Capital.** If an entity needs equity capital, a general partnership is not a suitable organizational form. No sophisticated investor (whether an individual or an institutional investor) will invest funds in an enterprise that exposes their wealth and assets to unlimited personal liability.

IV. CORPORATIONS

A. **Brief History of Corporations.**

1. **Historic Distrust.** As the common law developed and commerce grew, a need arose for an organizational form that protects the owners from individual liability. However, there was a distrust regarding the creation of non-corporeal "persons" and a fear that wealth and power could be misused.

2. **Creation by Statute.** Therefore, the first corporations could be created only by an act of the king or queen or, in the United States, by state legislation. This method of incorporation was followed by all of the states in the United States through the nineteenth century.

3. **Why Do We Hear So Much About Delaware Corporations?** In the early twentieth century, the small and relatively insignificant State of Delaware saw an opportunity to create a liberal corporations code to attract organization of corporations which could then be taxed based on the number of shares of stock the corporation was authorized to issue. This was very attractive to corporate management. Therefore, many of the oldest and largest corporations are Delaware corporations.

4. **The Race to the Bottom.** The liberal Delaware corporation law touched off the "race to the bottom" as the other states tried to create more liberal corporation codes and make it easier to incorporate. Today, it is very easy to incorporate in almost any state, but Delaware law continues to be the most influential body of business law. Delaware corporation law is regarded to be the most "liberal" because it is perceived to provide the greatest protection of management and management decisions.

5. **Model Business Corporations Act.** The corporations code in most states is based on a uniform act known as the Model Business Corporations Act, but this Act is largely ignored in Delaware as well as California and New York.

B. **What Are the Essential Elements of a Corporation?**

1. **Articles of Incorporation.** A corporation is formed by filing Articles of Incorporation with a state's Secretary of State. Although Articles of Incorporation were formerly required to contain many specific provisions, little information is now required. For example, many states formerly required the Articles to set forth both a specific purpose and a minimum amount of equity capitalization (to protect the public against "thinly capitalized" companies). Now, states rarely require either. The Articles describe the amount and classes of authorized shares of stock. Amendments require the filing of a new document with the Secretary of State. Copies of a corporation's Articles of Incorporation are publicly available.

2. **By-Laws.** The by-laws set forth the general terms and conditions of corporate governance and can usually be revised by resolution of the Board of Directors. In contrast to Articles of Incorporation, by-laws are not recorded with the Secretary of State.

3. **Shares of Stock.** The corporation issues shares of stock to its shareholders. There may be more than one class of shares (for example, common stock and preferred stock), and a class of stock may have different characteristics (such as voting and non-voting common stock).

4. **Governance Structure.** In a corporation, ownership and management are separated. Shareholders elect directors, which have the power to direct the actions of the corporation. Directors in turn elect officers, and the officers manage the day to day affairs of the corporation. In general, the primary duty of the officers is to maximize shareholder wealth. In a closely held corporation, all roles may be filled by the same persons, but a closely held corporation still needs to follow corporate formalities to maintain "corporate integrity" and prevent a "piercing of the corporate veil," which makes individual corporate officers, directors, and shareholders personally liable for corporate obligations.

5. **Shareholders' Agreements.** Shareholders' Agreements generally place restrictions on the transfer of shares and corporate governance and are recommended for closely held corporations with multiple shareholders. Like partnership agreements, Shareholders' Agreements can also include restrictive covenants intended to protect and preserve the corporation.

C. **Who Can Form a Corporation?** Corporations can be formed and owned by either individuals or other corporations, but, as described below, ownership structures are influenced by tax considerations.

All corporations are formed in the same way with the Secretary of State, regardless of their tax status. Once formed, a corporation can elect to be taxed under several different chapters of the Internal Revenue Code, the most common of which are subchapter "C" and subchapter "S." These designations merely signify how a corporation is taxed, not how it is organized under state law.

D.   **C Corporation.** The C corporation is the traditional form of taxable entity for large, public businesses. The term "C corporation" refers only to how a corporation is taxed, not how it is organized under state law.

1.   **What Are the Advantages of a C Corporation?** The C corporation offers several advantages, including limited liability for the owners (shareholders), few limitations on the number and type of shareholders allowed, permissive transfer of ownership interests, and easy access to capital in both the public and private markets. Both individuals and any kind of business organization (such as a corporation, limited partnership, trust, or limited liability company) can own shares of stock in a company that is taxed as a C corporation. The C corporation is also the most established and recognized form of business entity and thus enjoys a wealth of case law interpreting the intricacies of corporate transactions, governance, and operations.

2.   **What Are the Disadvantages of a C Corporation?** The major drawback of the C corporation is double taxation. First, the C corporation pays corporate tax on its profits. Second, shareholders are taxed when they receive distributions such as cash dividends. While a smaller corporation may be able to practically eliminate double taxation by paying out profits as reasonable salaries, Social Security, Medicare, Obamacare, and other taxes must be paid on such salaries, again reducing after-tax return of C corporation shareholders. Third, in order to ensure that the shareholders are insulated from personal liability, corporate formalities should be followed, such as keeping current records of all corporate action taken and having regular meetings of shareholders and directors. Last, because corporations are managed by a Board of Directors elected by the shareholders and officers elected by the Board of Directors, shareholders have no direct authority to manage the affairs of the corporation.

E.   **S Corporation.** Again, the term "S corporation" refers to how a corporation is taxed, not how it is organized under state law. Consequently, much of the above analysis with respect to C corporations also applies to S corporations. There are, however, important differences.

1.   **What Are the Advantages of an S Corporation?** The "S" in S corporation means that the shareholders have unanimously elected to have the corporation taxed under Subchapter S of the Internal Revenue Code. This election allows the S corporation shareholders to receive pass-through taxation of profits and losses without taxation of the corporation itself. At the same time, the shareholders of an S corporation enjoy the limited liability of a C

corporation. Also, some tax deduction benefits are provided to S corporation shareholders under the Tax Cuts and Jobs Act of 2017, but the S corporation tax deduction is less than the potentially 20% tax deduction for limited liability companies that are taxed as partnerships. Since there are few material differences between limited liability companies taxed as partnerships and S corporations, availability of the tax deduction may cause formation of more limited liability companies.

2. **What Are the Disadvantages of an S Corporation?** An S corporation can have no more than 100 shareholders, no foreign investors, and no more than one class of stock (although voting rights may differ within the class), and shareholders are restricted to individuals, their estates, and certain trusts. In other words, if a corporation's shares of stock are owned by another business organization such as another corporation or limited liability company, the corporation cannot qualify for "S" tax status. Also, the 100 shareholder and no foreign owner limitations prohibit an S corporation from being a publicly traded company.

F. **"Not "for Profit" Corporations.** "Not for profit" or "non-profit" corporations make profits, but the profits are retained by the corporation and not distributed to equity owners. Consequently, all "not for profit" corporations are classified as "C corporations" for tax purposes but may be exempt from taxation as described below. This organizational form is appropriate when there is no expectation that the corporation will have profits or when there is no expectation of distribution of proceeds to individuals from the corporation's profits. In other words, all of the corporation's profits are retained by the corporation and taxed to the corporation at that level.

1. **Governance Models.** The Board of Directors has the power to direct the actions of a "not for profit" corporation, and, like "for profit" corporations, the Board of Directors appoints officers to manage the day to day affairs of the "not for profit" corporation. There are two different "not for profit" corporation governance models for election or appointment of a Board of Directors:

a. **Member Model.** The "not for profit" corporation has "members" who, like shareholders, elect directors, and the directors elect officers. The "not for profit" corporation may create several "membership" classes that have different voting or governance rights.

b. **Self-Nominating Board Model.** The by-laws provide for a nominating committee, usually consisting of current directors, which nominates a slate of directors to be voted on by the existing Board of Directors.

2. **Importance of the Articles and By-Laws.** Unlike "for profit" corporations, which typically have standard Articles of Incorporation and by-laws, "non-profit" Articles of Incorporation

and by-laws are highly customized because the terms and conditions typically described in a "for profit" corporation shareholders' agreement are described in a "non-profit" corporation's by-laws (because, obviously, a "not for profit" corporation has no shareholders).

3.   **Tax Exempt Status.** "Non-profit" corporations are created under state law, and profits of "non-profit" corporations are taxable under state and federal tax laws unless the corporation receives "tax exempt" status under the federal Internal Revenue Code. Tax exempt status is generally available only to entities that qualify under the Internal Revenue Code as "charitable" organizations (which can accept charitable contributions) or social or trade organizations (which cannot accept charitable contributions). Only "not for profit" corporations (or other entities that are organized as being "not for profit") can apply for tax exempt status. To obtain tax exempt status, a "non-profit" corporation must submit IRS Form 1023 and receive a determination letter from the federal Internal Revenue Service that confirms the entity's charitable purpose. Without this, a "non-profit" corporation's profits are taxable to and become earnings of the entity.

4.   **Advantages of "Not for Profit" Corporations.** When an organization is not organized for purposes of making a profit and distributing earnings, the "not for profit" corporation is a suitable organizational form. For example, a "not for profit" corporation is suitable for a trade association that has numerous members in the same industry. A "not for profit" corporation may be a suitable organizational structure for any entity that exists more to promote its members or participants than to promote the business of the corporation itself. Also, as stated above, it is also the only kind of corporation that can apply for tax exempt status.

5.   **Disadvantages of "Not for Profit" Corporations.** The obvious disadvantage is that all "not for profit" corporation profits are retained by the "not for profit" corporation and taxed at C corporation levels (unless the Internal Revenue Service provides tax-exempt status) and cannot be distributed to the corporation's members or participants.

G.   **Professional Corporations.** Although the "race to the bottom" in the late 19th and early 20th centuries took hold early for general business corporations, the states continued to distrust the practice of the "learned professions" through corporations. For example, dating back to the nineteenth century, most states had laws prohibiting the "corporate practice of medicine," which developed in the 19th century and early 20th century in response to the increasing provision of medical care by corporations and the resulting encroachment upon the traditional private physician based practice of medicine. The same rules generally applied to all of the "learned professions," such as medicine, law, accounting, and architecture. However, in the early 1970s, most states began enacting "professional corporations" codes, which allow "learned professionals" to practice in a corporate form. Therefore, in most states, while a profession like the practice of law or medicine cannot be organized as a general corporation, it can be organized as a professional corporation subject to restrictions and limitations that are not imposed on general corporations.

1. **Ownership and Governance Limitations.** Typically, shares of stock in a professional corporation (PC) can be owned only by professionals who are active in the practice; once a professional stops actively practicing the profession, the professional's shares of stock must be redeemed by the corporation or sold to other actively practicing professionals. Also, the President must be an actively practicing professional. However, there are typically no restrictions on who may serve as a director of the professional corporation.

2. **Restrictions on Limited Liability.** Typically, a professional who practices under a professional corporation is still individually responsible for his or her professional services. Therefore, the PC does not provide its shareholders with the same broad limitation on liability as a standard business corporation.

3. **Evolution of Professional Corporations Codes.** Some states, such as Arizona, have revised their professional corporations codes to permit investment interests in a professional corporation by non-professionals, recognizing that the old restrictions may prevent a professional enterprise from raising the capital necessary to compete in a changing economy.

4. **Taxation of Professional Corporations.** Like all business corporations, a professional corporation can be taxed as either a C corporation or an S corporation.

V. LIMITED LIABILITY COMPANIES

A. **Limited Liability Company Acts.** The limited liability company (LLC) is a relatively new form of entity that has quickly gained popularity because of its flexibility. LLCs are organized under state Limited Liability Company Acts. The first LLC statute was enacted in the late 1970s, but many states did not enact LLC statutes until the early 1990s. Today, most closely held ventures are organized as LLCs rather than corporations.

B. **Who Can Form an LLC?** Any person or entity can be a member of an LLC. This instantly makes an LLC more flexible than an S corporation because an organized entity such as a corporation, partnership, or another LLC can acquire an ownership interest in an entity that has the tax pass through benefits of an S corporation plus limited liability for the investors. It is also possible to have a single member LLC.

C. **How Is an LLC Formed?** An LLC is formed by filing Articles of Organization with a state's Secretary of State. While Articles of Organization can include specific and detailed provisions regarding governance and operations of an LLC, most Limited Liability Company Acts also permit LLCs to file "bare bones" Articles of Organization that describe no more than the name, principal place of business, and registered agent for service of process, leaving all details regarding governance and operation of the LLC to its "Operating Agreement" described below. Filing bare bones Articles of Organization is usually preferable because amendments to the Articles of Organization require filing a public document with the state's Secretary of State while amendments to the Operating Agreement are subject only to amendments to the private contract.

D.   **How Is an LLC Owned?** The equity owners of an LLC are called "members." This is a somewhat awkward term because, in common parlance, "membership" connotes a voluntary act, such as being a "member" of a country club or church congregation. However, when used by an LLC, its meaning is analogous to "shareholder." "Membership interests" can have almost any desired characteristic without affecting the tax status of the LLC. For example, membership interests may be voting or non-voting for governance purposes or may be merely a "profits interest" that provides an interest in profit distribution but not as "participating" in a liquidation event such as a sale of the LLCs assets or all membership interests.

E.   **How Is an LLC Governed?** Unlike a corporation, whose governance structure is dictated by the applicable corporations code, an LLC can be governed in almost any way that it wants. For example, an LLC can be either "member managed" or "manager managed;" can be managed by a "Board of Directors" or "Board of Managers" like a corporation; or managed by a single "managing member." This list is not exhaustive; there are as many governance variations as imagination permits.

F.   **How Is an LLC Operated?** The heart and soul of an LLC is its Operating Agreement (in some states, such as Delaware and Texas, called the "Company Agreement"), which looks substantially similar to a partnership agreement and includes terms and conditions such as the following: qualification for purchase of a membership interest; governance; transferability of membership interests; events of disassociation; and restrictive covenants. Also, most LLC statutes permit an LLC to have an oral Operating Agreement. However, if the members do not enter into a written Operating Agreement, important aspects of the LLC are governed by the default provisions in the LLC code. For example, some written Operating Agreements require either unanimous or super-majority approval of some acts such as a sale of all or substantially all of an LLC's assets, but LLC codes typically provide that all actions of the members can be taken by majority vote of the members unless the Operating Agreement provides otherwise.

G.   **How Is an LLC Taxed?** There are several ways that an LLC can be taxed. In general, most LLCs are taxed like partnerships as "pass through" entities. To isolate operating risk, corporations or LLCs frequently form separate LLCs in which the parent organization is the sole "member." A single member LLC is a "disregarded entity" for tax purposes, so its finances are consolidated with the parent person or entity for taxation. The LLC is also a hybrid entity that can, if it so desires, elect to be taxed like either a C corporation or an S corporation. Last, an LLC that is taxed as a partnership qualifies for the 20% tax deduction under the Tax Cuts and Jobs Act of 2017 described above for sole proprietorships and general partnerships. Consequently, organization of an LLC requires consultation with a qualified tax advisor.

H. **What Are the Advantages of a Limited Liability Company?** Advantages include the following: an LLC can be organized for virtually any purpose; an LLC offers investors limited liability and flow through taxation without limited partnership management restrictions described below, S corporation ownership restrictions, and the corporate formalities typically required of S and C corporations; and an LLC provides investors the opportunity to customize a business entity through a detailed Operating Agreement that meets their individual needs without many of the constraints imposed by the previously discussed business entities. In particular, an LLC permits entities like corporations and other LLCs to have tax pass-through advantages that they cannot have in a corporation because S corporation status can be given only to corporations that have only individual members.

I. **What Are the Disadvantages of a Limited Liability Company?**

1. **Lack of Legal Precedent.** One disadvantage of the LLC is the lack of precedent interpreting the rules that govern the entity. Because the LLC can be crafted to meet individual needs, there is no typical LLC. This has caused courts to struggle when applying traditional business concepts, like fiduciary duties, power of a member to bind the entity, and choice of law, to LLCs.

2. **Inability to "Go Public".** An additional concern for companies in need of capital is that the LLC is not the form of business entity principally used when seeking private equity or venture capital or in public securities offerings. Even though it is theoretically possible to engage in a public offering of LLC membership interests, there are practical difficulties associated with it, and the general corporation form is highly preferred. This can limit the ability of the company to raise capital and create adverse tax consequences if a switch to the corporate form is made without adequate planning.

J. **Use of LLC for Professional Services Company.** Most state LLC laws provide that the LLC organizational form can be used for any profession covered by the state's professional corporations code. In many states, the LLC law does not include any further specific provisions regarding "professional LLCs," so it appears that a profession such as the practice of law or medicine can organize as an LLC without the PC restrictions on active professional ownership. In some states, this is implied. In others, this is openly acknowledged. Some states, however, have enacted professional limited liability company or PLLC statutes, and these laws include many of the same ownership and governance restrictions as professional corporation codes. Specifically, membership interests in most PLLCs can be owned only by licensed professionals who are active in the practice, which limits equity capital sources and makes a PLLC suitable only for the professional services practice and not for any other business venture.

VI. LIMITED PARTNERSHIPS

A.   **Uniform Limited Partnership Act.** A limited partnership (LP) is an organizational form that provides limited liability to some of its partners, thereby reducing the investment risk of those "limited" (as opposed to "general") partners. In the evolution of business organizations, the LP form is quite old. The original Uniform Limited Partnership Act ("ULPA") was published in 1916, and it was replaced by the Revised Uniform Limited Partnership Act ("RULPA") in 1976. When it first came into effect, it was the only alternative to either a general partnership or a corporation. ULPA and RULPA have been legislatively tweaked in many states.

B.   **How Is a Limited Partnership Organized?** An LP is composed of at least one general partner (usually a corporation) who has unlimited liability for the debts and obligations of the LP and at least one limited partner who enjoys limited liability for partnership debts. The limited partner's risk is limited to the amount of the investment. If the LP fails, the limited partner loses his or her investment money, but the limited partner is not exposed to any other risk related to operation of the LP. While unlimited liability for the general partner can seem daunting to an individual, a corporation can be used as a general partner, resulting in limited liability to its individual shareholders.

C.   **What Are the Advantages of a Limited Partnership?**

   1.   **"Pass Through Entity".** Like other partnerships, LPs enjoy flow through taxation from the limited partnership to the partners.

   2.   **Limited Liability.** The limited partners enjoy limited liability but the general partner does not. Only the limited partner's equity investment is at risk. However, in most states, in exchange for limited liability, limited partners cannot participate in the management of the business.

   3.   **Suitability.** An LP is a suitable organizational form when a general partner with business expertise seeks investment from strategic investors to promote a business concept. For example, many of the early ambulatory surgery center syndications were formed with a corporate general partner and physician limited partners who provided services at the ASC. Also, private equity funds are typically organized as limited partnerships: a corporate general partner with investment expertise raises funds through capital contributions by individual investors. The private equity fund has a duty to maximize the wealth of its investors, but the investors are not involved in the private equity fund's investment decisions.

D.   What Are the Disadvantages of a Limited Partnership?

1.   Reliance on the General Partner. A general partner is permitted to withdraw from the limited partnership at any time. This can leave a limited partner who relied upon the general partner to manage the LP in a precarious situation. The withdrawal of a general partner can also result in dissolution of the LP, which can result in loss of important contracts, strained financial resources, and general uncertainty during critical times. Conversely, it is frequently difficult to remove a general partner who is not meeting performance expectations.

2.   Taxation Limitations. While general partners may enjoy the benefits of "flow through" taxation, "passive activity" and "at risk" restrictions in the Internal Revenue Code may prevent limited partners from deducting certain losses passed through to them from the LP.

3.   Limited Management Involvement. As stated above, in most states, limited partners are prohibited from participating in management of the LP: management is controlled entirely by the general partner.

VII. LIMITED LIABILITY PARTNERSHIPS

A.   Use of Limited Liability Partnerships. The limited liability partnership (LLP) is the newest form of entity and, while rarely used, is most often used by professional entities like medical practices or law firms in which all partners actively participate in the management of the firm. In essence, a partnership that would otherwise be treated as a general partnership can acquire limited liability for its partners by merely filing a document declaring that it is a "limited liability partnership," usually in a state court.

B.   What Are the Advantages of a Limited Liability Partnership? An LLP combines the tax advantages of a general partnership with the limited liability of a corporation or limited liability company (LLC). In essence, an LLP allows partners to escape the control restrictions of a limited partnership, the ownership restrictions of an S corporation, and the double taxation of a C corporation and is virtually identical to a limited liability company. Because an LLP is virtually the same as an LLC that elects partnership taxation and organization of an LLC is a more formal process, an LLP is rarely used.

C.   What Are the Disadvantages of a Limited Liability Partnership? Whether the partners truly have limited liability can differ depending on the basis of the claim and the state in which the claim arises. In addition, states vary on whether a partner is personally liable for the contractual debts of the LLP. There is virtually no market for the purchase and sale of partnership interests, and, while perhaps suitable for a professional services organization, an LLP is generally not advisable for a commercial enterprise.

VIII. HOW ARE BUSINESS ORGANIZATIONS USED IN ASSET PROTECTION STRATEGIES?

A. **What Is the General Rule for Asset Protection?** The general rule is that each revenue producing asset should be in a separate limited liability entity.

B. **What Can You Do to Protect Your Personal Assets from Professional Liability Claims?** Many physicians use Delaware Asset Protection Trusts or Family Limited Partnerships (or LLCs) to preserve and protect personal assets.

CHAPTER 4

FUNDAMENTALS OF EQUITY FINANCING

I. HOW ARE BUSINESS VENTURES CAPITALIZED?

A.   **How to Finance a Business.** All businesses need financing. There are a variety of financing options. The type of financing appropriate for the particular business will depend in large part upon the company's financial characteristics, such as whether the company has adequate cash flow to service a commercial loan or whether the cash generated by the business must be reinvested to build the business.

B.   **What Is a "Security"?** Capitalization of any venture except a "not for profit" enterprise involves the purchase and sale of "securities". The following are the common elements involved in defining what a "security" is: (1) the investment of money; (2) in a common enterprise; (3) with an expectation of profits; (4) to be earned through the efforts of others. As interpreted in the federal courts and most state courts, the test is intended to be broadly construed and to meet the economic realities of the investment and business world. As soon as there is an offering of a security, state and federal securities laws are implicated.

C.   **Regulation of the Purchase and Sale of Securities.** The federal government, primarily through the Securities Act of 1933 and the Securities Exchange Act of 1934, and all of the states separately regulate the purchase and sale of "securities." The federal laws are administrated by the United States Securities and Exchange Commission (the "SEC"). The state securities regulation laws, commonly referred to as the "Blue Sky Laws," are administered by securities regulators in each state. In other words, securities regulation is an area in which federal and state laws function in parallel: federal law does not preempt state law.

D.   **Securities Fraud.** Under federal Securities and Exchange Commission Rule 10b-5, securities fraud arises from the misrepresentation or concealment of a material fact in connection with the offering or sale of a security. Consequently, the securities rules apply as soon as there is an offering of a security, regardless of whether there is acceptance of the offer and a corresponding sale. Therefore, compliance with securities laws relies heavily on disclosure of all material facts and risk factors as soon as there is an offering of a security. This is frequently a challenge for entrepreneurs, who are inclined to characterize businesses in the most favorable manner possible without acknowledging weaknesses in the business plan.

E. **Equity.** Businesses raise equity capital by selling ownership interests in the venture, from which the investors expect a return on investment.

    1. **Organization of the Business Entity.** All businesses issue ownership interests when they are organized (for example, shares of stock in a corporation, membership interests in an LLC, or partnership interests in a partnership).

    2. **Adequacy of Initial Equity Capitalization.** Virtually no successful business, and especially businesses that have a significant growth strategy, can be completely capitalized with organizational equity contributions. Typically, there is a search for deeper pockets.

F. **Debt.** Equity capital is rarely adequate to entirely fund the enterprise's business plan. The venture will likely need to borrow funds with a promise to repay the debt at some rate of interest. Debt can also be used to leverage a business's profits. Debt is usually the only capital funding that a "not for profit" enterprise (like many health care delivery systems) can obtain.

G. **Hybrids of Debt and Equity.** Some forms of capital investment have features of both equity and debt, such as preferred stock and convertible debentures.

H. **Business Plan.** Regardless of whether a company obtains financing through debt or equity, the company will need a business plan designed to "sell" the company to its potential funding sources. The business plan should: describe the company, the product it makes or the services it provides, and the market for its products or services; present a compelling argument for investing in or lending to the company; demonstrate the potential for rapid growth in the business; provide projections of the future financial condition of the company and assumptions to explain how it anticipates achieving the targeted level of growth; assess the risks associated with the business; and explain how the financing will be used and how it will assist the company in meeting its projections. Projections of future financial condition based on historical financial statements that have been audited will enhance the credibility of the projections, but start-up enterprises rarely have audited financial statements. One key to any successful business plan is to determine how the goods or services will be distributed. While private equity and venture capital companies frequently say that a unique and scalable product or service and effective management are more important in making investment decisions than the business plan, every well-organized entrepreneurial enterprise needs a well prepared business plan.

II. WHAT ARE THE TYPICAL EQUITY CAPITAL SOURCES?

A. **Founders.** Typically, most business enterprises are initially capitalized by having the founders invest their own resources. As a general rule, the more capital invested by the founders, the more likely other sources of capital will invest in or loan funds to the company.

B. **Friends and Family.** The next likely source of investment capital is "friends and family." Warning: be sure to document the investment correctly if you expect to preserve your relationship and protect your company against claims in the future if the company prospers and grows.

C. **Crowdfunding.** A relatively new way to raise equity capital, "crowdfunding" means getting small amounts of capital from a large number of individuals, usually through Internet based networks and social media. Crowdfunding provides start-ups with an alternative to the traditional sources of equity capital. Entrepreneurs and early stage start-ups that are unable to undertake traditional methods of capital financing may choose to take advantage of using crowdfunding to reach an expansive group of investors through a seemingly user-friendly access point: the Internet. However, the extensive reporting requirements and regulatory restrictions, as well as the practical difficulties associated with having numerous minority investors, are likely to make crowdfunding an expensive and time-consuming exercise for both issuers and intermediary funding portals. Also, it is frequently advantageous for emerging companies to obtain equity capital from strategic investors who can help the enterprise implement its business plan, which is sometimes referred to as "smart money." Crowdfunding cannot be characterized as "smart money."

D. **Incubators.** In many places, either local government or academic institutions sponsor and promote "incubators" which may provide space for the business and consulting advice as well as access to capital for business start-ups.

E. **Private Placement of Securities to Outside Investors.** If the company is not sufficiently capitalized by the initial equity capital and commercial loans, the next step up the investment line is the private offering of securities (which are offerings made solely by the issuer). At this stage, there are three typical financing sources.

    1. **Angel Investors.** An "angel" investor is typically a high net worth individual who provides capital for early stage businesses or business concepts, usually in exchange for stock or equity ownership but sometimes for convertible debt. While statistics show that the average angel investment is around $500,000, the range may run from several thousand dollars to several

million dollars. Angel investors usually do not get involved in management of the venture. In some areas, angel investors have organized into networks and groups, and a business can make a presentation to several potential investors at one time at an angel network meeting.

2. **Private Equity Funds.** A private equity fund raises capital from a series of investors and then looks for investments to make that capital grow. Typically organized as limited partnerships, the funds are intended to exist for a limited period of time (typically ten years). If successful, the private equity company will raise new funds every three to five years. A typical private equity fund looks to put at least $10,000,000 to work in each target company either at the closing or within two years after the closing with the expectation that the capital will be used for substantial target company growth. Unlike angel investors, private equity funds are rarely interested in early stage or start-up businesses. While private equity funds are typically not involved in day to day management, the funds expect representation on the target company's Board of Directors. At this investment level, the private equity company will impose restrictions on the target company's ability to raise equity and debt capital from other sources. Generally, the private equity fund will be looking for a two critical characteristics: (a) a proven business concept that has generated actual revenue; and (b) a competent management team.

3. **Venture Capital.** A company that has several years of operating history and plans to increase in size in order to implement a growth and liquidation strategy or to go public may want to consider venture capital financing. Venture capital financiers generally invest larger amounts of money and require a greater percentage of the equity of the business for their investment, but may not want to have a 50% or more interest for tax and securities reporting reasons. In addition, venture capitalists usually insist on Board of Directors representation. Venture capitalists are experienced money managers who, as Board members, can also add valuable assistance in growing the company. In many ways, there are few material distinctions between private equity and venture capital investors.

F. **Public Offering of Securities.** The last source in the equity capital chain is the public offering of securities, after which the securities can be traded on a public exchange. Public capital is expensive, and it exposes the company to a wide array of securities regulation, including reporting requirements under the federal Securities Acts and responsibility requirements under Sarbanes-Oxley. The rules governing public offering of securities are beyond the scope of this work.

III. WHAT ARE THE FUNDAMENTALS OF EQUITY CAPITAL INVESTMENT?

A. **Partnerships and Limited Partnerships.**

1. **General Partnerships.** Ownership structures in general partnerships can be designed and implemented in almost any manner. However, as stated in Chapter 3, general partnerships

are rarely used and in fact are unsuitable for any commercial enterprise, especially an enterprise with a growth strategy.

2.   **Limited Partnerships.** Limited partnerships have passive limited partners and an active general partner but are funded almost entirely by monetary contributions of the limited partners. Typically, the general partner is a special purpose entity, usually a corporation, formed by the developer or promoter of an enterprise, that brings a core expertise or asset to the limited partnership as its contribution. As described in Chapter 3, the limited partnership interests give investors an interest in the profits of the enterprise but no governance rights.

B.   **Shares of Stock in a Corporation.** One very common investment interest is shares of stock in a corporation. In general there are two types of stock: common stock and preferred stock.

1.   **Common Stock.** Holders of common stock are pure equity holders and, as such, bear the greatest risk of loss. In a liquidation of the company, common stockholders will be paid only after debt and preferred equity is paid in full. On the other hand, if the business is successful, common stock will generally appreciate faster than the other types of investment securities.

    a.   **Return on Investment.** A stockholder receives a return on investment in two ways: (i) appreciation of the value of the stock as the company grows; and (ii) dividends. The appreciation of the value of the stock can only be realized upon a liquidity event (sale of the stock or the business), and the gain may be taxed at favorable capital gains rates if the stock is held for a year or more. Dividends are subject to double taxation (after tax profits of the corporation are distributed to the shareholders, and the shareholders pay tax at their individual tax rates). Growth company stock ownership focuses on stock value appreciation, not dividends.

    b.   **Voting and Non-Voting Common Stock.** The common stock shareholders have the power to elect the directors of the corporation. A corporation can also issue non-voting common stock for governance purposes. Any corporation that issues more than one class of stock with differing rights to distributions and liquidation proceeds cannot qualify for S corporation status, but shares of stock can have different voting rights without exposing the corporation to loss of "S" tax status.

    c.   **Tracking Stock.** Stock can be issued that "tracks" the performance of a separate division of a business enterprise.

2.   **Preferred Stock.** Holders of preferred stock receive dividend and liquidation priority over holders of common stock. There are three characteristics attributable to preferred stock: (a) cumulative, noncumulative, or partially cumulative dividend payment obligations; (b) convertible or nonconvertible, usually into shares of common stock; and (c) participating or nonparticipating in the proceeds of a sale of the company. This is the most utilized investment vehicle for private equity funds and venture capitalists.

C.   **Membership Interests in Limited Liability Companies.** Equity ownership interests in limited liability companies are called "membership interests," and the owners are called "members." This can be confusing because the common meaning of the word "member" does not connote "ownership." In other words, the term "member" when used in the context of limited liability companies is analogous to the term "shareholder" in the context of corporations. However, LLCs have substantially more flexibility in defining rights of membership interests as opposed to shares of stock in a corporation. As stated in Chapter 3, LLC membership interests can have any characteristics that the LLC desires. For example, some LLCs find it beneficial to issue "profits interests" in the LLC or a division of the LLC that require no capital contribution and have no rights upon liquidation of the enterprise to reward key management personnel.

D.   **Convertible Debentures.** A convertible debenture is a debt instrument that may be changed or converted into another form of security (often common stock but can be membership interests in a limited liability company) generally at the insistence of the investor. It is typically evidenced by a promissory note or bond and is generally unsecured, being backed simply by the full faith and credit of the company. Convertible debentures are very similar to preferred stock and are also commonly used for early stage and venture capital investment.

E.   **Warrants.** A warrant is a contractual right to purchase a certain number of shares of a particular class of stock or membership interests in a limited liability company at a stated price, known as the "strike price." Warrants are often issued in connection with debt financing as a means of inducing lenders to accept terms which would otherwise be unacceptable to such lenders. The "strike price" is usually higher than market value at the time of issuance and is an inducement to create a long term relationship. A warrant provides considerable upside to the holder if the company is successful. Accordingly, a company that issues warrants in connection with debt financing may be able to negotiate for lower financing costs up front, either on a loan with its commercial lender or on a debenture.

F.   **Options.** An option is a contract in which one party agrees to sell stock or membership interests in a limited liability company for a specified price at a specified time in the future. An option to buy is a "call;" an option to sell is a "put." A warrant is a type of option.

IV. WHAT RULES GOVERN PRIVATE PLACEMENT OF SECURITIES?

A. **What Laws Govern the Purchase and Sale of Securities?** The sale of securities is regulated by both federal and state law. Federal and state securities laws focus on three primary variables: (1) the security itself; (2) the persons selling the security; and (3) the disclosures made to investors about the security. In general terms, every sale of a security in the United States must either be registered with the Securities and Exchange Commission and the securities regulators of each state where investors reside or qualify for an exemption from such registration requirements.

B. **Exemptions From Registration.** Registration of the sale of a security with the SEC is an expensive and time-consuming process. Therefore, an exemption from registration is often critical, especially for start-up and emerging companies. Two of the most important exemptions from the registration requirements of the federal securities laws are the *private placement exemption* contained in Section 4(a)(2) of the Securities Act of 1933, as amended (the "Act"), and the safe harbor thereunder provided by SEC Rule 506 of Regulation D.

   1. **The 4(a)(2) Private Placement Exemption.** Section 4(a)(2) of the Act exempts from the registration requirements of the Act "transactions by an issuer not involving any public offering." This section usually is referred to as the "private placement exemption," but the statute does not define what constitutes a "non-public offering." The SEC and the courts have interpreted the exemption to be available for offerings involving sophisticated offerees and purchasers who have access to or are provided the same kind of information that a registered offering would provide and who are able to "fend for themselves" as knowledgeable investors, and when the offerings are conducted in a non-public manner. Section 4(a)(2) also provides that the sophistication level of both the offerees and the purchasers are important in determining the availability of the exemption.

   2. **Regulation D Offerings.** Because of the great uncertainty in determining when the private placement exemption was available under Section 4(a)(2), the SEC adopted Rule 506 of Regulation D, which provides a "safe harbor" under Section 4(a)(2). Section 4(a)(2) is sometimes used when an offering is made to a small number of sophisticated investors. However, most issuers attempt to employ the Rule 506 exemption and use the Section 4(a)(2) exemption as a back-up in the event one of the conditions of the Rule is not met.

   3. **Impact of the JOBS Act on Private Placement of Securities.** The Jumpstart Our Business Start-ups Act of 2012 (the "JOBS Act") included material changes to the law governing private placement of securities. The intended purpose of the JOBS Act is to stimulate job growth in small companies and "start-up" enterprises by relaxing regulatory burdens on raising

capital. The JOBS Act both (a) modified the rules governing private placements under Rule 506 and (b) created a new exemption from registrations for "crowdfunding" transactions.

C. What Are the Limitations on the Manner of a Rule 506 Offering? Prior to enactment of the JOBS Act, neither the issuer of the securities nor any person acting on its behalf could offer or sell the securities by any form of general solicitation or advertising, including any advertisement, article, press release, mass mailing, notice or other communication published in a newspaper, magazine, or similar media or broadcast over television or radio. The JOBS Act, however, included a radical departure from prior law regarding solicitation of investors in private placements that rely on the exemption from securities registration under Rule 506.

1. **Permissible General Solicitation Under Rule 506(c).** After the JOBS Act, issuers can elect to rely on Rule 506(c), which permits general solicitation and advertising of securities offering under certain circumstances. Under Rule 506(c), issuers are free to advertise securities offerings in any medium provided that the ultimate purchasers are "accredited investors", which requires issuers to take "reasonable steps" to verify that the purchasers are accredited investors. The intention of Rule 506(c) is to provide an issuer with access to a deeper pool of accredited investors. While Rule 506(c) offers a flexible approach to permit an issuer to ascertain whether an investor is "accredited," issuers will need to maintain adequate documentation of the verification process to carry the burden of proving that the issuer is entitled to the Rule 506(c) registration exemption. To receive the relaxed solicitation benefits, the issuer will need to indicate on Securities and Exchange Commission Form D that the offering is being made under Rule 506(c).

2. **What If the Issuer Does Not Elect to Proceed Under Rule 506(c)?** If the issuer does not select Rule 506(c), then the old non-solicitation rules apply. In practice, Rule 506(c) and the broader solicitation rights are rarely used. Most offerings continue to rely on the old Rule 506. To maintain the Rule 506 registration exemption when Rule 506(c) does not apply, the issuer must control the number and kind of offerees to be able to show that no general solicitation occurred. Practical steps include a determination that (a) the prospective investor is an "accredited investor," or otherwise meets the standards established by the issuer and (b) investment in the securities would be suitable investment for the prospective investor. Ideally, each prospective investor should have a pre-existing relationship with the issuer and its officers, directors, or affiliates of sufficient contact to determine suitability.

D. How Many Offerees and Purchasers May There Be? Rule 506 places no limitation on the number of persons to which the issuer may offer the securities. However, offers to a significant number of persons may be deemed a prohibited general solicitation. Rule 506 does restrict the number of purchasers. The issuer must reasonably believe that no more than 35 "sophisticated" investors (as discussed in more detail below), plus a theoretically unlimited number of "accredited investors," become purchasers. However, some transactions are structured for sale only to accredited investors because certain additional protections from potential liability are obtained thereby and requirements with respect to the information that must be provided to investors are more flexible.

E.   **Who Is an "Accredited Investor"?** "Accredited investor" means any person who comes within any of the following categories or who the issuer reasonably believes comes within any of the following categories at the time of the sale of the securities to that person:

1.   **Certain Institutional Investors.** Generally applies to banks, registered investment companies, broker-dealers, insurance companies, and other financial institutions.

2.   **Tax Exempt Organization With Total Assets in Excess of $5,000,000.** Any organization described in Section 501(c)(3) of the Internal Revenue Code (dealing with tax-exempt organizations), any corporation, Massachusetts or similar business trust, or partnership not formed for the specific purpose of acquiring the securities offered, with total assets in excess of $5,000,000. Any corporation, whether publicly or privately held, will be accredited under this section if it has total assets (not net worth) in excess of $5,000,000.

3.   **Directors, Executive Officers, and General Partners.** Any director, executive officer, or general partner of the issuer of the securities being offered or sold, or any director, executive officer, or general partner of a general partner of that issuer (if the issuer is a limited partnership).

4.   **High Net Worth Individuals.** Any natural person whose individual net worth or joint net worth with that person's spouse, at the time of purchase, exceeds $2,000,000, or has assets under management in the amount of $1,000,000 or more, excluding the value of the person's primary residence. Also, any amount of indebtedness secured by the primary residence that is in excess of the residence's value is to be considered a liability and deducted from the investor's net worth accordingly. Net worth of a spouse may be included even when the property is held solely by that spouse. Partnerships, corporations, or other entities may not take advantage of this category.

5.   **Income Test.** Any natural person who had an individual income in excess of $200,000 in each of the two most recent years or joint income with that person's spouse in excess of $300,000 in each of those years and who reasonably expects at least the same income level in the year of purchase.

6.   **Certain Trusts.** Any trust with total assets in excess of $5,000,000 not formed for the specific purpose of acquiring the securities offered whose purchase is directed by a sophisticated person.

7.   **Entities Made Up of Accredited Investors.** Any entity in which all of the equity owners are accredited investors.

F.   **What Information Must Be Disclosed?** If the issuer is not relying on Rule 506(c) and securities are sold to non-accredited investors, certain specified information (similar to that contained in a registration statement) must be delivered to such purchasers, usually in the form of a Private Placement Memorandum (PPM). Offerings in which securities are sold exclusively to accredited investors allow significant flexibility in the form of offering documentation to be used in the offering. Theoretically, it is not necessary to provide a PPM if all of the investors are "accredited," but it is a "best practice."

1.   **Material Information.** State and federal securities laws require the issuer to provide the purchasers with full, fair, and complete disclosure of all "material" facts about the offering and the issuer, its management, business, operations, finances, and most importantly, the risks associated with the offering. Information is deemed "material" if a reasonable investor would consider the information important in making an investment decision. Omissions of material facts, even if inadvertent, can lead to liability for "securities fraud."

2.   **Ability to Ask Questions.** Last, all purchasers must be given the opportunity to ask questions and receive answers about the offering and to obtain information reasonably obtainable by the issuer to verify the information furnished.

G.   **What Sophistication Must the Purchasers Possess?** If the issuer is not relying on Rule 506(c) and the purchaser is not an accredited investor, the issuer must reasonably believe immediately prior to making any sale that each purchaser (except for accredited investors), either alone or with a purchaser representative, has such knowledge and experience in financial and business matters that the investor is capable of evaluating the merits and risks of the prospective investment.

H.   **How Does the Issuer Determine That a Prospective Purchaser That Is Not an Accredited Investor Is Capable of Evaluating the Merits and Risks of the Investment?** A commonly used approach is to require that the prospective investor complete a questionnaire that elicits responses concerning education, investment background, net worth, investment experience, and other matters. Only after review of the completed questionnaire and a determination that the person qualifies as being "sophisticated" is the person accepted as a purchaser.

I.   **What Limitations Are Imposed on Resale of the Securities?** Securities acquired in a transaction under Rule 506 must be acquired for investment purposes only and may not be resold for an indefinite period, which for persons not closely associated with the issuer is generally not less than two years. These securities will be deemed restricted and cannot be resold without registration under the Act or an exemption therefrom. The issuer must exercise reasonable care to assure that the purchasers of the securities do not intend to immediately redistribute the securities acquired. Such reasonable care includes, but is not limited to, an inquiry as to whether the purchaser is acquiring the securities for his or her own account; written disclosure to each purchaser prior to the sale that the securities have not been registered under the Act and therefore cannot be resold unless they are registered under the Act or unless an exemption is available; and the placement of a legend on any certificate or document that evidences the security stating that the security has not been registered under the Act and setting forth the restriction on transferability and sale of the securities.

J.   **What SEC Filings Are Necessary for a Regulation D Offering?** The issuer should file with the SEC five copies of a notice on Form D no later than 15 days after the first sale of securities in a Regulation D offering, although the failure to file the Form D on time may not affect the availability of the exemption.

K.   **What Is the "Crowdfunding" Exemption to Securities Registration?** The JOBS Act created a new exemption from securities registration for "crowdfunded" offerings under a new Section 4(6) to the Securities Act of 1933 and the SEC adopted final crowdfunding rules in 2015. The final rules provide that securities issued pursuant to the crowdfunding exemption are restricted securities that must be held for at least one year and are not be required to be registered with any state securities commission. The following are the criteria of the SEC's crowdfunding regulation:

1.   **Crowdfunding Issuer Requirements.** Issuers who intend to use the crowdfunding exemption must meet the following requirements:

a.   The issuer must be a United States company;

b.   The issuer must not be either a company that is required to submit reports to the Securities Exchange Act of 1934 or an investment company; and

c.   The issuer is limited to selling a maximum of $1,000,000 in crowdfunded securities in a twelve month period.

2.   **Crowdfunding Investor Requirements.** The following restrictions are imposed on the amount the issuer can raise from any individual investor.

a.   Investors with an annual income or net worth below $100,000 may only invest, in the aggregate, the greater of $2,000 or 5% of such investor's annual income or net worth; and

b.   Investors with both an annual income and net worth greater than $100,000 may only invest 10% of such investor's annual income or net worth, with a maximum aggregate investment through all crowdfunding offerings capped at $100,000.

3.   **Crowdfunding Information and Disclosure Requirements.** Crowdfunding issuers are registered to both file certain information with the Securities and Exchange Commission and provide the same information to potential investors and intermediaries or funding portals, the requirements for which are as follows:

a.   The initial filing with the SEC must contain basic information related to the issuer, including: the issuer's business; the officers, directors, and significant holders of the company's securities; financial information; and the size and scope of the offering.

b.   Offerings of $100,000 or less require financial statements certified by the company's principal financial officer; offerings of $100,000 to $500,000 require financial statements reviewed by an auditor when relying on the crowdfunding exemption for the first time (if audited financial statements are unavailable) and audited financial statements thereafter; and audited financial statements for offerings from $500,000 to $1,000,000.

c.   At least once per year, the issuer must file with the SEC and provide to investors financial statements and reports of results of operations as the SEC deems appropriate.

4.   **Restrictions on Crowdfunding Issuers.** Issuers are subject to the following restrictions.

a.   Issuers are prohibited from advertising the terms of the offering except for directing investors to the funding portal or broker that is managing the offering;

b.   Issuers may not compensate any third party promoter of the offering unless the compensation is disclosed to the investors; and

c.   Issuers may be subject to liability for misleading communications to investors as well as for misrepresentation or concealment of material facts under Rule 10b-5.

5.   **Intermediaries or Funding Portals.** Crowdfunding transactions can be funded only through a qualified broker or "funding portal" that is registered with the SEC. Under the JOBS Act, a "funding portal" is defined as any person acting as an intermediary in a transaction

involving the offer or sale of crowdfunded securities for the account of others. Intermediaries of crowdfunding transactions have significant responsibilities under the JOBS Act, including providing certain disclosures regarding the offering and undertaking actions both to prevent fraud and to ensure investor and issuer compliance. Funding portals are subject to the following requirements:

a. Funding portals may not offer investment advice or recommendations;

b. Funding portals are restricted from soliciting purchases, sales, or offers to buy the securities offered or displayed on its web site or portal;

c. Funding portals may not compensate employees, agents, or other persons based on the sole securities displayed or referenced on its web site or portal;

d. Funding portals may not hold, manage, possess, or otherwise handle investor funds or securities; and

e. Funding portals must otherwise comply with SEC regulatory requirements.

L. **What Are the State Securities Laws Considerations?** An exemption from federal registration pursuant to Rule 506 does not generally exempt offerings from the qualification requirements of state Blue Sky Laws. The Blue Sky Laws of every state where the securities are being offered must be reviewed to determine the effect and applicability of such laws on the transaction.

M. **Broker-Dealer Issues.**

1. **Registration of Broker-Dealers.** Persons or entities selling the issuer's securities, and particularly when a commission or compensation is received in connection therewith, may be required to register as "brokers," "dealers," or "agents" under federal or state securities laws. However, if the issuer is going to sell the stock without a broker-dealer, then the issuer and related individuals may fall within a federal exemption and avoid having to register as "brokers," "dealers," or "agents."

2. **Exemption from Broker-Dealer Registration for Directors and Officers.** Directors and officers of the issuer may qualify for an exemption from broker-dealer registration if they: (a) have not relied on the issuer exemption in the preceding twelve months; (b) are not subject to a "statutory disqualification;" (c) are not compensated (directly or indirectly) by paying commissions or other compensation based on sales of the securities; and (d) are not at the time of the sales of the securities an "associated person of a broker or dealer," nor

were they "a broker or dealer, or an associated person of the broker or dealer" within the prior 12 months, all as defined under applicable SEC rules.

V. HOW ARE PRIVATE EQUITY FUND AND VENTURE CAPITAL TRANSACTIONS NEGOTIATED?

A. **Overview of the Private Equity Venture Capital Industry.**

1. **General Description of Private Equity and Venture Capital Funding.** Private equity and venture capital is money provided by professionals who invest alongside management in growing companies that have the potential to develop into significant enterprises. Professionally managed private equity and venture capital firms generally are private partnerships or closely-held corporations funded by institutional investors, including private and public pension funds, endowment funds, foundations, corporations, wealthy individuals, foreign investors, and the venture capitalists themselves. It is difficult to distinguish between two sources in many ways, but the principal difference is that private equity funds are typically interested in transactions involving $10,000,000 to $100,000,000 and venture capital funds are generally interested in investing $100,000,000 or more. However, these are not hard rules.

2. **What Is the Typical Target Company?** Private equity funds and venture capitalists generally invest in companies that represent the opportunity for a high rate of return within two to seven years. An equity fund or venture capitalist may look at several hundred investment opportunities before investing in only a few selected companies. Typically, they are not passive investors. Equity funds and venture capitalists encourage growth in their portfolio companies through their involvement in management and strategic planning. The usual target has some unique, core asset or service that is frequently protected by intellectual property (patent, trade secret, copyright, or trademark).

3. **Investment Focus.** Equity funds and venture capitalists may be generalist or specialist investors depending on their investment strategy. While equity funds and venture capital firms may on occasion invest in companies that are in their initial start-up modes, they expect to invest in companies at various stages of the business life cycle. Some venture capitalists focus on later stage investing by providing financing to help a company grow to a critical mass to attract public financing through a stock offering. Alternatively, a venture capitalist may help a company attract a merger or acquisition with another company by providing liquidity and an exit for the company's founders.

4. **Types of Equity Fund and Venture Capital Firms.** The most common type of venture capital firm is an independent firm that has no affiliation with any other financial institution.

Equity fund and venture capital firms also may be affiliates or subsidiaries of a commercial bank, investment bank, or insurance company and may make investments on behalf of outside investors or the parent firm's clients. Still others may be subsidiaries of non-financial, industrial corporations making investments on behalf of the parent itself. These latter firms typically are referred to as "strategic investors" or "corporate venture investors."

B.   **Uniform Venture Capital and Private Equity Investment Documents.** To reduce legal fees and facilitate venture capital and private equity fund transactions, many funds require use of publicly available model documents developed for the National Venture Capital Association found at https://nvca.org/resources/model-legal-documents/ as a starting point. The forms are annotated with substantive footnotes that describe alternative terms and conditions, many of which are mutually exclusive, and include the following documents that are common to virtually every venture capital or private equity fund transaction:

- Term Sheet;

- Stock Purchase Agreement;

- Voting Agreement;

- Investor Rights Agreement;

- Right of First Refusal and Co-Sale Agreement;

- Indemnification Agreement; and

- Amended and Restated Certificate of Incorporation.

C.   **Guidelines and Checklists for Entrepreneurs.**

1.   **Evaluating Project Risks.** An entrepreneur should understand and be able to address the project's risks before approaching an equity fund or venture capitalist. These risks should be clearly articulated in the company's business plan. Equity funds and venture capitalists typically will review the following four risks of a project before investing in it. Thus, if a target company understands and addresses these risks up front, financial backing will be much easier to obtain.

    a.   **Market Risk.** What problem is this product solving? This helps equity funds and venture capitalists determine whether the product or technology addresses a significant problem in the marketplace, what the competitive alternatives are, and whether the market is large enough to yield a significant return on the investment.

b.   **Technology Risk.** Who owns the idea? Considering this risk requires investors to evaluate the proprietary aspects of the technology, including patent position and ownership; further development work needed to produce the first product or service; manufacturability; and the potential breadth of the protected technology's application.

c.   **Financial Risk.** How much money will it take? The investors will evaluate the amount of capital needed to achieve a sustainable market position, the potential sources of capital required by the project in addition to initial capital investments, and the possible investment withdrawals that may occur.

d.   **Management Risk.** Can the market opportunity be exploited? The investors will assess the strengths and weaknesses of the entrepreneur or founding management team, whether additional management is needed, whether effective working relationships can be established, and whether the commercial objectives and expectations of the entrepreneur and the venture capitalist match.

2.   **The Entrepreneur's Checklist.** The following is a checklist for approaching an equity fund or venture capitalist.

a.   **Type of Security.** Companies typically sell convertible preferred stock to investors, which provides a preference payment to the preferred stockholder if the company is acquired or otherwise liquidated and other preferences over the common stock held by the founders. These preferences help justify a much higher price for the preferred stock than the price paid by founders for the common stock.

b.   **Price/Valuation.** Investors use a number of different methods to determine a company's value and the price they will pay for their investment, from a discounted revenue stream approach based on business plan projections, to a more arbitrary figure based on a desire to own a predetermined percentage of the company in return for the anticipated level of funding needed to achieve a certain milestone.

c.   **Liquidation Preference.** Upon liquidation of the company, the preferred stock will receive a certain fixed amount before any assets are distributed to the common stock. A "participating preferred" stock will not only receive this fixed amount, but then also will participate in some manner with the common stock in further distributions.

d. **Dividend Preference.** Generally, a dividend must be paid to the preferred stockholder before any dividend is paid to the common stockholders. This dividend may be non-cumulative and discretionary, or it may be cumulative so that it accrues from year to year until paid in full.

e. **Redemption.** Preferred stock may be redeemable, either at the option of the company or the investors or mandatorily on a certain date, perhaps at some premium over the initial purchase price of the stock.

f. **Conversion Rights.** Preferred stock will be convertible into common stock at some conversion ratio, which is typically expressed as the initial purchase price of the preferred stock divided by a "conversion price" which initially equals the purchase price but is subject to adjustment upon the occurrence of certain events. Conversion is generally available at any time at the option of the stockholder and may be automatically triggered by certain occurrences, such as an initial public offering.

g. **Anti-Dilution Protection.** The conversion price of the preferred stock will be subject to adjustment for diluting events, such as stock splits or stock dividends, and will probably also be subject to "price protection," which is adjustment upon future sales of stock at prices below the conversion price. Price protection can take many forms, from an extreme "ratchet" protection which lowers the conversion price to the price at which any new stock is sold, regardless of the number of shares, to a broad-based "weighted average" protection which adjusts the conversion price based on a formula incorporating both the number of new shares being issued and their price. The issuance of a certain number of shares is generally excepted from this protection to cover anticipated issuances to key employees, consultants, and directors. Price protection is sometimes subject to a "pay-to-play" provision, which makes the continuation of such protection for a given investor contingent on that investor purchasing at least its pro-rata share of any future issuances priced below the conversion price.

h. **Voting Rights.** On general matters, preferred stock usually votes along with common stock and has a number of votes equal to the number of shares of common stock into which it is convertible. The preferred stock also typically has special voting rights, such as the right to elect one or more of the company's directors or to approve certain types of corporate actions, such as amendments of the articles of incorporation, mergers, or creation of a new series of preferred stock.

i. **Right of First Refusal.** Holders of preferred stock generally will have a right to participate, usually at up to an investor's current aggregate ownership percentage, in any future issuance of securities by the company.

j.   **Co-Sale Right.** Preferred investors often will require founders to enter into a co-sale agreement. A co-sale right provides some protection against founders selling their interest in the company to a third party by giving investors the right to sell a portion of their stock as part of any such sale.

k.   **Registration Rights.** Preferred investors generally will receive registration rights as a part of their investment. These rights provide liquidity to investors by allowing them to require the company to register their shares for sale to the public, either as part of an offering already contemplated by the company ("piggy-back rights") or in a separate offering initiated at the investors' request ("demand rights").

l.   **Vesting on Founders' Stock.** As a protection against founders leaving the company after the investment money is in, investors generally insist on some sort of "vesting" on founders' stock, so that a percentage of such stock, decreasing over time, is subject to repurchase by the company at cost if a founder terminates his or her employment.

CHAPTER 5

FUNDAMENTALS OF DEBT FINANCING

I. WHAT LAWS GOVERN DEBT FINANCING TRANSACTIONS?

A. **Debt Financing.** While the previous chapter describes the general role of debt financing in a capital plan, this chapter covers the specifics of debt financing. Virtually every commercial debt transaction includes the following documents: Loan Agreement; Promissory Note; Security Agreement; and Guaranty Agreement. Some forms of debt financing, such as bond financing, include additional agreements.

B. **Debt Financing is Governed by Both the State Law of Contracts and the Uniform Commercial Code.** Unlike contracts for the purchase and sale of "goods," which are governed entirely by Article 2 of the Uniform Commercial Code (UCC), debt financing transactions are governed by a combination of the general state law of contracts as well as Article 3 of the UCC, which governs "commercial paper," and Article 9 of the UCC, which governs "secured transactions."

C. **Medical Practice Debt Financing.** Because the only available source of equity financing for medical practices organized as either professional corporations or professional limited liability companies (and, in fact most medical practices) is the physicians who are active in the practice themselves, most medical practices are undercapitalized by equity capital funding and rely principally on debt financing. Consequently, many medical practices are highly leveraged.

II. WHAT ARE THE TYPES OF DEBT TRANSACTIONS?

A. **Term Loans.** A term loan is generally a longer term form of financing, typically three to five years, which is amortized over the term of the loan, often at a fixed interest rate.

1. **What Is the Purpose of a Term Loan?** Term loans generally provide capital asset financing for the borrower such as to purchase or develop real estate or to purchase equipment or other fixed assets, but also may be used to provide operating capital. As a fundamental part of an enterprise's capital plan, term loan debt can be used as "leverage" to enhance the value of the enterprise's stock or other ownership interests.

2. **What Is the Cost of a Term Loan?** Although term loans can have a variable interest rate, they typically have a fixed rate of interest that reflects the credit worthiness of the borrower and market rates. Sometimes the interest rate is based on an objective rate such as the bank's "prime rate" (the rate available to the bank's best customers) or the Intercontinental Exchange London Interbank Offered Rate, commonly referred to as "LIBOR."

3. **How Is a Term Loan Secured?** Term loans are generally senior loans secured by real estate, equipment, or other fixed assets, but can also be secured by additional types of collateral, including accounts receivable, personal property, and intellectual property.

B. **Revolving Credit Loans.** Revolving credit loans are usually made by commercial banks and provide short-term financing for a company to meet its working capital requirements. A revolving credit loan is a line of credit that may be drawn down, paid back, and drawn down again, but is generally not intended to provide long-term capital financing. Most revolving loans also require a zero balance for some period of time during each year, typically 30 days. Most revolving credit loans have a one year term that is renewable at the election of the lender from year to year.

1. **What Is the Purpose of a Revolving Credit Loan?** A revolving credit loan is used when a business has short term working capital needs. For example, if a business pays its employees every two weeks, occasionally there is a month in which the business has three payrolls but does not have available cash. Having a revolving credit loan can fill this short term working capital deficiency. Also, working capital loans can support a business's purchase of inventory needed for the business to produce its goods or services or help to carry accounts receivable until they are paid.

2. **What Is the Cost of a Revolving Credit Loan?** The interest rate for a revolving credit loan is generally a floating interest rate set at a certain percentage above the lender's prime rate. Lenders generally also require that the borrower pay a quarterly commitment fee which is a percentage of the amount of the revolving credit facility not used by the borrower.

3. **How Is a Revolving Loan Secured?** A revolving credit facility may be secured solely by the borrower's accounts receivable, inventory, or equipment, in which event the lender will generally lend up to the lesser of the commitment or a borrowing base, which is generally

a percentage of eligible accounts receivable, inventory, or equipment. Alternatively, a line of credit may be secured by all the assets of the business and may not be tied to a specific borrowing base.

C. **SBA Financing.** Banks and other financial institutions are common sources of debt financing. However, banks in the current economy have tight credit requirements, and, without substantial collateral, it may be difficult for early stage enterprises to obtain commercial bank financing. The United States Small Business Administration (the "SBA"), a governmental agency that is dedicated to the growth of entrepreneurial businesses, assists start-up and early stage enterprises that may not qualify for a loan under a bank's typical credit standards to obtain loans by guarantying repayment of the loan, which reduces the bank's lending risk. Thus SBA guaranteed loans may provide start-up and early stage enterprises with a path to debt financing that might otherwise be available.

D. **HUD and Other Federal Loan Programs.** The United States Department of Housing and Urban Development (HUD) has special loan programs for financing assisted living facilities, senior care facilities, skilled nursing facilities, continuing care retirement centers, memory care facilities, rehabilitation hospitals, and similar enterprises. Both "for profit" and "not for profit" enterprises can qualify for HUD loans. Similarly, other federal government departments, such as the United States Department of Agriculture through its Rural Development Loan program, can be sources of debt financing.

E. **Tax Exempt and Industrial Revenue Bonds.** By definition, "not for profit" corporations do not have equity investors. Consequently, the only way that "not for profit" corporations can raise capital is through debt financing transactions. "Not for profit" corporations that have qualified as "tax exempt" under Section 501(c)(3) of the Internal Revenue Code can borrow from the issuance of the tax exempt bonds issued by or on behalf of a state or local governmental unit. Similarly, Industrial Revenue Bonds (IRBs) are tax-exempt loans issued by state or local governments to finance private company projects, particularly those with the prospect of stimulating the local economy and creating jobs for local residents.

1. **What Are the Characteristics of Bond Financing?** Bond financing is usually amortized over a longer period of time than commercial term loans, with most having terms of ten, twenty, or thirty years.

2. **How Are Bond Financings Managed?** In addition to fundamental loan documents including a Loan Agreement, Promissory Note, and Security and Mortgage Agreements, bond financing also requires a "Trust Indenture" or "Trust Agreement" that appoints a "Trustee," usually a division of a commercial bank, to manage the flow of funds related to the borrower's

operations and obligations to repay the bonds. Under the terms of a bond financing Loan Agreement, the borrower pledges all of its revenue to be transferred to the Trustee. The Trustee is obligated to establish a series of internal funds, including, for example, a Revenue Fund, Debt Services Reserve Fund, Operating and Maintenance Fund, Renewal and Replacement Fund, and Depreciation Reserve Fund. The Trustee then manages the revenue received from the borrower in accordance with a prescribed "flow of funds."

3. **How Are Bond Financings Secured?** Bond financings are typically secured in every manner possible. Not only are all gross revenues transferred to the Trustee, security will include accounts receivable, furniture, fixtures, equipment, and all other personal property that can be secured under UCC Article 9 as well as mortgage security interests in any borrower owned real property.

III. WHAT ARE THE FUNDAMENTAL TERMS OF LOAN AGREEMENTS?

A. **Nature of Loan Agreements.** A commercial lender will require execution of a Loan Agreement in connection with a credit facility. The Loan Agreement is a private contract that is governed by the state law of contracts. Many commercial Loan Agreements are form documents prepared by a commercial lender. You must read them carefully to ensure that they fit your entity. Loan Agreements typically include the provisions described below.

B. **Positive Covenants.** One purpose of positive covenants is to require that the borrower provide the lender financial and other information in the future. For example, the borrower may be required to deliver to the lender quarterly and annual financial statements. In order to remain informed about the borrower's condition, the lender may require that the borrower give it notice of certain events such as the threat of litigation or instigation of a governmental investigation. Otherwise, positive covenants are a list of borrower's promises to take such actions as: maintain its corporate or other existence; pay all its debts when due; keep proper records; maintain adequate insurance; and comply with laws.

C. **Negative Covenants.** Negative covenants are the most heavily negotiated provisions of a Loan Agreement. It is through negative covenants that the lender imposes on the borrower restrictions that protect the lender's interest in being paid but may interfere with the borrower's unfettered conduct of its business and may not be clearly understood when an enterprise executes a bank's standard form of loan agreement. The lender reasonably wants to ensure that its loan is paid and the borrower reasonably wants to conduct its business in a manner that results in a successful enterprise. Sometimes these positions, although each may be "reasonable," clash. Standard negative covenants for a borrower to make to a lender include the following: not to merge, consolidate, liquidate, or dissolve itself without lender prior written permission (often excepting mergers of, into, or among wholly-owned subsidiaries); not to enter into a new business without the lender's prior permission; not to sell assets without using the proceeds to pay down the principal amount of the loan; not to sell stock or other ownership interests; not to pay dividends (possibly qualified by whether or not the borrower maintains certain financial ratios); not to increase executive compensation; and other promises tailored to particular borrowers.

D. **Financial Covenants.** Financial covenants generally cause borrowers the most headaches. The lender wants to ensure that the borrower maintains substantially the same financial condition as it had when the Loan Agreement was executed, produce substantially the same results of operations in the future as it had produced in the past, or some combination of both. Lenders frequently require that borrowers maintain certain financial ratios to ensure these results.

E. **Financial Representations and Warranties.** Any credit facility, whether a term loan or revolving loan, will have a representations and warranties section that describes a borrower at a particular moment in time. For example, the borrower represents and warrants that the financial statements provided to the lender are true and accurate, prepared in accordance with GAAP, and fairly represent the financial condition of the company. There will generally also be a representation that no material adverse event has occurred since the date of the financial statements.

F. **Non-Financial Representations and Warranties.** The non-financial representations and warranties usually include statements that the borrower is a validly formed corporation (or other entity), is engaged in a specific business, and does not engage in some other types of businesses. The borrower will have to list all of its subsidiaries and make statements about what types of entities they are and where they are validly formed. The lender is probably going to ask the borrower to make statements about some or all of the following: litigation; labor matters; compliance with ERISA; compliance with environmental laws; payment of taxes; and ownership of property (whether real, personal, or intellectual property).

G. **How Do You Manage the Risk of Potential Breach of Warranty?**

1. **Knowledge.** Try to precisely define "knowledge" to actual, not constructive, knowledge, and try to limit knowledge to specific borrower representatives.

2. **Material Adverse Effect (MAE).** Limit representations and disclosures to those that have a material adverse effect.

3. **Time Limit.** Limit the duration of the representation.

4. **Schedules.** Schedules to the Loan Agreement disclose exceptions to the representations and warranties.

H. **Events of Default.** "Events of Default" typically include not only failure to make timely payment but also a breach of the other terms and conditions of the Loan Agreement (such as representations and warranties, positive and negative covenants, and other contract terms), insolvency of the borrower, and any false statement made to induce the lender to make the loan. That is why reading the bank's standard form of Loan Agreement is so important: Loan Agreements sometimes include representations and warranties that it is impossible for the borrower to make because it is difficult to force a "one size fits all" document into applying to individual borrower circumstances.

IV. WHAT IS A PROMISSORY NOTE?

A. **History of "Commercial Paper".** A promissory note is a form of "commercial paper" that is governed by the UCC Article 3 and is referred to in law as a "negotiable instrument." As the commercial common law developed in the 17th and 18th centuries, while the courts would enforce "bills of exchange" (analogous to modern "checks"), the courts did not enforce notes that promised payment in the future. However, a law was passed in England in 1704 that made promissory notes enforceable, and the modern law of negotiable instruments is based on English law developments after that enactment. Today every state, including Louisiana, has enacted a form of UCC Article 3.

B. **Definition of Promissory Note.** A "Promissory Note" is defined in Article 3 of the UCC to be a written document in which a borrower unconditionally promises to pay to the order of a specific person or to the bearer a certain sum to a lender on demand or at a definite time, usually with interest accruing on the outstanding principal amount. It is more than mere acknowledgment of a debt like an "I.O.U." A Promissory Note is actually a separate agreement from other loan documents that in many ways stands on its own.

C. **What Makes a Promissory Note a "Negotiable Instrument"?** To be "negotiable," an instrument must (1) be in writing, (2) be signed by the maker, (3) contain an unconditional promise to pay a fixed sum of money on demand or at a definite time, (4) contain "words of negotiability," and (5) be free from unauthorized promises (like conditioning payment on the delivery of goods or services, which makes the agreement a simple contract, not a negotiable instrument). A negotiable instrument can be enforced by a "holder in due course." In other words, it can be transferred from the original holder to a successor holder. For example, a bank that is the "holder" of a Promissory Note payable over a long period of time, such as five or more years, can sell the note to a "holder in due course" for a discounted present value, exchanging payout over time for present cash. This is the foundation for the 2008 financial collapse. Mortgage lenders "securitized" mortgage loan instruments by bundling many Promissory Notes into one security and then selling an interest in that security to the public. However, when the underlying mortgage loans began going into default, the bundled loan securities lost their value.

D. **What Are the Typical Provisions in a Promissory Note?** Promissory Notes generally have the following terms:

1. **Financial Terms.** The principal amount, interest, and term.

2. **Payment Terms.** The payment schedule (for example monthly or annual installments) and how payments will be allocated to the loan amortization (typically first to interest and then to principal). If permitted under the terms of the Promissory Note, payments in an amount greater than the required interest and principal payment are allocated to unpaid principal, which results in faster repayment of the loan.

3. **Prepayment Penalty.** While most Promissory Notes permit prepayment at any time without penalty, some require a prepayment "penalty" to compensate the lender for expected interest income and some do not permit prepayment at all.

4. **Late Charges.** Promissory Notes typically charge a late payment fee which might be either a percentage of the unpaid amount or a flat fee.

5. **Interest After Default.** Upon a default, interest will increase substantially, sometimes to as much as 21%.

6. **Events of Default.** In addition to nonpayment, commercial Promissory Notes sometimes permit a lender to declare a default on less objective grounds, such as (a) the occurrence of a material adverse change in the financial condition of the borrower or a guarantor or (b) the lender in good faith believes itself insecure regarding repayment of the Promissory Note.

7. **Lender's Rights Upon Default.** When a Promissory Note is in default, commercial Promissory Notes typically provide lenders with an array of assertable rights, all of which a lender can pursue without exclusion (provided that, as with any contract action, the lender's remedies end when the lender is "made whole," meaning that the lender makes a full financial recovery under the terms of the Promissory Note). Rights and remedies available to a commercial lender upon default typically include the following: (a) accelerate full payment of the outstanding principal and interest plus attorneys' fees, costs, expenses, and other fees and charges (such as late fees and default interest) permitted under the Promissory Note; (b) if the borrower has more than one loan or credit facility with the lender, declare all other loans and obligations in default, even if there is no independent default on those loans; (c) proceed directly against guarantors of the Promissory Note; and (d) take such action as may be permitted under a related Security Agreement. These same rights are also typically described in the Loan Agreement.

8.   **Attorneys' Fees.** Commercial Promissory Notes typically require a defaulting borrower to be responsible for the lender's attorneys' fees that accrue as soon as the Promissory Note is referred to an attorney for collection. Because this may be a relatively open-ended financial risk, borrowers may want to negotiate for a cap on potential attorneys' fees, such as a percentage of the outstanding principal amount or a fixed monetary cap.

9.   **Collateral.** The collateral for the Promissory Note is generally described in the Promissory Note but more particularly described in the Security Agreement.

E.   **How Is a Promissory Note Enforced?** With the possible exception of "fraud," which requires evidence of a factually specific misrepresentation or concealment of a material fact, if the signature on a Promissory Note is authentic, there is virtually no defense to a lawsuit to enforce payment on a Promissory Note. Once the authenticity of the signature is proved, the holder can get a judgment against a maker in default. Note: Whenever a transaction involves a Promissory Note, the maker should sign only one original. While it is customary to have several originally executed transaction documents so each party has a set of originals, that practice does not apply to Promissory Notes.

F.   **What Happens When a Promissory Note Is Fully Paid?** When a Promissory Note is fully paid, the original Promissory Note should be returned to the borrower marked "SATISFIED."

V. WHAT IS A "SECURED TRANSACTION" AND WHAT IS THE IMPORTANCE OF A SECURITY AGREEMENT?

A.   **What Is A "Secured Transaction"?** A Security Agreement makes a Loan Agreement a "secured transaction." Consequently, the word "security" is relevant to both equity capital and debt capital transactions, but with completely different meanings. In the context of equity financing, a "security" is an investment interest in which the investor expects to profit from the efforts of others. In a debt capital transaction, the meaning of the word "security" is closer to its common dictionary usage: it refers to making the lender more "secure" when loaning money to an enterprise. A promise to repay the loan as embodied in the Promissory Note is typically not enough to induce a bank or other lender to make a loan because the only remedy the lender has for repayment is to file a lawsuit and go through the entire judicial process to obtain a judgment against the defaulting borrower. However, if the borrower already cannot repay the loan, judicial proceedings are useless and futile. The lender wants other ways to be "made whole" in the event of a loan default. In other words, the lender wants to enter into a "secured transaction," meaning that the lender takes a "security interest" in the borrower's "personal" (as opposed to "real") property, including, for example, accounts receivable, furniture, fixtures, equipment, inventory, and any other moveable good such as a motor vehicle as well as "intangible" property such as patents, copyrights, and trademark goodwill.

B.   **What Law Governs Secured Transactions?** Secured transactions are governed by Article 9 of the UCC, which has been enacted in all of the states. Security interests in real property through a real property "mortgage" are governed by state real property law and are not covered in this discussion of "secured transactions."

C.   **What Is a "Security Interest"?** A "security interest" is a consensual "lien" granted by a borrower to a lender in specifically identifiable personal property that secures payment or performance of a contracted obligation.

D.   **What Is a Security Agreement?** A "Security Agreement" is a contract between a lender and borrower that states that the lender can repossess the property a person has offered as collateral if the loan is not paid as agreed. After acquiring security interests through the Security Agreement, the lender must "perfect" the security interest. It is important to understand that, without proper security, a lender is unlikely to make a loan. This makes it particularly difficult for a start-up enterprise with no accounts receivable or other valuable assets to obtain debt financing.

E.   **What Are the Typical Provisions in a Security Agreement?** Security Agreements generally have the following terms:

1.   **Grant of the Security Interest.** The Security Agreement must grant a security interest in specifically described collateral as required for perfection of the security interest. Without limitation, as described elsewhere in this chapter, the security interest governed by Article 9 of the UCC may be granted in the following personal property: accounts receivable; inventory; furniture; fixtures; equipment; intellectual property and other intangible property; bank accounts and cash; and borrower books and records.

2.   **Representations and Warranties.** Like the Loan Agreement, a Security Agreement typically includes representations and warranties on which the lender relies, including, for example, that the borrower:

   a.   Has clean title to the collateral;

   b.   Has not granted another security interest that has higher priority than the security interest granted under the Security Agreement; and

   c.   Has not stored the collateral at any location not disclosed to the lender.

3.　**Covenants.** Again like the Loan Agreement, the Security Agreement includes positive covenants that focus on protection and preservation of the collateral, including, for example, that the borrower will:

    a.　Not change its principal office or locations where the collateral is maintained without the lender's prior written consent;

    b.　Keep and maintain satisfactory books and records related to the collateral and make them available to the lender on request;

    c.　Keep and secure goods and inventory in a careful, secure, and commercially reasonable manner;

    d.　Not transfer the collateral except as permitted in the Loan Agreement;

    e.　Maintain the collateral free of all other liens, claims, and encumbrances;

    f.　Pay all taxes, assessments, and fees related to ownership and use of the collateral as and when due;

    g.　Maintain the collateral in good condition and repair and replace it when necessary;

    h.　Procure and maintain suitable insurance on the collateral; and

    i.　Execute all documents required to perfect security interests in the collateral upon the lender's request.

4.　**Default and Remedies.** Upon occurrence of an Event of Default as defined in the Loan Agreement, the Security Agreement sets forth specific remedies related to the security interest in the collateral, such as stating that the lender can:

    a.　Require the borrower to assemble and send the collateral to the lender;

    b.　Enter the defaulting borrower's premises and take possession of the collateral;

    c.　Ask a court to appoint a receiver to take possession of or manage the collateral;

    d.　Sell the collateral; and

e.   Have the borrower's power of attorney to, in essence, take over all management of the collateral, to which the borrower is powerless to object.

F.   How Are Rights in a Security Interest Perfected? After a security interest is granted in a Security Agreement, the creditor such as a commercial bank needs to take certain actions to "perfect" the creditor's lien on the collateral.

1.   **UCC-1 Financing Statements.** Perfecting security interests in collateral governed by UCC Article 9 requires the filing of financing statements either centrally (with the Secretary of State) or locally (for example, in a county Superior Court) for security interests in property that is not characterized as real property, including the following: furniture; fixtures; equipment; accounts receivable; general intangible property, such as copyrights, patents, and trademarks; and inventory. UCC-1 financing statement have terms of five years and need to be periodically renewed.

2.   **Real Estate as Collateral.** If the lender is taking real estate as collateral, the lender will also require the following:

a.   deed to secure debt or mortgage;

b.   UCC-2 notice filing in order to perfect a security interest in fixtures;

c.   mortgagee title insurance policy;

d.   appraisal; and

e.   survey.

3.   **Perfecting a Security Interest in Cash.** The only way to perfect a security interest in cash is by possession. Consequently, commercial bank loans typically require the borrower to maintain its bank accounts with the lending bank and provide the bank with the power to seize the funds in the borrower's bank account upon an Event of Default.

4.   **What Other Capital Financing Transactions Are Governed by Article 9 of the UCC?** Some businesses raise capital by selling certain assets that can potentially be liquidated into cash proceeds, like accounts receivable and promissory notes, and such transactions are governed by Article 9 of the UCC. For example, an enterprise may have substantial accounts receivable but may not expect to receive payment of the accounts receivable in a manner that meets the enterprise's cash flow needs. Rather than borrowing funds granting a security interest

in accounts receivable, an enterprise can sell its accounts receivable to an independent purchaser at a discount. This is commonly called "factoring" accounts receivable. The advantage to factoring is that it provides ready cash with no corresponding liability. The disadvantage is that factoring discount rates are typically higher than commercial loan interest rates. As discussed above, the holder of the promissory note can also sell the note to a "holder in due course" at a discounted rate, which might also be a cash source. Since virtually all enterprises have accounts receivable, factoring is a commonly used capital financing method.

VI. WHAT IS A GUARANTY AGREEMENT?

A.   **Definition of a Guaranty.** A "guaranty" is an independent party's agreement to be responsible for the payment obligations of a third party and, in the context of debt financing, is manifested in a Guaranty Agreement. For example, commercial lenders typically require individual owners of a borrower to "guaranty" the borrower's payment obligations and performance under a Loan Agreement and Promissory Note.

B.   **What Special Laws Govern Guaranty Agreements?** First, a guaranty is a form of "surety" agreement, and, under the Statute of Frauds, must be in writing to be enforceable. Second, Guaranty Agreements are "strictly construed," which means that the language of the guaranty and how it can be enforced must be precisely and unambiguously described.

C.   **What Are Typical Provisions in a Guaranty Agreement?** Some provisions are relatively standard and found in virtually all Guaranty Agreements, while some provisions may be customized to fit the specific facts underlying the guaranty obligation.

　　1.   **Description of the Guaranty Obligations.** Typically, the guaranty is tied specifically to a borrower's indebtedness.

　　2.   **Joint, Several, and Solidary Liability With the Borrower.** Guaranty Agreements typically provide that the guarantor's obligations and liability are "solidary" or "joint and several" with the borrower to the same degree and extent as if the guarantor is a co-borrower or co-signer on the core indebtedness.

　　3.   **Joint, Several, and Solidary Liability With Other Guarantors.** There are two ways that a guarantor can be obligated. One way is to have "joint and several" liability with all guarantors. This means that, if there is more than one guarantor, each guarantor guaranties the borrower's entire indebtedness, permitting, for example, a lender to proceed against only one guarantor for the entire amount due to the lender from the borrower. However, multiple guarantors can negotiate to guaranty only a portion of the borrower's indebtedness.

For example, a limited liability company with four members might negotiate to have each member guaranty only a pro rata portion of the borrowing LLC's indebtedness.

4. **Cancellation or Termination of Guaranty Obligation.** Most Guaranty Agreements provide that the guaranty obligation remains in effect until the underlying borrower has paid the debt in full and cannot be terminated except by the lender. This can lead to difficulties when a co-guarantor of the borrower's debt is no longer involved with the borrower. For example, a medical practice may have four physician-owners, each of whom guaranties the medical practices debt. Even if one physician leaves the medical practice, the guaranty obligation continues unless the lender, at the lender's sole discretion, releases the guarantor from the Guaranty Agreement.

5. **Bank Deposit Accounts.** The commercial lender may require the guarantor to maintain personal bank accounts with the lender against which the lender may proceed to confiscate the amounts in the bank accounts if there is an event of default.

VII. WHAT OTHER FORMS OF SECURITY MAY BE REQUIRED BY A LENDER?

A. **Stock or Other Ownership Interest Pledge.** The guaranties of individual owners might be enhanced by a pledge of the individual owner's stock or other ownership interest in the borrowing entity. This is another way to make individuals responsible for the debts of the borrowing entity.

B. **Commercial Lender Bank Accounts.** As stated above, commercial bank lenders frequently require borrowers to maintain bank accounts at the lending brank and take a security interest in the bank account deposits.

VIII. LENDER REMEDIES WHEN A LOAN IS IN DEFAULT

A. **Choice of Remedies.** As stated above, typically, upon occurrence of an Event of Default, the lender may: accelerate payment of the loan in full plus principal, interest, costs, expenses, and attorneys' fees; file a collection lawsuit against the borrower; file a lawsuit against a guarantor; and proceed to seize collateral and exercise all rights under the Security Agreement. It is important to understand that the remedies are not mutually exclusive and the lender has the right to take whatever action sit wants to exercise the lender's rights under the loan documents.

B. **"Work Out" of Loan Default.** In practice, lenders typically do not go directly to court or proceed to seize collateral: a loan in default is assigned to the lender's "work out" department. For example, even if the lender secures a loan through a stock pledge upon an Event of Default, the lender is unlikely to exercise its rights and assume ownership and operation of a business. A lender would rather find a way to receive money and mitigate its monetary damages. However, when in a "work out" situation, borrower's management typically loses virtually all control and authority over business operations, and the additional costs of the "work out" will be allocated to the borrower under the loan documents.

IX. OVERVIEW OF BANKRUPTCY LAW

A. **Bankruptcy Court Protection.** When a borrower goes into default under a Loan Agreement and the borrower is insolvent, the borrower may consider filing a petition with the United States Bankruptcy Court for protection to prevent the lender from exercising all of the lender's rights under the loan documents. "Insolvency" generally means either the inability for an entity to pay its debts as they become due or an entity's liabilities are greater than its assets. This is called "voluntary bankruptcy." Under certain circumstances, creditors can force an insolvent business into "involuntary bankruptcy."

B. **What Law Governs Bankruptcy?** Bankruptcy is governed by the federal Bankruptcy Code. There are no state bankruptcy courts, although it is possible for an entity to go into "receivership" under state law. Nevertheless, the most common way that an insolvent entity seeks protection from creditors is through the federal Bankruptcy Code.

C. **What Forms of Bankruptcy Code Protection Are Available to Insolvent Entities?** There are two forms of Bankruptcy Court relief that are used more commonly than others: petitions filed under Chapter 7 and Chapter 11 of the Bankruptcy Code.

   1. **Chapter 7 Bankruptcy Petitions.** Chapter 7 is used for a complete liquidation of the debtor's assets, with net proceeds being distributed first to secured creditors and then, if there are any funds remaining, to unsecured creditors.

   2. **Chapter 11 Bankruptcy Petitions.** Chapter 11 protection permits an insolvent entity to "reorganize" under the protection of the Bankruptcy Court and emerge as an enterprise that has an opportunity to continue its operations. In the typical situation, debts are reduced or sometimes eliminated, so, even if a lender may believe it is fully secured, the lender may not receive payment in full. Chapter 11 requires Bankruptcy Court approval of a "plan of reorganization" that involves input from creditors, but the Court can force the creditors to accept a plan even if the creditors do not approve.

   3. **The Automatic Stay: a Potential Lifeline for an Insolvent Enterprise.** When an enterprise is not making timely payments on its obligations, it is likely to be sued by its creditors. Virtually all litigation is time consuming and expensive. The last thing an insolvent company wants to do is pay attorneys to defend the company in litigation. A bankruptcy

petition can throw the insolvent enterprise a lifeline through the "automatic stay," which immediately stays virtually all creditor collection activities, including without limitation, the following:

a.   any attempt to collect on a debt, including phone calls and letters;

b.   any lawsuit to collect a debt;

c.   repossession of the debtor's assets; and

d.   any attempt to perfect a security interest.

5.   **When Should a Debtor Consider Seeking Bankruptcy Court Protection?** As long as an enterprise is able to work out its debt obligations outside of the Bankruptcy Court, it is not in an enterprise's best interest to seek Bankruptcy Court protection. However, when the enterprise starts getting sued, survival may require filing a petition in bankruptcy to obtain the benefits of the automatic stay.

CHAPTER 6

FUNDAMENTALS OF MERGERS AND ACQUISITIONS

I. BAKER'S RULES OF BUSINESS TRANSACTIONS

A. **Most Deals Don't Happen.** Inertia is against consummation of transactions, particularly complex transactions. Multiple parties with multiple advisors need to be looking in the same direction at the same time. Therefore, we need to be aware of the inertia and remove obstacles that might prevent completion of the transaction.

B. **All Transactions Take More Time Than Intended or Desired by the Parties.** Time is a constant enemy. Also, there is a direct correlation between time and cost of closing the deal because delays almost always result in higher legal, accounting, and consulting fees.

II. WHAT ARE THE TYPICAL ACQUISITION FORMS?

A. **Generally Used Forms.** Although there are numerous forms that negotiated acquisitions can take, they are generally accomplished by means of one or more of the following methods: (1) a stock or limited liability company membership interest purchase; (2) an asset purchase; or (3) a merger under state law (including subsidiary mergers and other variations). For purposes of this material, the symbol "T" will be used to denote the acquired or target company; the symbol "P" will be used to denote the acquiring or parent company; and the symbol "S" will be used to denote a subsidiary of P, the parent company. Also, this chapter will refer only to transactions involving corporations and limited liability companies since these are the most common forms of business organization, and these materials assume that there are no restrictions on transfer of stock or membership interests in the entity's organizational documents.

B. **Stock or Limited Liability Company Membership Interest Purchases.** The stock or membership interest purchase is probably the simplest method of acquisition. P purchases the stock or membership interests of T from its shareholders or members, each of whom makes his or her own decision whether to sell. P can acquire all or less than all of the outstanding T stock or membership interests. Following the acquisition, T will continue in existence as a subsidiary of P. P will pay the purchase price directly to T's shareholders. As a general rule, stock or membership interest purchases are favored by sellers because of potentially favorable capital gains tax treatment and few post-closing issues. However, purchasers generally may not prefer ownership interest acquisition because the liabilities of the selling entity are assumed by the purchaser and the purchaser will not receive a "stepped up basis" on the assets of the selling entity for purposes of depreciation.

C.   **Asset Purchases.** Rather than acquire T's business by purchasing its outstanding stock or membership interests, P could instead purchase all or substantially all of T's assets. In contrast to an ownership interest purchase, the purchaser does not acquire the liabilities and other obligations of the seller unless they are specifically identified and assumed, and an asset purchase will provide the purchaser with a "stepped up basis" in the assets of the target company, which creates value for the purchaser through the ability to depreciate the acquired assets at their purchase price. Although T continues in existence as a corporation or limited liability company, this transaction differs from the stock or membership interest purchase in at least two important respects.

   1.   **Continued Existence of the Target Company.** First, T does not become a subsidiary of P; it is still owned by its shareholders or members. Similarly, what had formerly been T's assets are now owned directly by P, which is also now responsible for those liabilities and obligations of T assumed by it. T, by contrast, no longer holds what had been its assets or (to the extent P has agreed to take them) its liabilities, absent third party releases. However, T generally will remain liable for its obligations, with rights against P if P fails to discharge the liabilities assumed by P.

   2.   **Payment of the Purchase Price to the Target Company.** Second, the purchase price has been paid to T, not to its shareholders or members, who, in order to receive such consideration, will have either to (a) liquidate T or have T declare a dividend on its outstanding stock if T is a corporation or (b) distribute the proceeds through the Operating Agreement if T is a limited liability company.

D.   **Mergers.** Mergers are creatures of, and governed in large part by, the laws of the states of incorporation of the companies that are to be merged (often referred to as the "constituent organizations") and by the charters and by-laws or Operating Agreements of such constituent organizations. Thus, the ability of two companies to merge is entirely dependent on a statutory enabling provision. In these materials, we are assuming that the merging entities are corporations, but the same principles generally apply to a merger involving limited liability companies.

1. **Direct Merger.** As a matter of law, the merger of T into P results in P automatically succeeding to all of the assets and liabilities of T, which disappears into P. At the corporate level, therefore, a merger is similar to a sale of all of T's assets to P and P's assumption of all of T's liabilities, although in the latter case T remains in existence, still owned by its former shareholders. At the shareholder level, however, the merger operates more like a stock purchase in which T's shareholders all participate (except to the extent that any such shareholder exercises in the merger any available dissenters' appraisal rights). As a result of the merger, the T stock held by T's shareholders is converted automatically into the consideration to be paid by P in the transaction. Under the law of most states, this consideration can be securities, cash, or other property. Both of the constituent corporations are parties to the acquisition agreement.

2. **Three-Party Mergers.** Two important variations on the direct merger transaction are the "forward subsidiary merger" and the "reverse subsidiary merger."

    a. **Forward Subsidiary Merger.** In a forward subsidiary merger, T merges into S, a wholly-owned subsidiary of P. S succeeds to all of T's assets and liabilities, T goes out of existence, and the T stock formerly held by T shareholders is converted into the same consideration which the T shareholders would have obtained pursuant to a merger of T directly into P. The only structural difference between a direct and a forward subsidiary merger (although an important one) is that, following consummation, the assets and, particularly, the liabilities of T have been assumed by a subsidiary of P, not by P itself. This procedure permits P to acquire T using the merger technique for tax or other reasons without having to obtain the vote of P's shareholders or triggering dissenters' rights in those holders, while largely preserving the historical attributes of T.

    b. **Reverse Subsidiary Merger.** If a forward subsidiary merger is similar at the corporate level to an asset acquisition by S and at the shareholder level to a stock sale, a reverse subsidiary merger is similar from both the corporate and shareholder viewpoints to a stock purchase of T by P. In a reverse subsidiary merger, S merges into T (S, rather than T, ceasing to exist), and T succeeds to all of S's assets and liabilities. If, as is often the case, S were a newly created shell corporation with no assets or liabilities, then after the merger T would be the same entity practically as well as legally as T pre-merger. The outstanding shares of the common stock of S are converted into shares of common stock of T; accordingly, T becomes a wholly-owned subsidiary of P, and the T stock held by the former shareholders of T is converted into the acquisition consideration. The effect is the same as a purchase by P of all of the outstanding stock of T from its shareholders. This procedure may make possible a merger without the risk of having the transaction treated as an "assignment" which may be prohibited by various contracts and licenses to which T is a party, which is frequently important in the health industry.

3. **Short-Form Mergers.** In order to simplify those transactions where T is entirely, or almost entirely, owned by P, states have adopted so-called "short-form" merger statutes. Short-form mergers can be accomplished between parents and subsidiaries without the approval of the Board of Directors or a vote by shareholders of the subsidiary being acquired if (a) P owns at least a specified percentage (90% in most jurisdictions) of the outstanding shares of each class of T and (b) the Board of Directors of P adopts a resolution approving the merger. Parent shareholder approval is generally not required.

E. **Board or Management Approval.**

1. **Corporate Board Approval.** Generally speaking, every corporation that is a party to the acquisition agreement must obtain the approval of the transaction its Board of Directors. This will be required either specifically by statute or by the bylaws of the corporation.

2. **Limited Liability Company Management Approval.** In the absence of a modifying provision in the Operating Agreement, any fundamental organizational change, such as a merger or acquisition, will require approval by a majority of the members as described below. However, many Operating Agreements have customized approval processes, such as delegating approval of a transaction to either a single managing member or to a management committee.

F. **Shareholder or Member Approval.** The question of whether shareholder or member approval is required in a particular acquisition is significantly more complicated than the issue of Board approval. For corporations, whether such approval is required and, if so, what the requisite vote will be varies from jurisdiction to jurisdiction and depends to a significant degree on the method of acquisition. Indeed, the issue of shareholder approval (or, rather, a desire to avoid the need to obtain such approval) often helps determine the method of acquisition. For limited liability companies, as stated above, the approval process may be customized. As a general rule, in the absence of an Operating Agreement provision to the contrary, majority member approval is required for a fundamental organizational change such as a merger or acquisition. However, some Operating Agreements require super-majority member approval. Therefore, you will always need to review the terms and conditions of the Operating Agreement.

1. **Stock or Membership Interest Purchases.** Stock or membership interest purchase acquisitions are the easiest transactions to consummate. In the absence of restrictive provisions in a Shareholders' Agreement or Operating Agreement, no vote by the shareholders or members of T is required since T is not engaged in any transaction. The acquiror is viewed

as purchasing assets (from the viewpoint of the acquiror, stock of the target is really just another asset) and, except where the acquiror's securities are listed or quoted on a stock exchange or association and their rules provide otherwise, no shareholder or member vote is necessary. As always, this general rule can be modified by the agreement of the shareholders or members.

2. **Mergers.** The general rule is that, except for statutory short-form mergers, the shareholders or members of both constituent organizations in a merger must approve the transaction. In most jurisdictions, the required vote is a majority of the outstanding shares, but this can be modified by agreement of the shareholders or members.

3. **Asset Sales.** If a target company is selling all or substantially all of its assets, approval by its shareholders or members is required in virtually all jurisdictions. In most of these jurisdictions, the required vote is a majority of the outstanding shares or membership interests. The critical, and often very difficult, question is determining when a sale is of "substantially all" of the entity's assets. The acquiror's shareholders or members are rarely given a statutory right to vote on acquisitions of assets from another entity (even when they constitute all or substantially all of its assets), regardless of the form of consideration paid by the purchaser.

4. **Dissenters' Rights.** As a general rule, when shareholder or member approval is required for a transaction, shareholders or members who do not give their approval and who follow the statutory procedures are generally entitled to claim dissenters' rights of appraisal and receive in cash the value of their shares in lieu of participating in the transaction. Under the normal statutory provisions, shareholders or members who exercise such rights must vote against, or fail to vote for, the transaction and claim their rights in a timely fashion.

   a. **No Dissenters' Rights in Stock or Membership Interest Transactions.** Dissenters' rights are not available to target company shareholders or members in connection with a straight stock or membership purchase. A target company shareholder or member who does not wish to sell remains as a shareholder or member in the target.

   b. **Shareholders or Members of the Acquiror.** Shareholders or members of the acquiror are generally not entitled to appraisal rights except in connection with a direct merger of the target into the acquiror, although in many jurisdictions, shareholders or members of the acquiror will not be entitled to appraisal rights with respect to a transaction in which they were not entitled to vote.

   c. **Market Exception.** Many states create an exception to appraisal rights with respect to shares or other equity interests listed on a national securities exchange or held of record by more than a statutorily prescribed minimum number of shareholders or members subject, in certain instances, to the satisfaction of other conditions.

G. **Other Structuring Issues.** In addition to the differences in board approval requirements and shareholder or member voting and appraisal rights discussed above, there are other important aspects of structuring a transaction that may influence the nature of the transaction.

    1. **Third Party Consents.** The ability of the target to retain the benefits of a material agreement to which it is a party is often an important consideration in an acquisition. This issue normally arises where the consent of the other party to the contract is required to waive a provision that prohibits its assignment by the target. A purchase of all of the outstanding stock of the target, whether by a negotiated stock purchase or pursuant to a share exchange, if permitted under the target's (and acquiror's) jurisdictions of incorporation, does not constitute a transfer of any assets of the target; accordingly, any non-assignment provision would not be violated and no consent or waiver would be required. A sale of assets by the target, however, would constitute an assignment of the contract and would require the consent of the other party to the contract.

    2. **Governmental Consents.** Whether any particular consent, approval, or filing with a governmental or regulatory body is required in connection with a given structure depends, as with third party consents, on the exact wording of the particular statutory provision or regulation.

III. HOW DOES THE ACQUISITION PROCESS USUALLY FLOW?

A. **Initial Discussions.** The first step in any acquisition is a realization by the parties that there may be a deal to be made. Sometimes investment bankers for one or both parties are involved at this stage; sometimes not. Lawyers are generally not involved at this stage except, perhaps, to give some advice about the process to their clients or to draft or negotiate an appropriate confidentiality agreement. The steps outlined below are fairly typical of many transactions in terms of "what happens when" and "who does what." Obviously, significant variations can (and often do) occur in any particular transaction.

B. **Confidentiality Agreement.** When parties begin discussions, it is advisable to enter into a simple confidentiality agreement to create a fiduciary relationship and preserve certain rights, such as trade secret and patent rights. The parties usually commence their business and legal due diligence during this period, the scope of which will vary from deal to deal.

C. **Term Sheet.** As the parties continue to negotiate, it is sometimes advisable to develop a term sheet that outlines the fundamental terms and conditions of the transaction. One benefit of a term sheet is that it may describe fundamental terms and conditions that lead to an early decision not to proceed with the transaction, which may save the parties substantial time and resources.

D. **Memorandum of Understanding.** The term sheet may evolve into a detailed memorandum of understanding of the transaction. Again, preparation of a memorandum of understanding is not absolutely necessary, but it may reveal material issues that lead to an early decision not to proceed with the transaction.

E. **Letter of Intent.** The parties also might, but need not, enter into a letter of intent or agreement in principle. There is some dispute among practitioners as to whether a letter of intent is a desirable document in an acquisition transaction and, if so, what its provisions should be. Whether the execution of such a document may be beneficial in a given factual setting cannot be definitively answered in the abstract.

    1. **Advantages to Executing a Letter of Intent.**

        a. **Facilitating a "Meeting of the Minds".** The process of preparing and executing a letter of intent makes it possible for the parties to determine, at least in broad outline, whether in fact there is a basic agreement as to the terms and structure of a transaction. This consideration may be of particular significance in transactions in which (i) one party (or both) is relatively inexperienced in these types of transactions and, therefore, may more easily misunderstand some of the consequences of the process or (ii) there are particularly complex or intricate elements to the transaction that may lead to mutually inconsistent interpretations in the absence of a written statement.

        b. **Obtaining Some Binding Agreements.** Second, it may be the desire of one party or the other that at least some elements of the preliminary understanding are to be binding. In such a situation, a written agreement is obviously necessary to reflect those understandings, and the other party is unlikely to agree to a separate written agreement unless there is at least an expression of the parties' understanding of the principal terms of the acquisition itself. Examples include "no shop" clauses (which restrict the target company from "shopping" the transaction to other potential purchasers), confidentiality (if not subject to a separate confidentiality agreement), earnest money and its application, and matters related to the due diligence process.

        c. **Initiating Regulatory Approvals.** Third, required regulatory approvals for the transaction can delay the transaction and can be initiated at an earlier stage if a letter of intent, memorandum of understanding, or some comparable writing has been executed. In this context, execution of such a document may mean that proceedings seeking the required approval and negotiation of the definitive agreement can proceed along parallel tracks, thus reducing the total elapsed time until consummation of the transaction.

    d.   **Facilitating Public Disclosure.** Finally, if other factors compel the conclusion that public disclosure of the proposed transaction is appropriate, either or both of the parties may be more willing to make that disclosure if the transaction is sufficiently firm that the parties are willing to sign the letter of intent.

    2.   **Disadvantages of a Letter of Intent.**

    a.   **Obligations Arising from Execution of a Formal Letter of Intent.** A letter of intent may have sufficient elements of a contract to bind the parties and will almost certainly obligate them to carry on further negotiations in good faith. Furthermore, with a publicly-held entity on one side or the other of the transaction, the execution and announcement of a letter of intent will bring to bear significant pressures to complete the transaction. Given that there are always significant variables that cannot be resolved at the letter of intent stage and that will be thoroughly negotiated in connection with a definitive agreement, it is not unusual for a party to refuse to commit to a transaction until a full definitive agreement is in a form acceptable for execution.

    b.   **Potential for Wasted Time and Effort.** The second principal disadvantage is related to the first. In a transaction with complex elements, trying adequately to define them in a letter of intent may prove counterproductive to the total effort. The letter of intent may itself become a lengthy, involved document that tries to do too much. In such an environment, negotiations over the letter of intent may make the entire process more, rather than less, cumbersome and may unnecessarily jeopardize the ability of the parties to negotiate a definitive agreement.

F.   **Due Diligence.** "Due diligence" is the part of the negotiation process during which each party is able to analyze non-public and sometimes confidential or proprietary information about the other party that is material to closing the transaction. There is no absolutely fixed place where due diligence fits into the transaction process. However, due diligence generally begins with an analysis of fundamental target company information by the purchaser after execution of the confidentiality agreement, and it will continue in earnest after execution of a memorandum of understanding or letter of intent (if any) and the definitive agreement.

1. **Stock Purchase Due Diligence.** Because a stock purchase requires the purchaser to assume all of the actual and contingent liabilities of the seller, stock purchase due diligence can be expected to be detailed and time consuming.

2. **Asset Purchase Due Diligence.** Since an asset purchase is focused on the assets acquired and liabilities assumed, due diligence is generally more focused and streamlined from stock purchase due diligence.

G. **Execution of the Definitive Agreement.** Regardless of whether a letter of intent has been executed, the next step in the acquisition process is the negotiation, approval, and execution of a definitive acquisition agreement. During the course of negotiating and finalizing the acquisition agreement, the parties will be continuing and, in most cases, essentially completing their due diligence. When the agreement is fully negotiated, or almost finalized, the parties will usually obtain the necessary board approvals. Fairness opinions, if a part of the transaction, will typically be delivered at the board meeting at which the execution of the definitive agreement is approved.

IV. WHAT ARE THE TYPICAL TERMS AND CONDITIONS OF DEFINITIVE ACQUISITION AGREEMENTS?

A. **Typical Terms and Conditions in the Definitive Agreement.** The definitive agreement is typically a lengthy document replete with representations, warranties, other protective mechanisms, conditions to the closing (because the closing usually will occur after the signing of the definitive agreement), and the like. With the exception of the first portion of the agreement, which will generally set forth the basic economics and form of the transaction and identity of the parties, acquisition agreements are generally very similar in structure regardless of whether they are for an asset purchase, a stock purchase, or a merger.

B. **Description of the Transaction.** The initial provisions of the definitive agreement will generally describe the deal.

1. **Stock Sale Description.** If it is a stock purchase, they will describe the stock being transferred. If there are numerous shareholders, the purchaser may request appointment of a "shareholders representative" who will have power of attorney to execute documents on behalf of all of the shareholders.

2. **Asset Sale Description.** If it is an asset sale, the definitive agreement will describe the assets being transferred as well as specifically excluded assets. Also, the definitive agreement will describe any liabilities to be assumed by the purchaser.

C.   **Consideration.** Of course, the consideration and payment provisions are critically important. These provisions may be simple, as is usually the case in a simple stock purchase agreement for a fixed cash amount, or very complicated, as, for example, in a cash election merger or a transaction that includes an "earn-out" that provides future consideration depending on the post-closing performance of the business enterprise or a closing balance sheet adjustment. Although it is impossible to describe every possible permutation, the consideration and payment provisions might include the following:

1.   **Purchase Price.** The overall purchase price will be described, which may include cash, stock, or other consideration. Frequently, however, the total purchase price is not paid at the closing.

2.   **Purchase Price Escrow.** A portion of the purchase price may be held in escrow or paid in installments, with the amount held in reserve used for payment of indemnification claims as described below. This protects the purchaser from undisclosed liabilities and other unforeseen circumstances. If the parties negotiate a formal escrow arrangement, the transaction documents will include a separate Escrow Agreement.

3.   **Earn-Out.** An "earn-out" provision permits the seller to obtain additional consideration if, after the closing, the target company achieves certain performance objectives. Although this may seem appealing to a seller, many sellers experience difficulty in achieving the goals once the company is under control of the purchaser. Therefore, in most situations, a seller is well advised to determine whether the transaction is acceptable based on the purchase price paid at closing and not on contingent consideration like an earn-out.

4.   **Employment Agreements.** Continuing employment of the seller's principal management is usually a critical deal point. Consequently, formal Employment Agreements and Restrictive Covenant Agreements are typically executed as part of the transaction documents.

D.   **Representations and Warranties.** Each party to the agreement makes representations concerning its business and the effect of the transaction on it. Representations and warranties are statements made by a party about itself or the company it owns. Representations can cover such matters as the due incorporation of a party; its qualifications to conduct business; its authorization of the transaction; receipt of any regulatory approvals or third party consents it must obtain prior to consummation; compliance with generally accepted accounting principles with respect to its financial statements; the absence of material adverse changes in its business; compliance with the statutes and regulations governing the health industry; and many other matters.

1.   **Responding to Representations and Warranties Through a Disclosure Schedule.** Typically, the representations and warranties will provide, for example, that "except as otherwise provided in the Disclosure Schedule to this Agreement, the seller is not

involved in any litigation." If the seller is involved in litigation, it needs to be disclosed on the Disclosure Schedule. Therefore, the Disclosure Schedule becomes the heart and soul of the acquisition agreement and forms the foundation for determining what the purchaser is acquiring.

2. **The Seller Typically Carries the Burden of Substantial Representations and Warranties.** Usually, and almost certainly in a cash transaction, the seller's representations and warranties will be lengthy and all-inclusive while the purchaser's representations will be relatively few and limited in nature. If the purchaser is paying cash, the only concern the seller should have is whether it will be prevented from keeping the cash (i.e., whether there are any potential claims that the transaction or the payment of the consideration was improper). If a significant part of the consideration consists of debt or equity securities of the purchaser, additional representations may be appropriate; when the quantity of equity securities being issued is such as to make it unclear who is "acquiring" whom, there is good reason to argue for parallel representations and warranties from each party to the other.

3. **Responsibility for Accuracy of the Representations and Warranties.** Once all of the representations and warranties have been negotiated and included in the agreement, the questions become who is liable for them, for what period of time, how are damages to be measured, and what security is to be provided to ensure payment. These questions can create significant obstacles to the completion of an acquisition, and some of the questions that are raised may not be easily resolved.

4. **Managing Risks Related to Representations and Warranties.** Like loan agreements, risk arising from representations and warranties can be mitigated by the following:

   a. **Knowledge.** Trying to precisely define "knowledge" to actual, not constructive, knowledge, and try to limit knowledge to specific borrower representatives.

   b. **Material Adverse Effect (MAE).** Limiting representations and disclosures to those that have a material adverse effect.

   c. **Time Limit.** Limiting the duration of the representation.

   d. **Disclosure Schedule.** Paying careful attention to preparation of the Disclosure Schedule.

5. **What Happens When There is a False Representation?** If a representation is false when made (for example, when the agreement is executed), the representing party may be liable for damages regardless of whether the transaction closes. If any representation becomes false

by the time of the closing, the other party will generally be allowed to refuse to close. This is the crucial "bring-down" condition. If the representation is false at closing and this is not disclosed to the other party and the acquisition is consummated, the other party might be entitled to indemnification for losses or damages as a result.

E.   **Restrictive Covenants.** Purchase agreements typically restrain the selling entity, if an asset transaction, and the owners of the target enterprise in both asset and stock purchase transactions, from competing with the purchasing enterprise. Like restrictive covenants in employment agreements described in Chapter 3, restrictive covenants in acquisition agreements must be reasonable as to time, territory, and activity restrained. However, it is generally easier to enforce a restrictive covenant in an acquisition agreement than an employment agreement, and the restrictions are typically more broad. For example, while the time restraint in an employment agreement is usually one or two years, the time restraint in an acquisition agreement is typically five years.

F.   **Other Covenants.** Just as representations and warranties serve to establish the condition of the entity when the acquisition agreement is executed and, frequently, at the time of the closing if they are reaffirmed then, covenants establish what the owner of the business will do between execution of the definitive agreement and the closing and, sometimes, after the closing. At least as to the pre-closing covenants, the goal is usually to create a contractual obligation on the part of the seller to preserve the business, operations, and conditions of the entity substantially as they were at the time of execution of the agreement and to preclude actions that would adversely affect the buyer (such as paying dividends, redeeming stock, increasing salaries, issuing warrants or options, or committing to material obligations). These obligations are particularly important when there are elements of the transaction that could be affected by activities of the seller between execution of the agreement and closing.

G.   **Conditions to Closing.** The conditions to close determine whether a party must consummate the transaction. These conditions may include receipt of any necessary shareholder, member, or Board of Director approval; satisfaction with detailed due diligence; delivery of the opinions of opposing counsel as to various matters; receipt of a tax ruling or opinion; receipt of an accountant's letter; third party and governmental consents and approvals; availability of financing; absence of litigation; in non-cash transactions, conditions relating to securities and stock exchange matters; satisfactory completion of due diligence; and reaffirming representations and warranties at the closing as though made again at that time.

H.   **Indemnification.** Most acquisition agreements will provide for indemnification. These provisions grant either party (particularly, the purchaser) the right to recover post-closing for misrepresentations and noncompliance with covenants by the other party. Because these provisions have real economic substance, they are among the most highly negotiated aspects of the agreement.

1. **Liability.** Liability arises from a breach of a representation, warranty, or covenant.

2. **Limitation of Exposure.** There are several aspects of indemnification clauses that should be vigorously negotiated. First, negotiate a "basket," which is a minimum amount in indemnification claims that must accrue before a claim is made. Second, negotiate a time limit for survival of the representations and warranties and indemnification claims. Third, negotiate a precise procedure for making an indemnification claim.

3. **The Danger of "Materiality Scrapes".** Increasingly, purchasers are preparing agreements that, in essence, remove "materiality" qualifications in representations and warranties for purposes of indemnification, under the theory that the seller is protected from material claims by the "basket." This "scrapes" materiality qualifications from the agreement, resulting in more exposure to the seller. Therefore, if the purchaser insists on a materiality scrape, the seller needs to increase the "basket."

4. **Representation and Warranty Insurance.** Increasingly, especially in larger transactions, purchaser representation and warranty indemnification insurance is leading to walkaway transactions with no indemnification obligations, leaving all reliance on the insurance. For example, it is estimated that 50% to 60% of all private equity transactions use representation and warranty insurance. A sell side transaction request for proposal might say that proposals that include representation and warranty insurance in the purchase price will be favored or sometimes even require representation and warranty insurance for the bid. In practice, escrow of 10% of the purchase price for a year or two is relatively standard. When the buyer has representation and warranty insurance, the escrow amount can be reduced to 1% or less or sometimes entirely eliminated. However, representation and warranty insurance is relatively expensive. It is rarely seen under the level of private equity fund mergers and acquisitions, the floor for which is typically $10,000,000, and is more prevalent in transactions of $100,000,000 or more. Also, there is usually some buyer "retention" that is similar to a "basket" for indemnification obligations: indemnification insurance does not kick in until some threshold amount of indemnification obligations is reached. Retention is determined by enterprise value, so it can be quite high. Because liabilities travel with stock and membership interest transactions, representation and warranty insurance is more useful in stock transactions. The key to whether representation and warranty insurance is appropriate may depend upon what is excluded in the insurance policy. For example, most representation and warranty insurance policies exclude allegations of fraud (misrepresentation or concealment of material facts). To underwrite the insurance, the insurer will conduct its own due diligence to ascertain indemnification risk.

J.   **Miscellaneous Matters.** The concluding sections of the agreement typically deal with a number of miscellaneous matters, including choice of law, consent to jurisdiction, termination rights, and, not infrequently, "lock-up" options, "bust-up" fees, "no-shop," and "go shop" covenants, and expense reimbursement, all of which latter provisions will, if challenged, be closely scrutinized by the courts and should be agreed to only after the most careful and deliberate consideration by target directors. The agreement will also include many of the "boilerplate" provisions described in Chapter 1, which must not be overlooked in your contract negotiations.

V. WHAT HAPPENS AFTER THE DEFINITIVE AGREEMENT IS EXECUTED?

A.   **The Post-Signing/Pre-Closing Period.** The length of this time period will often primarily be a function of many factors, some of which are described as follows:

1.   **Due Diligence.** Each party will complete the due diligence process to fulfill any conditions to closing set forth in the definitive agreement.

2.   **Preparation of Schedules.** Every acquisition agreement, and especially an asset purchase agreement, will require the seller to complete numerous schedules to the definitive agreement. For example, the seller will be required to complete schedules describing insurance, real and personal property leases, pending litigation, retirement and benefit plans, and many other items, most of which relate to the covenants, representations, and warranties set forth in the definitive agreement. An asset purchase agreement will include a detailed description of the assets being acquired and the liabilities being assumed by the purchaser. This can be a painstaking and time consuming process.

3.   **State Corporations or LLC Law Requirements.** There likely will be an additional waiting period under state corporate or limited liability company law if a vote is required by shareholders or LLC members on a merger or a sale of all or substantially all of a corporation's or limited liability company's assets. At the end of the applicable period, the shareholders' or members' meeting will be held and the vote taken. By contrast, if the transaction is a stock or membership interest purchase, then (subject to the time necessary to allow shareholders or members to review any necessary disclosure document) no additional time is needed.

4.   **Securities Law Requirements.** If the buyer is required to register securities under the Securities Act of 1933 or if the target is required to file a proxy or consent statement with the SEC pursuant to the Securities and Exchange Act of 1934 (the "1934 Act") in connection with obtaining shareholder approval of the sale, the period between signing and closing could be substantial. It could easily take up to 20 days or longer to prepare the registration

statement or proxy statement to be filed with the SEC and an additional 30 to 60 days to complete the SEC review process and mail to shareholders.

5. **Hart-Scott-Rodino Act Notification Requirements.** Another time variable is the Hart-Scott-Rodino Act, which, if applicable to the acquisition, will require a waiting period of 30 days (15 days in the case of a stock purchase by cash tender offer rather than a privately negotiated stock purchase asset acquisition or merger) from the filing of the requisite forms before the transaction can be consummated. If the Federal Trade Commission ("FTC") or the Antitrust Division of the Department of Justice (the "Justice Department") requests additional information before the expiration of the waiting period, the period will be extended until 20 days (10 days in the case of a cash tender offer) following "substantial compliance" by the parties with the request for additional information. If the FTC or Justice Department has concerns about the anti-competitive effects of the transaction, they will often ask the parties to voluntarily extend the waiting period beyond the statutory limits; failure to voluntarily extend the waiting period could result in the commencement of litigation by the applicable government agency.

6. **Request for Audited Financial Statements.** The period of time necessary between signing and closing also may be significantly affected by the pre-signing status of financial statements of the business being acquired. If the statements are unaudited, the buyer or its financing source may well demand that an audit be performed prior to closing, sometimes accompanied by a physical inventory.

B. **Closing.** At the closing, the buyer will purchase the selling shareholders' stock (in a stock purchase transaction), the selling company's assets (in an asset purchase transaction), or effect the merger (in a merger transaction). Whatever documents of transfer are needed (in the first two cases) or are to be filed in the appropriate Secretary of State's office (in the merger situation) to accomplish the transaction will be delivered or filed at closing as well as any officers' certificates, opinions of counsel, and accountant's letters required by the acquisition agreement. The closing will usually occur as soon as possible. In many transactions, this will mean as soon as practicable after the expiration of the Hart-Scott-Rodino Act waiting period and the obtaining of all requisite shareholder and regulatory approvals. Following the closing, a press release will be issued in many transactions.

VI. HOW IS A BUSINESS VALUED FOR MERGERS AND ACQUISITIONS?

A. **Valuation Methods.** There are three basic approaches to valuation of on-going businesses: income approach; "asset approach;" and market approach.

B. **Income Approach.** The income approach is a general way of determining value using one or more methods that convert anticipated economic benefits into a present single amount. The income approach may involve either a discounted cash flow approach, which combines the organization's estimated free cash flows, terminal value, and the value of assets not required for operations (for example, cash and short-term investments) or a discounted earnings approach, which takes debt-free earnings for a given number of years and capitalizes them to estimate the current value of the organization. The discounted cash flow or earnings are multiplied by a capitalization rate (a market multiple) that reflects the relative risk of the business as a going concern.

1.   **Typical Issues Related to the Income Approach.** If the seller is an owner who will be employed by the buyer post-transaction, then the available cash flow to the purchaser will be reduced by the amount of the seller's on-going compensation and will reduce the value of the transaction. Payment for a restrictive covenant or non-compete provision may double count cash flow since the income approach already assumes that cash flow will remain with the purchased practice. Revenue growth rate assumptions can have a significant impact on the valuation. In addition, the need for capital investment (for example, for information technology, communications systems, or new space or equipment) will reduce value under an income approach. Last, small businesses are inherently riskier than large businesses because they are dependent on the health, availability, and performance of only a few key principals who have fewer resources to respond to market conditions and so, in general, will command a lower market multiple.

C.   **Asset Approach.** The asset-based approach uses one or more methods based on the value of the assets net of liabilities. This approach may involve an estimate of the value of property and equipment based on replacement cost new, less depreciation, an estimate of the value of current assets and liabilities at book values, and calculation of the adjusted debt-free net asset value of the organization based on individual asset values and non-interest bearing liabilities.

D.   **Market Approach.** The market approach determines value by using one or more methods that compare the target business to similar businesses or business ownership interests that have actually been sold. This approach involves looking for comparable transactions. However, it is sometimes difficult to define precisely what is "comparable" because of, for example, different geographic regions and revenue sources, and there is no ready market for the stock or ownership interests of small businesses.

VII. WHAT OTHER STRUCTURING ISSUES MUST BE CONSIDERED?

A.   **Allocation of Purchase Price.** Asset transfers require an allocation of purchase price among the various assets or types of assets being sold. This is critical for obtaining a stepped up basis for purposes of depreciation. Both parties must agree on the allocation of the purchase price and report it to the IRS in the same manner.

B.   **Bulk Sales of Assets.** Asset transfers have other complications. Virtually all states have enacted what are known as "bulk sales" laws which require the purchaser of a "major portion" of the inventory of a seller whose principal business consists of the sale of inventory to give advance notice of the sale to each creditor of the seller and, in some jurisdictions, to ensure that the proceeds of sale are used by the seller to pay its existing debts.

CHAPTER 7

UNDERSTANDING FUNDAMENTAL ANTITRUST LAW

I. WHAT IS "ANTITRUST LAW"?

A. **Common Law Foundation.** Antitrust, like many bodies of law, has its foundation in the English common law, under which contracts in general restraint of trade are unenforceable. For example, contracts that create a monopoly are unenforceable under the common law because they constitute a general restraint of trade. However, contracts in partial restraint of trade may be enforceable under the common law if they are "reasonable." Consequently, a core principle of the United States legal system, stretching far back into its common law roots, is promotion of "free trade."

B. **What Is the Purpose of Antitrust Law?** In general, the purpose of antitrust law is to protect economic competition for the benefit of the public under the theory that unfettered competition is in general the best system for allocation of scarce economic resources. The United States Supreme Court has consistently held that the antitrust laws protect individual consumer welfare by promoting lower prices, higher output, higher quality, efficiency in production and distribution, innovation, and consumer choice. Antitrust law does not protect competitors from each other; antitrust law operates for the benefit of consumers, not to insure that competitors such as small businesses remain in the market.

C. **What Conduct Is "Anticompetitive"?** There are several schools of antitrust thought. The more populist "liberal school," in general, takes the position that "big is bad" and favors possible governmental regimentation of some portions of the economy. If size leads to squeezing out competition and thereby increasing prices, decreasing quality, or both, big can certainly be bad. However, sometimes larger size leads to economies of scale that permit distribution of goods and services at lower prices and higher quality. The more conservative "Chicago school" (named because of prominent economists at the University of Chicago) promotes incentives to compete and provide the best products or services at the lowest cost to consumers based on the belief that unfettered competition leads to market efficiency. In either case, there are no clear lines for determining whether conduct is anticompetitive. Consequently, antitrust law is difficult to understand and at some point becomes counterintuitive.

D.   **The Role of Economics.** Antitrust law and economics are intimately intertwined: you cannot understand antitrust law without understanding economics because, in essence, antitrust law is applied microeconomics and industrial economic theory. In most markets, there are no market dominant forces so there is open competition. Other markets, however, constitute an oligopoly in which there are five or six enterprises that control the market. When there are fewer competitors, concerns regarding potential anticompetitive conduct increase. When only one enterprise is market dominant it can be alleged to have a "monopoly." However, simply having monopoly power alone may not be illegal, but the manner in which monopoly power was obtained may be impermissibly anticompetitive. Therefore, antitrust law compliance requires economic analysis, and legal proceedings alleging antitrust law violations require expert witness testimony from economists.

E.   **Federal Antitrust Law.** The federal government has enacted a series of laws intended to prevent unfair restraints on competition. The general purpose of the federal antitrust laws is to prevent conduct that weakens or destroys competition in the marketplace. Generally stated, federal antitrust law prohibits (a) agreements or actions that unnecessarily restrain trade or commerce and (b) unilateral monopolistic activity. Federal antitrust laws do not preempt state antitrust laws, but most antitrust enforcement arises under federal antitrust law.

F.   **What Are the Three Principal Federal Antitrust Laws?** There are three principal federal antitrust laws: the Sherman Act; the Clayton Act; and the Federal Trade Commission Act. There are other federal laws that have antitrust-related provisions, such as the Robinson-Patman Act that makes certain forms of price discrimination illegal, but for purposes of obtaining a fundamental understanding for the impact of the federal antitrust law on business transactions we will focus on the three principal antitrust laws:

1.   **The Sherman Act.** The Sherman Act prohibits (a) contracts, combinations, or conspiracies in restraint of trade and (b) monopolization, attempts to monopolize, and conspiracies to monopolize.

2.   **The Clayton Act.** The Clayton Act prohibits (a) mergers, acquisitions, and the formation of joint ventures which may substantially lessen competition and (b) certain types of exclusive and conditional dealing.

3. **The Federal Trade Commission Act.** The Federal Trade Commission Act prohibits unfair methods of competition and unfair or deceptive trade practices. Actions that violate the Sherman Act also violate the Federal Trade Commission Act, but the Federal Trade Commission Act includes other prohibitions.

G. **What Federal Agencies Enforce Federal Antitrust Law?** There are two principal federal enforcement agencies: the Federal Trade Commission (FTC) and the Antitrust Division of the Department of Justice (DOJ). This leads to some confusion regarding whether the FTC or DOJ is responsible for any specific arrangement, but the agencies have historically cooperated in their enforcement activities.

H. **State Antitrust Laws.** Each state except Pennsylvania has enacted an antitrust law that generally codifies the common law principles regarding restraint of trade. While state laws generally follow federal antitrust law precedent, some state law is particular to the governing state. State antitrust laws may provide broader remedies for anticompetitive behavior than the common law does and are primarily enforced by state attorneys general.

II. WHAT ARE THE ESSENTIAL CONCEPTS FOR UNDERSTANDING AND APPLYING ANTITRUST LAW?

A. **Federal Law Regulates Interstate Commerce.** As stated in the Introduction, the "Commerce Clause" in the United States Constitution permits Congress to pass laws that regulate commerce between the states. The federal antitrust laws rely on the Commerce Clause for their passage. For the federal antitrust laws to apply, the subject conduct must either be in interstate commerce or substantially affect interstate commerce. Conduct that is entirely intrastate is subject only to state antitrust laws, and the federal antitrust laws do not apply. However, in modern commerce it is difficult to find commercial conduct that does not at least substantially affect interstate commerce.

A. **The Importance of Market Power.** Virtually all antitrust analysis is focused on two kinds of "market power." First, the most familiar is "seller market power" that gives a seller (or, through collusion, a group of sellers) the ability to raise prices above those that would exist in a competitive market. Seller market power depends on an organization's market share in the "relevant market" and the number of alternative sources of goods or services available to consumers. "Monopoly power" is a high degree of market power but does not necessarily mean a 100% market dominance. Second, there is the less familiar "buyer market power" (sometimes called "monopsony power") gives a buyer (or group of buyers) the power to reduce the amount they pay for a good or service below the competitive price by a significant amount.

B. **What Is the "Relevant Market"?** Before determining market share, you need to define the "relevant market." "Relevant market" has two components: the "relevant product market;" and the "relevant geographic market." Therefore, two fundamental questions must be answered. First, what is the product or service in question? Second, what is the geographic area in which the subject product or service is provided? Each question has the same purpose: to identify significant competitors. Businesses tend to see the "relevant market" very broadly, while regulators frequently see a much more narrow market. Determination of the "relevant market" frequently requires the expert testimony of economists.

1. **How Is "Relevant Product Market" Determined?** In general, the scope of the relevant product market includes all firms selling, from the consumer's perspective, "reasonably interchangeable" products or services that are good substitutes for one another from the consumer's perspective. That can be difficult to define because the regulatory agencies need to present the perspective of the "reasonable consumer." Again, commercial enterprises will define the product or service as broadly as possible. For example, the FTC or DOJ might allege that a merger of orthopedic medical practices in a particular market is anticompetitive based only on an assessment of medical practices that are presented as practicing orthopedic medicine. However, the orthopedic medical practices might counter by asserting that the service is much broader and includes podiatrists (which perform orthopedic procedures in a specific area of the body), neurosurgeons who perform spine surgery such as spinal fusion, and physical therapists, chiropractors, or acupuncturists who provide alternative treatments to orthopedic procedures. Nevertheless, the FTC and DOJ use the "smallest market principle" in determining relevant product market, which seeks to define competitors that, by themselves, would restrain the selling enterprise in question from raising prices.

2. **How Is "Relevant Geographic Market" Determined?** In general, relevant geographic market is the area in which the enterprise in question operates and to which its customers could practically turn to obtain the relevant product or service. It is impossible define the relevant geographic market without first defining the relevant product or service market. The FTC and DOJ also apply the "smallest market principle" for determining relevant geographic market using the "hypothetical monopolist" methodology. The smallest market in which the subject enterprise as a "hypothetical monopolist" could profitably raise prices above competitive levels is a "relevant geographic market." If, however, consumers would react to increased prices by purchasing products or services from outside the region, then the geographic market expands. Therefore, determining relevant market is an iterative process, starting with the smallest market and expanding outward as the hypothetical monopolist methodology is applied. For example, in a hospital merger, a health care delivery system took the position that the relevant geographic market should be as far as the hospital's emergency helicopter service flies, which naturally was an expansive area. The FTC and DOJ, however, took a different approach and applied the "smallest market principle" to determine whether the merger might be anticompetitive.

D. **What Are "Horizontal" and "Vertical" Integration?** Under universally accepted economic theory, inefficient markets consolidate, requiring development of integration strategies in the pursuit of market efficiency. Business plans may follow either a "horizontal" or "vertical" integration strategy (or both), each of which has antitrust implications.

1. **What Is Horizontal Integration?** "Horizontal integration" refers to market consolidation of enterprises that are in the same relevant product or service market in order to gain market strength, which may, in some instances lead to monopoly power and anticompetitive conduct. The proposed merger of oligopoly telecommunications enterprises Sprint and T-Mobile is an example of a horizontal merger.

2. **What Is Vertical Integration?** "Vertical integration" refers to market consolidation of enterprises in different but interrelated product or service markets. For example, "vertical integration" may involve acquisition of a supplier to assure a source of materials for producing a consumer product or service or by a hospital system of physicians and other ancillary service providers. Vertical integration can also result in increased prices, decreased quality, or other conduct that is harmful to consumers.

III. WHAT ARE THE ESSENTIAL CHARACTERISTICS OF THE SHERMAN ACT?

A. **What Is the Purpose of the Sherman Act?** With the advent of the Industrial Revolution in the 19th century and the evolution from an agrarian to a manufacturing economy, commerce, and in particular commerce among the states of the United States, changed. Steel, coal, and soon automobile and other manufacturing that required substantial amounts of capital became dominant. It was an era of "trusts" and business or capital "combinations" organized and developed to control markets and suppress competition in the marketing of goods and services, leading to enterprises attaining monopoly power in manners that were not previously of collective public concern. It was perceived that this anticompetitive conduct placed an undue burden on free competition in interstate commerce, but there were no federal laws to address the problem. That changed with the passage of the Sherman Antitrust Act in 1890. As stated in the United States Supreme Court decision in *Apex Hosiery Co. v. Leader*, the goal of the Sherman Act was to prevent restraints of free competition in business and commercial transactions that tended to restrict production, raise prices, and otherwise control the market to the detriment of consumers of goods and services. Note that the Sherman Act, at its core, prohibits unreasonable "restraint of trade," a concept that was well developed under the common law.

B. **What Are the Fundamental Elements of the Sherman Act?** There are two core parts of the Sherman Act: (1) Section 1 declares illegal every "contract, combination, or conspiracy in restraint of trade;" and (2) Section 2 provides sanctions for "monopolization" or attempts at monopolizing any aspect of interstate trade or commerce.

C.   What Are the Fundamental Elements of Sherman Act Section 1? As stated above, Section 1 of the Sherman Act prohibits contracts, combinations, and conspiracies that unreasonably restrain trade or commerce and is the antitrust statute that is used most frequently in enforcement proceedings.

1.   **What Is an "Agreement" Under the Sherman Act?** Although there is some legal authority to the contrary, in general the terms "contract," "combination," and "conspiracy" are synonymous, meaning merely an "agreement," "understanding," or "concerted action." "Agreement" is very broadly defined and construed. An "agreement" under the Sherman Act does not have to be an explicit, formal agreement and does not have to be written. It is not necessary that there have been a handshake or even a knowing wink. An "agreement" can be an informal, loose knit arrangement. However, the existence of the agreement must be supported by factual evidence, and the agreement must unreasonably restrain trade.

2.   **An Agreement Can Be Implied Based on Facts and Circumstances.** An "agreement" can be, and frequently is, implied from all the facts and circumstances. It has been found that there was a "meeting of the minds" as to concert of action sufficient to constitute an "agreement" when competitors, in the course of a meeting, on the golf course, at a reception, or at a trade association meeting, have discussed that "prices are too low," or that "cost increases in the industry certainly justify a price increase," or, with respect to purchasing, that "prices are too high," or that "it would be foolish to purchase from a manufacturer that does not offer a five year warranty," or similar statements and have thereafter acted consistently with the views expressed. In such cases, "agreements" for purposes of antitrust enforcement have been found, despite the presentation of evidence that the pricing or other actions were taken for sound business and market reasons. Consequently, every trade association meeting or gathering of competitors leads to antitrust sensitivity.

3.   **Internal Agreements Are Not "Agreements" for Purposes of Sherman Act Enforcement.** There must be two or more parties in an agreement to support a violation of Sherman Act Section 1. For example, agreements between an organization and its employees or between a parent organization and its subsidiaries cannot violate Section 1 of the Act. Also, arrangements between corporations or other entities and their stockholders or other equity owners, directors, officers, and employees generally are not "agreements" for purposes of Sherman Act Section 1, although a Sherman Act violation may be alleged if an individual otherwise has an "independent personal stake" in the organizational action.

4.   **Unilateral or Independent Acts Are Not "Agreements" or "Conspiracies" for Purposes of Sherman Act Enforcement.** Sometimes, competitors in a relevant product or service market take actions that are substantially identical. We have all seen consumer gasoline prices rise and fall in near unison in geographic markets. However, "conscious parallelism" in which,

for example, competitors raise prices because they believe their competitors will do so, standing alone, is a unilateral act that does not constitute an impermissible conspiracy. Inference of a "conspiracy" requires evidence of certain "plus factors" that indicate that behavior was collective and not unilateral, including that the organizations involved (a) had a motive to conspire, (b) had an opportunity to conspire, (c) acted in a manner that was unlikely absent an agreement, (d) can offer no legitimate explanation or procompetitive business justification for the action, or (e) presented only pretextual justifications for their actions. Consequently, proving whether there was an impermissible conspiracy is very fact specific and difficult to prove with certainty.

5. **What Kind of Conduct Violates Sherman Act Section 1?** There are generally two types of violations of the Sherman Act: (a) *per se* violations; and (b) conduct that constitutes an "unreasonable" restraint of trade under the "Rule of Reason." However, the courts also apply a third rule, the "Quick Look Rule of Reason," which is an intermediate standard somewhere between the *Per Se Rule* and the Rule of Reason on the enforcement spectrum.

6. **What Are *Per Se* Violations of Sherman Act Section 1?** A *per se* violation of a law requires only that the prohibited conduct occur: the intent of the parties is not taken into consideration. Certain arrangements are considered to be so indefensible under any circumstances that they are presumed to be "unreasonable restraints of trade" and, therefore, illegal. *Per se* violations of the Sherman Act include the following:

   a. **Price Fixing.** Any agreement or understanding between competitors to raise, lower, or stabilize prices is illegal. Price fixing applies to the price at which goods or services will be purchased, as well as the price at which they will be sold. Agreements that affect price or an element of price are also illegal (for example, agreements on terms of sale, credit terms, price changes, profit margins, warranties, discounts, or rebates). An agreement or understanding between a supplier and customer as to the price at which the customer will resell the goods purchased from the supplier is also illegal. Such an agreement is commonly referred to as vertical price fixing or resale price maintenance.

   b. **Limitation of Supply or Demand.** An agreement or understanding between competitors to restrict the volume of goods or services they will produce or make available for sale or to restrict the amount of a product or raw material which they will purchase is illegal.

   c. **Allocation of Business.** An agreement or understanding between competitors that each will confine its business to a different geographic area, to a different line of products or services, or to different customers or classes of customers is illegal. Such an agreement is sometimes called market division or customer allocation.

d. **Boycotts.** An agreement or understanding between competitors that they will not sell to a particular customer or purchase from a given supplier or that in some manner they will not deal with another is generally illegal, although many boycotts are now treated under the Rule of Reason.

e. **Tying Arrangements.** An arrangement in which a customer is required to purchase an unwanted product or service in order to obtain a desired product or service is illegal if the seller controls a substantial part of the market for the desired product or service.

7. **What Kind of Conduct Violates the "Rule of Reason"?** Numerous types of business conduct other than *per se* conduct may become "unreasonable" restraints of trade in light of surrounding facts and circumstances. For example:

a. **Refusal to Deal.** A supplier or purchaser of goods or services generally may determine with whom it will or will not do business. However, a supplier may not cut off a customer in furtherance of a *per se* violation such as price fixing.

b. **Reciprocity.** The practice of purchasing goods from another on condition that the other purchase different goods from you may be an antitrust offense. It is more likely to be condemned if done systematically and enforced through coercion.

c. **Exclusive Dealing.** An agreement to purchase from only one supplier or sell to only one customer may be illegal if it has a substantial adverse impact on competition. However, exclusivity may also be procompetitive under certain circumstances.

d. **Other Non-Price Vertical Restraints.** This category includes practices such as territorial and customer restraints on dealers. Such restraints may be illegal if they have a substantial adverse impact on competition.

D. **What is the "Quick Look Rule of Reason" for Enforcement of Sherman Act Section 1?** As stated above, antitrust law is difficult to apply and is very fact specific. In that regard, the *Per Se* Rule and the Rule of Reason for determining what constitutes an "unreasonable restraint of trade" sit on opposite ends of the enforcement spectrum. Over time, the "Quick Look Rule of Reason" has emerged as an intermediate standard. The Quick Look Rule of Reason provides that certain actions involving competitors that directly affect price or output are conclusively presumed to have anticompetitive effects, but the courts permit the competitors to rebut the presumption by producing evidence of plausible procompetitive justification for the agreement that is allegedly in restraint of trade.

E. **What Are the Fundamental Elements of Sherman Act Section 2?** Section 2 of the Sherman Act prohibits monopolization, attempts to monopolize, and conspiracy to monopolize. Contrary to Sherman Act Section 1, no "agreement" is required to find a Sherman Act Section 2 violation: a single legal entity can engage in conduct that violates Sherman Act Section 2. In general, Section 2's monopolization and attempted monopolization provisions apply to "exclusionary" or "predatory" conduct exercised by organizations with substantial market power.

1. **What Is "Monopolization"?** Monopolization has two separate elements. First, monopolization requires "monopoly power." However, monopoly power alone does not constitute illegal monopolization. More is required. Second, monopolization requires "predatory," "unreasonably exclusionary," or "anticompetitive" conduct resulting in willful acquisition or maintenance of monopoly power as distinguished from legitimate reasons for attaining monopoly power such as a superior product or service, business acumen, or historically fortuitous circumstances and a deliberateness in the acquisition, use, or preservation of such power.

1. **What Is "Monopoly Power"?** The legal definition of "monopoly power" is the power to control prices or exclude others from the market. This definition is broad and imprecise. Rationally, an organization cannot control prices unless others are excluded from the market. However, mere ability to exclude competition, without more, is not sufficient to give an organization monopoly power. In essence, "monopoly power" is a substantial degree of "market power." "Market share" is often used as a shorthand for market power. For example, control of 90% of a market is generally considered to be enough to establish monopoly power, while control of 65% or more of the market is generally enough to constitute "monopoly power."

b. **What Is "Predatory," "Unreasonably Exclusionary," and "Anticompetitive" Conduct for Purposes of Constituting "Monopolization"?** This element of monopolization focuses on how an organization interacts with competitors, not consumers, and is an area in which antitrust analysis becomes obtuse. It defies definition. For example, it is difficult to distinguish aggressive, but procompetitive, conduct from predatory or unreasonably exclusionary anticompetitive conduct. For purposes a fundamental understanding, conduct is "predatory" for purposes of Sherman Act Section 2 if (a) it has exclusionary effect on an organization's competitors and contributes significantly to an organization's ability to maintain market power but generates none of the benefits of competition, such as lower prices, greater productivity, more choice, increased market access, innovation, and efficiency in production or distribution and (b) there is no legitimate business interest that renders the conduct non-predatory. In other words, "predatory" conduct is fact specific and difficult to define, but one type of conduct typically found to constitute predatory conduct is "predatory pricing," which results when an organization (i) charges a price below its cost of market production for a significant period of time to drive its competitors from the market and (ii) can recoup its losses after competitors are driven from the market by charging higher prices.

c.   **Refusals to Deal With Competitors.** A predominant amount of Sherman Act Section 2 cases involve an organization with substantial market power refusing to deal in some form with its competitors who allegedly need the organization's cooperation to compete effectively against the organization. However, there is no clear duty for a market dominant organization to deal with competitors, so there are no bright lines for determining monopolization.

2.   **What Is an "Attempt to Monopolize"?** An attempt to monopolize requires a specific intent to monopolize, predatory conduct pursuant to that intent, and a "dangerous probability" that the attempt will succeed if the predatory conduct continues. The only difference between "monopolization" and "attempt to monopolize" is the necessary share of the perpetrator's market share.

a.   **What Is the Meaning of "Specific Intent to Monopolize"?** This element is typically satisfied by an organization engaging in "predatory conduct," and thus this element is typically collapsed unto the "predatory conduct" element.

b.   **What Is the Meaning of "Predatory Conduct"?** The definition of "predatory conduct" for attempts to monopolize is the same as for "monopolization."

c.   **What Is the Meaning of "Dangerous Probability of Actual Monopolization"?** Even if an organization has a specific intent to monopolize and has engaged in predatory conduct, Section 2 of the Sherman Act is not violated unless the conduct results in a dangerous probability of actual monopolization, given the market's structural characteristics and the type of alleged predatory conduct. The critical criteria for this element of the test is the perpetrating organization's market share. While there is no specific market share percentage for purposes of the test for an attempt to monopolize, it is generally agreed that a market share of at least 40% to 50% is sufficient to support a violation.

3.   **What Is a "Conspiracy to Monopolize"?** A conspiracy to monopolize has three essential elements: (a) a conspiracy; (b) two or more concerns acting with the specific intent to monopolize; and (c) an overt act in furtherance of the conspiracy. Like Section 1 of the Sherman Act, a

"conspiracy" requires two different entities that are not financially integrated. In reality, any alleged "conspiracy to monopolize" under Section 2 can be alleged as a violation of Section 1, under which claims are more commonly made.

IV. WHAT ARE THE ESSENTIAL CHARACTERISTICS OF THE CLAYTON ACT?

A.   **What Is the Purpose of the Clayton Act?** As the Industrial Revolution progressed, large organizations continued to develop in the United States economy, and, even after passage of the Sherman Antitrust Act in 1890, there were concerns regarding the anticompetitive impact of large enterprises on interstate commerce. While the Sherman Act provided sanctions for conduct that restrained trade, that presupposes that the arrangement exists. So the question was posed: what can be done to prevent anticompetitive conduct? From those concerns, Congress enacted the Clayton Antitrust Act of 1914. Instead of policing existing organizations and arrangements, the Clayton Act, as a supplement to the Sherman Act, attempts to thwart anticompetitive conduct in its incipiency by prohibiting certain anticompetitive conduct.

B.   **What Is the Clayton Act Prohibition of Arrangements that May Have Anticompetitive Effects?** Section 7 of the Clayton Act provides that no person engaged in any activity affecting interstate commerce shall acquire, directly or indirectly, the ownership interests or assets of another person in any line of commerce in any geographic area if a reasonable probability of such acquisition may be to lessen competition or to tend to create a monopoly. In essence, Chapter 7 of the Clayton Act prohibits arrangements that *may* have significant anticompetitive effects, including, without limitation, mergers, acquisitions, joint ventures, leases, licenses, partial acquisitions, and even employment. No actual lessening of competition is required to violate the Clayton Act: only reasonable probability of an adverse effect on competition, and doubts are resolved against the arrangement.

    1.   **What Are the Market Thresholds for Applying the Clayton Act?** If a merger, acquisition, or other consolidation results in an organization having a "high market share" or" high market concentration," there is a rebuttable presumption that the transaction will be anticompetitive, and it is *prima facie* unlawful. The general rule is that the rebuttable presumption applies if the merging firms have a post-merger market share that is 30% or more. If that threshold is reached, then the burden shifts to the organization to introduce evidence that the merger, acquisition, or consolidation is not anticompetitive.

    2.   **How Are Clayton Act Merger Challenge Actions Brought?** Although private plaintiffs may challenge mergers, almost all merger challenges are enforcement actions brought by the FTC or DOJ Antitrust Division as pre-transaction injunctions to block the transaction, which requires prediction of the post-transaction anticompetitive effects.

3.   **Pre-Merger Notification Requirements.** Acquisitions, mergers, and formations of joint ventures which exceed certain "size of the transaction" and "size of the parties" thresholds are subject to reporting requirements to both the FTC and the DOJ Antitrust Division under the Hart-Scott-Rodino (HSR) Act, which amended the Clayton Act, to enable the FTC and DOJ to examine the legality of the transaction before it is consummated. The thresholds required to trigger the HSR filing requirement are quite substantial: the size of the transaction must be greater than $80,000,000.00; and, alternatively under the size of the parties test, one party to the transaction must have assets or annual revenues of at least $170,000,000.00 and the other party must have assets or annual revenues of at least $17,000,000.00. Consequently, only the largest transactions require HSR pre-transaction notification; most transactions do not.

C.   **What Is the Clayton Act Prohibition on Exclusive Dealing?** Section 3 of the Clayton Act prohibits exclusive dealing arrangements, requirements contracts, and tying arrangements if the effect of the arrangement may be to substantially lessen competition or tend to create a monopoly.

D.   **What Is the Clayton Act Prohibition of Interlocking Officers and Directors?** Section 8 of the Clayton Act prohibits any person from simultaneously serving as an officer or on the Board of Directors of competing organizations, commonly referred to as "interlocking" relationships, if the organizations are engaged in interstate commerce and exceed certain capital, surplus, and profits thresholds as established and annually revised by the FTC. Like HSR reporting, the "interlocking" relationships thresholds are quite substantial. In general, the Clayton Section 8 prohibitions apply if each of the interlocking organizations has capital, surplus, and undivided profits in excess of $35,000,000 and the competitive sales of each organization are greater than $3,500,000. The actual thresholds are greater, and they increase annually. Even without application of Clayton Act Section 8, as explained in the Chapter on Corporate Governance and Fiduciary Duty, officers and directors cannot engage in conflicts of interest arrangements, cannot usurp corporate opportunities for their own benefit, and must maintain confidentiality of an organizations trade secret and otherwise proprietary information. Therefore, "interlocking" relationships are dangerous regardless of whether they violate the Clayton Act.

V. WHAT ARE THE ESSENTIAL CHARACTERISTICS OF THE FEDERAL TRADE COMMISSION ACT?

A.   **What Is the Purpose of the Federal Trade Commission Act?** Again during the early days of the Industrial Revolution, the need for a federal agency that could police anticompetitive conduct became apparent. Consequently, in the same year that the Clayton Act was enacted, Congress passed the Federal Trade Commission Act of 1914, through which the FTC was created.

B. **What Conduct Does the Federal Trade Commission Act Cover?** In general, the Federal Trade Commission Act prohibits unfair methods of competition and deceptive acts or trade practices. For example, the FTC has been actively involved in investigating trade associations such as independent physician associations that try to collectively negotiate price terms with health care payors even if the trade association is not clinically or financially integrated. The Act reaches a bit deeper than the Sherman Act and Clayton Act and is intended to protect consumers in other ways, such as deceptive advertising. Also, one emerging FTC power is protection of consumer privacy, which the FTC shares with the United States Department of Health and Human Services, Office of Civil Rights, the agency responsible for enforcing the Health Insurance Portability and Accountability Act of 2010 privacy rules.

C. **What Are the Federal Trade Commission Regulatory Powers?** The Act authorizes the FTC to bring actions against every trade practice which: (1) restrains competition in violation of the Sherman Act; (2) may lessen competition in violation of the Clayton Act; (3) is contrary to the public policy underlying the Sherman and Clayton Acts; (4) is contrary to broad principles of ethics or "fairness;" or (5) might deceive the public. Under the Federal Trade Commission Act, the FTC is empowered to (a) prevent unfair methods of competition, (b) seek monetary sanctions and other relief arising from conduct that injures consumers, (c) promulgate rules that describe specific conduce that is by definition "unfair" or "deceptive" and establish requirements intended to prevent such conduct, (d) conduct investigations related to potentially anticompetitive conduct of entities engaged in interstate commerce, and (e) provide reports and recommendations to Congress.

D. **How Does the Federal Trade Commission Work with the DOJ Antitrust Division?** Although there are no clear lines of delineation, because any violation of the Sherman Act is also a violation of the Federal Trade Commission Act and the FTC can act on matters that violate each Act, the FTC and the DOJ Antitrust Division work collaboratively through interagency protocols. However, only the DOJ Antitrust Division can prosecute criminal misconduct, although the FTC may assist the DOJ Antitrust Division with a criminal investigation.

VI. WHAT CONDUCT IS EXEMPT FROM APPLICATION OF THE FEDERAL ANTITRUST LAWS?

A. **What Conduct or Persons Are Exempt or Immune From Antitrust Law Enforcement?** There are various persons, actions, and situations that are exempt or immune from antitrust enforcement. Most exemptions are "express" and described in the federal antitrust laws. Some exemptions are created by judicial decisions and are described as "implied," but they are disfavored. The following is an overview description of several of the more important express exemptions or conduct that is beyond coverage of the federal antitrust laws.

B. **What Is the "State Action" Exemption?** Basically, the United States Supreme Court many years ago established the rule that the Sherman Act was not intended to restrain state actions or official action directed by a state. There are some state laws that directly restrain competition and create barriers for competitors to enter the market, but those laws are not subject to federal antitrust law enforcement. For example, some states have enacted "Certificate of Need" (CON) laws which permit the states to develop a "need formula" for the provision of health services and require providers of new institutional health services to obtain a "certificate" before proceeding with development of the health service. This clearly protects holders of CONs from competition if the need formula developed by the state indicates that there is no need for the service, even if the new service might lead to lower consumer prices, higher quality, and greater consumer choice. Also, some states have "Certificate of Public Advantage" (COPA) laws that permit hospital mergers that create monopoly power. However, what a states permits or approves is not subject to federal antitrust law enforcement.

C. **What Is the "Noerr-Pennington" Exemption?** Commonly called the "Noerr-Pennington" exemption after the two United States Supreme Court decisions that created it, it has long been established that the antitrust laws do not apply to private parties' petitioning the government for anticompetitive action, for example, through filing litigation (unless the filing is either fraudulent or a "sham").

D. **What Is the Federal Governmental Immunity Exemption?** The federal antitrust laws do not apply to the federal government and its agencies or agents.

E. **What Is the Labor Exemption?** Even though labor unions are cartels that fix the price of the labor that they sell, labor unions are exempt from federal antitrust law enforcement.

F. **What Is the Health Care Quality Improvement Act (HCQIA) Exemption?** To protect hospitals from damages in antitrust lawsuits arising from denials of physician medical staff privileges, the HCQIA exempts hospitals from antitrust damages, but not liability, arising from a hospital's denial, revocation, or suspension of a physician's medical staff privileges. The exemption is limited to "professional review actions" of "professional review bodies" in the course of "professional review activities" and does not apply to other forms of allegedly anticompetitive conduct, such as a hospital's entering into exclusive contracts for provision of services such as anesthesia, radiology, and pathology.

VII. WHAT ARE THE PENALTIES FOR VIOLATING THE FEDERAL ANTITRUST LAWS?

A. **How Are the Federal Antitrust Laws Typically Enforced?** Although the FTC and the DOJ Antitrust Division have the ability to bring civil and criminal proceedings to enforce the federal antitrust laws, the overwhelming percentage of cases alleging federal antitrust law violation are brought by private plaintiffs, not governmental agencies.

B. **What Damages Can a Private Plaintiff Seek for Antitrust Law Violation?** The Clayton Act provides that a private party injured by any conduct that violates the federal antitrust law can sue to recover treble damages, costs, and attorneys' fees.

C. **What Can a Private Plaintiff do to Prevent Continuing Harm?** A private plaintiff can sue for injunctive relief against threatened losses and damages arising from antitrust law violations provided that the plaintiff can show irreparable harm; no adequate remedy at law (such as monetary damages); balancing the interests of the parties, equitable relief is warranted; and issuing the injunction will not harm public interest.

D. **What Criminal Sanctions, Civil Monetary Penalties, and Fines Can be Sought by Federal Antitrust Enforcement Agencies?** Violation of the antitrust laws can result in severe penalties: individuals may be convicted of a felony, with a maximum prison term of 10 years and a fine up to the greater of approximately $1,000,000 per violation or twice the defendant's gross gain or the victim's gross loss; a corporation may be fined up to the greater of $100 million per violation or twice the defendant's gross gain or the victim's gross loss.

VIII. HOW CAN YOU MITIGATE ANTITRUST RISK?

A. **Exercise Caution When Communicating With Competitors.** Any discussion among competitors, no matter how harmless it may seem at the time, may later be subject to antitrust scrutiny. You should assume that any conversation with a competitor, for example, at a trade association meeting, may later be the subject of testimony given under oath by your competitor and other participants in the conversation or meeting, who may be subpoenaed by government investigators to appear before a grand jury. The following topics should be strictly avoided in any communication between competitors:

1. Prices and pricing policies.

2. Terms or conditions of sale.

3. Credit terms and billing practices.

4. Suppliers' terms and conditions of sale.

5. Costs.

6. Profits or profit margins.

7. Advertising and marketing plans and practices.

8.   Bids, including your intent to bid or not to bid for a particular contract or program, and the timing or amount of your bid.

9.   Allocation of territories or customers.

10.   Refusals to deal with a supplier or customer.

B.   **How Is Antitrust Law Risk Managed in Horizontal Mergers, Acquisitions, and Consolidations?** As stated above, inefficient markets consolidate, and "horizontal" merger, acquisition, or consolidation of entities that are otherwise competitors in the market is a common integration or survival strategy. However, remember Baker's Rule of Business Transactions: Most Deals Don't Happen. If competitors engage in merger, acquisition, or consolidation discussions, at some point there must be an exchange of "price information" of a nature that might otherwise constitute a *per se* violation of Sherman Act Section 1. Consequently, parties are subject to strict scrutiny under both federal and state antitrust laws and must proceed cautiously to ensure antitrust law compliance. All communications should focus on the procompetitive aspects of the potential arrangement and if possible show awareness of and compliance with antitrust law. While the parties' legal counsel need to be involved and their advice followed, the following are suggestions on how to manage antitrust risk in horizontal mergers, acquisitions, and consolidations:

1.   **Confidentiality Obligations.** Each person or entity participating in the preliminary discussions should be party to a confidentiality agreement that states that the confidential and proprietary information exchanged by the parties is to be used only to evaluate the possibility of a merger, acquisition, or consolidation of the subject entities and will be disseminated only on a strict "need to know" basis within each organization.

2.   **Limitations During Preliminary Discussions.** At no time during the preliminary deliberations is it appropriate for the consolidating organizations to engage in discussions that contravene antitrust laws, including but not limited to: (a) discussions of prices charged by consolidating organizations for the provision products or services; (b) discussions of mutually agreed upon limitations on the products or services offered by consolidating organizations regardless of whether those limitations are defined by product, by geography, by customer segment, or by any combination thereof; and (c) discussions of mutually agreed upon refusals to conduct business with certain suppliers or customers.

3.   **Authorized Representatives.** Only designated representatives may prepare written communications, including, without limitation, e-mail and text messages, regarding the potential merger, acquisition, or consolidation.

4.   **Joint Defense Agreement.** The organizations' legal counsel should consider entering into a "joint defense agreement" with respect to antitrust law compliance in connection with the transaction. Under such an agreement, the parties state that they will jointly strive to comply with antitrust law, with the joint defense agreement being terminable if the interests of the parties on antitrust issues become divergent.

5.   **Involvement of Legal Counsel in Communications.** With respect to each communication from one party to the other, legal counsel should receive a copy. This gives an opportunity to characterize the communication as being "privileged" under the attorney-client communication privilege. It also gives legal counsel the opportunity to provide advice regarding how to proceed under the subject matter described in the communication in accordance with applicable law.

6.   **Involvement of Legal Counsel in Meetings Between the Parties.** Legal counsel for each party should also be involved in formal meetings between the parties at which issues such as structure and strategy are discussed. Attendance can be by telephone conference call, electronic communication services, or physical presence. This provides the triple benefits of (a) permitting legal counsel to read an antitrust compliance statement before the communications commence, (b) providing legal counsel with an opportunity to stop any line of discussion that might implicate the antitrust laws, and (c) being able to assert attorney-client communication and attorney work product privileges related to analysis and advice provided with respect to the antitrust laws. It is in this context that a "joint defense agreement" has specific value.

7.   **Tying Due Diligence Information Flow to the Status of the Negotiations.** Conducting due diligence and obtaining detailed information regarding a competitor in the market is a natural aspect of horizontal mergers. Because price and strategic information must be shared, policies and procedures need to be put into place that tie the flow of information to the status of the negotiations and restrict the information flow to a "need to know" basis. While it is impossible to state in advance what information must flow and when, the parties, with the advice of legal counsel, need to be sensitive to this overall objective.

8.   **Term Sheet.** There is no sense in investing time, effort, and energy in a potential transaction if there are insurmountable obstacles. Also, if there are such obstacles, then the parties can go their separate ways without getting into deep due diligence that might implicate the antitrust laws. An effective way to ferret out potentially insurmountable obstacles is to develop a Term Sheet that outlines the fundamental terms and conditions of the transaction. One benefit of a Term Sheet is that it may describe fundamental terms and conditions that

lead to an early decision not to proceed with the transaction, which may save the parties substantial time and resources.

9. **Engaging a Third Party for Purposes of Managing Price Information.** When price information begins to be exchanged, it may be beneficial to engage an independent third party, working with accounting and financial advisors, to assess the price information and prepare *pro forma* financial statements to predict what a merged or consolidated entity might look like.

C. **Maintaining Your Records.** The antitrust laws are concerned with substance, not form. Therefore, careful language will not avoid antitrust liability if the underlying conduct is illegal. On the other hand, conduct which is perfectly legal may become suspect if written documents are worded in a way that might be interpreted as indicating, contrary to fact, the existence of an antitrust violation. All documents should be written with the assumption that they may one day be required to be disclosed in connection with an antitrust investigation. In today's world, the greatest challenge is managing electronic communications, including electronic mail, text messages, and information sent through social media. If an arrangement provokes an antitrust law investigation, the FTC or DOJ Antitrust Division will engage in "e-discovery," permitting the regulators to perform an electronic search for "hot" words or phrases that might lead to antitrust compliance scrutiny. Consequently, all communications should focus on the procompetitive aspects of the potential arrangement and if possible show awareness of and compliance with antitrust law.

1. **Personal Notes.** Personal notes which record personal impressions rather than the facts of what occurred in a meeting or conversation, or which are based on recollection rather than being made at the time of the meeting, can be particularly dangerous. If personal notes are taken and retained, they should be carefully written to avoid misstatements of fact, complete so as to prevent statements from being taken out of context, and dated.

2. **Drafts of Documents.** Drafts of documents, after a final version of the document has been completed, are no longer necessary and could be confusing or subject to misinterpretation if examined by a third person. This is also true of notes that are not dated, do not clearly set out the context in which they were generated, provide only partial information, or relate to a completed transaction. Therefore, the parties should consider implementing a document retention policy that requires shredding of drafts and other documents once they are superseded. However, any document retention policy must be formally implemented and uniformly followed. This is what took Arthur Andersen down in the Enron scandal: documents were shredded in a manner that did not reflect customary practice, regardless of whether there was a written document retention policy.

D.   **Is It Possible to Acquire Antitrust Insurance?** With the increased scrutiny by the FTC and DOJ, liability insurance that covers antitrust is becoming increasingly difficult to obtain. Insurers are often requiring minimum deductibles in excess of $100,000 for antitrust claims or are excluding antitrust from liability policies altogether.

E.   **DOJ Business Review Letters and FTC Advisory Opinions.** Sometimes it is better to ask for permission than forgiveness, particularly when conduct is policed by powerful federal enforcement agencies. Recognizing that application of antitrust law is challenging and parties may be unwilling to engage in conduct if it will later bring antitrust law scrutiny, both the FTC and the DOJ Antitrust Division have developed protocols for obtaining pre-transaction permission to proceed. Under certain circumstances, an entity can request a Business Review Letter from the DOJ Antitrust Division or an Advisory Opinion from the FTC prior to engaging in conduct that might implicate the antitrust laws.

CHAPTER 8

UNDERSTANDING FUNDAMENTAL
INTELLECTUAL PROPERTY LAW

I. WHAT IS "INTELLECTUAL PROPERTY"?

A.   **Definition of Intellectual Property.** Land is called "real property." When you purchase a home or other real property in the form of land, title is passed in a deed, and the history of title to the land is recorded in a court. Material objects are called "personal property." You can see and feel personal property, and it can be possessed by only one person at a time. Under the law, original ideas, concepts, processes, and expressions are generally referred to as "intellectual property." One definition of "intellectual property" is "creative ideas and expressions of the human mind that have commercial value and receive the legal protection of a property right." These property rights arise from a person's intellect, and they are "property" even if you cannot feel or see it. The legal term for intellectual property is "intangible personal property." Like title to land, it is necessary to be able to trace the title to intellectual property so it can be protected from infringers. Unfortunately, many entrepreneurs unwittingly act in a manner that not only compromises ownership but results in a complete loss of intellectual property rights. For example, it is human nature to tell others about your great ideas, but even that simple act may have disastrously negative legal consequences. Also, every time a person or entity contributes to a business concept, intellectual property rights arise that may thwart a budding enterprise from implementing its business plan. Consequently, entrepreneurs need a fundamental understanding of intellectual property law before publicly disclosing the business plan to anyone.

B.   **What Bodies of Law Protect Intellectual Property?** The American dream is founded on entrepreneurial spirit and rewarding ingenuity and initiative. The bedrock for promotion of entrepreneurial spirit is in the seminal document that our Founding Fathers created at the birth of this great nation. The Constitution of the United States of America grants Congress the power *"To promote the progress of science and useful arts, by securing for limited times to authors and inventors* *the exclusive right to their respective writings and discoveries.*" In common parlance, this provision is known as the "patent and copyright clause." Other bodies of law have arisen from the common law to protect confidential proprietary information and the marks used to distinguish goods and services in the marketplace. Within this framework, the law has evolved to include four flavors of intellectual property protection: trade secret; patent; copyright; and trademark. Think of it as chocolate, vanilla, strawberry, and pistachio. Each is important for any business venture and are generally described as follows:

1.   **Trade Secrets.** Trade secrets protect confidential information from which a person or entity derives value or a competitive advantage.

2.   **Patents.** A patent grants to an inventor an exclusive right to exclude others from making, using, or selling the invention if it is a new and useful process, machine, method of manufacture, or composition of matter, or any new and useful improvements thereof.

3.   **Copyrights.** By contrast, copyrights protect the contents of original artistic or literary works and expressions, including books, magazines, newspapers, computer software, songs, and artwork.

4.   **Trademarks and Service Marks.** Trademarks protect words, phrases, symbols, or designs that identify and distinguish the source of goods and services of one party from those of another. Examples of famous trademarks include MICROSOFT®, NIKE®, COCA COLA® and MERCEDES BENZ®. (NOTE: Technically, trademarks identify goods or tangible products, while service marks identify services. For ease of reference, the term "trademark" is used to identify both trademarks and service marks in this work.)

C.   **Can More Than One Body of Law Apply to a Creative Work?** The ability to distinguish between the various rights can easily become blurred, particularly because several rights may be embodied in a single object. For example, the famous cartoon character "Mickey Mouse" is protected under copyright laws because it is an original artistic expression, but it also constitutes a trademark for Walt Disney's goods and services. Likewise, a golf club may be protected by patents for an element of the club that improves its performance (such as square grooves in the club face), while the club may also be identified by a trademark (like PING®).

D.   **Why Is Intellectual Property Protection Important?**

1.   **Every Business Enterprise Owns Intellectual Property.** Every business enterprise owns intellectual property, and every business enterprise should have an intellectual property protection plan.

2. **Intellectual Property Creates Value.** Intellectual property distinguishes business enterprises from their competitors, and it is frequently at the core of the value of a business. Conversely, failure to protect intellectual property devalues an enterprise and may prevent raising capital and implementing a business plan.

II. WHAT ARE THE FUNDAMENTALS OF TRADE SECRET LAW?

A. **What Is a "Trade Secret"?** It comes to you as if in a dream. There has to be a better way. There must be a product or service that satisfies a market need. You start sketching it out. You are excited. This will work. I know it. Even at this earliest stage in concept development, intellectual property rights arise. As long as you are the only person who knows the idea, it is a secret. "Trade secret" means information, without regard to form, including, but not limited to, technical or nontechnical data, a formula, a pattern, a compilation, a program, a device, a method, a technique, a drawing, a process, financial data, financial plans, product plans, or a list of actual or potential customers or suppliers which is not commonly known by or available to the public and which information (1) derives economic value, actual or potential, from not being generally known to, and not being readily ascertainable by proper means by, other persons who can obtain economic value from its disclosure or use and (2) is the subject of efforts that are reasonable under the circumstances to maintain its secrecy. Some businesses rely heavily on trade secret protection. Perhaps the most famous trade secret is the formula for COCA COLA®. Many competitors have tried to "reverse engineer" the Coke® formula, but none has been entirely successful. The safeguards on this trade secret are legendary.

B. **What Law Governs Protection of Trade Secrets?** Trade secret protection arises under the common law and is therefore principally governed by state and not federal law (although recent federal legislation described below provides some federal law trade secret protection rights). For example, under the common law, an employee must keep the employer's trade secrets confidential for all time, even in the absence of a written contract. An obligation to maintain trade secret confidentiality is usually held to be implied in independent contractor arrangements, but the best practice is to include confidentiality provisions in written independent contractor agreements. The common law of trade secrets has been codified in a "Uniform Act" called the Uniform Trade Secrets Act, which has been enacted in some form in every state or jurisdiction except three states: Massachusetts; New York; and North Carolina (although North Carolina law is very similar to the Uniform Trade Secrets Act). The Uniform Trade Secrets Act codifies the basic principles of common law trade secret protection, preserving its essential distinctions from patent law. As described in detail below, a valid patent provides a legal monopoly on certain "inventions" for a term of years in exchange for public disclosure of the invention, which, in essence, releases all trade secret rights. However, not all trade secrets are patentable, and, if the courts ultimately decide that the United States Patent and Trademark office (the "PTO") improperly issued a patent, an invention will have been disclosed to competitors with no corresponding benefit. In view of the substantial number of patents that are invalidated by the courts and the absence of a time limit for trade secret protection, many businesses now elect to protect commercially valuable information through reliance upon the state trade secret law.

C.   **How Are Trade Secrets Protected?** Basically, trade secrets must be kept confidential and secret. The common law is well settled that an entity must undertake reasonable precautions under the circumstances to maintain the secrecy or confidentiality of the information. The Uniform Trade Secrets Act also requires as an independent condition of trade secret protection that the information "is the subject of efforts that are reasonable under the circumstances to maintain its secrecy." The nature of the information sought to be protected, the nature of the enterprise, the nature of the market, and the costs and benefits of each possible precaution will determine what efforts are necessary to meet the reasonableness requirement.

D.   **What Remedies Are Available When Trade Secrets Are Misappropriated?**

1.   **State Law Remedies.** If a trade secret is misappropriated, a business can either recover monetary damages (a "remedy at law") or obtain an injunction or restraining order (an "equitable remedy") by filing a lawsuit in state court. Litigation in the state courts is the most commonly used method to seek remedies for trade secret misappropriation.

2.   **Federal Law Remedies.** Until 2016, trade secret remedies could be sought only in the state courts. That changed with the enactment of the Defend Trade Secrets Act of 2016 (the "DTSA"). The DTSA creates a federal cause of action for trade secret misappropriation similar to a state court action that can be asserted under the Uniform Trade Secret Act. However, the definition of "trade secrets" under the DTSA is generally more broad than under state law. The DTSA definition is as follows: all forms and types of financial, business, scientific, technical, economic, or engineering information, including patterns, plans, compilations, program devices, formulas, designs, prototypes, methods, techniques, processes, procedures, programs, or codes, whether tangible or intangible, and whether or how stored, compiled, or memorialized physically, electronically, graphically, photographically, or in writing if (a) the owner thereof has taken reasonable measures to keep such information secret; and (b) the information derives independent economic value, actual or potential, from not being generally known to, and not being readily ascertainable through proper means by, the other person who and obtain economic value from the disclosure or use of the information. Consequently, almost every type of information can qualify as a trade secret under the EEA so long as: (i) the information is actually secret; (ii) the owner took reasonable measures to maintain that secrecy; and (iii) independent economic value is derived from that secrecy.

E.   **What Should a Business Enterprise Do to Preserve Trade Secret Rights?** Every person to whom the trade secret is disclosed should be informed about the value of the company's protected confidential information and that the information should not be disclosed to persons not authorized to have it. For W-2 employees, the duty to maintain confidentiality of an employer's trade secrets arises under the law, even in the absence of a written contract. For independent contractors, this is typically accomplished through a written "Confidentiality Agreement," which is sometimes called a "Non-Disclosure Agreement" or "NDA." Also, an enterprise should use reasonable physical security measures, for example by marking the written information as "CONFIDENTIAL." In the absence of executed NDAs, there is a risk of loss of trade secret rights when proprietary concepts, programs, processes, and ideas are disclosed outside of a relationship that protects trade secret rights. If there are no NDAs in place, one way to mitigate the risk of disclosure, at least for patentable inventions, is filing of a patent application.

III. WHAT ARE THE FUNDAMENTALS OF PATENT LAW?

A.   **What Law Governs Patents?** Of the four major areas of law related to intellectual property (trade secrets, patents, copyrights, and trademarks), patent law is probably the most complex and confusing. Patents are governed exclusively by federal law; there is no common law of patents. Whoever invents or discovers any new and useful process, machine, manufacture, or composition of matter, or any new and useful improvement thereof, can obtain a patent from the United States Patent and Trademark Office (PTO) that gives the inventor an exclusive property right in the invention for a defined period of time.

B.   **What Is the Purpose of Patent Law?** By giving the Congress the right to enact patent laws in the United States Constitution, the Founding Fathers intended to provide citizens with the incentive to innovate and publicly disclose their innovations in exchange for a period of exclusive ownership. When Congress developed the United States patent system, it did so, in part, to encourage the development of technology in the United States by granting inventors exclusive rights to their inventions in the form of a limited monopoly lasting for a period of years in exchange for disclosure of the technology of their inventions to the general public through the publishing of issued patents. Patent rights are exclusionary rights: a patent gives the patent owner the right to exclude others from using the patentable claims. Without patent law, innovations are more likely to be kept secret, which could be detrimental to both the economic health of the nation and society in general.

C.   **What Is "Patentable"?** Patent protection can be obtained on new inventions and on new "improvements" to old inventions. An "improvement" generally is defined as adding to or altering an existing item resulting in an increased efficiency without destruction of identity. In other words, making an existing item better. To be entitled to patent protection, an invention or improvement must be: (1) new; (2) non-obvious; and, (3) useful.

1. **Definition of "New".** "New" generally means that the invention is not known, used, described, or patented by others.

2. **Definition of "Non-Obvious".** "Non-obvious" generally means that the differences between the subject matter sought to be patented and the prior art are such that the subject matter as a whole would not have been obvious, at the time the invention was made, to a person having ordinary skill in the art to which said subject matter pertains.

3. **Definition of "Useful".** "Useful" generally means that the invention will operate to perform a desired function to achieve an intended result.

D. **What Are the Types of Patents?** The United States Supreme Court has defined patentable subject matter as "anything under the sun that is made by man except "laws of nature, natural phenomena, and abstract ideas." There are three types of patents. "Utility" patents protect the physical structure of the invention (i.e., the "apparatus") or the function of the invention (i.e., the "process" or "method"). "Design" patents protect the ornamental appearance of an article. "Plant patents" protect distinct and new plant varieties.

E. **What Is a "Provisional Patent"?** Prior to June 8, 1995, the United States patent laws provided for only three types of patents and patent applications—the utility and design types previously described and the lesser-known "plant" type which protects new plants such as new roses or orchids. Since June 8, 1995, the less-expensive and simplified "provisional" patent application has been available to inventors and enables inventors to preserve their right to file utility and foreign patent applications within one year of the filing date of the provisional patent application.

    1. **What Are the Advantages of a Provisional Patent?** The provisional patent application has a number of important benefits. First, it places domestic patent applicants on even footing with foreign patent applicants because the filing of a provisional patent application does not trigger the start of the 20-year patent term. Second, unlike a utility patent application and as described in more detail below, the provisional patent application has minimal legal and formal requirements. Third, the provisional patent application provides a mechanism whereby applicants can quickly and relatively inexpensively establish an early effective filing date and a constructive reduction to practice for any invention described in the provisional patent application. Fourth, the filing of a provisional patent application provides up to 12 months to further develop an invention, to determine its marketability, to acquire funding or capital, to seek licensing, and to arrange manufacturing.

    2. **What Are the Disadvantages of a Provisional Patent?** While the provisional patent application is certainly of benefit to inventors, it is important to note that a provisional patent

application also has certain limitations. First, a provisional patent application cannot mature into an issued patent as it is not examined by an examiner at the PTO. The provisional patent application, once filed, merely sits idle at the PTO until it automatically becomes abandoned by law one year after its filing. Second, a provisional patent application is only available to disclose an invention which was formerly only the subject of a utility patent application. Therefore, an applicant cannot file a provisional patent application for an invention which should be the subject of a design patent application. Third, a provisional patent application is a regular national filing that starts the Paris Convention priority year (discussed below). Hence, international and foreign patent applications which claim priority on a provisional patent application must be filed within the 12-month period following the filing of the provisional patent application (unless they must be filed sooner due to sale, use, or publication of the invention prior to the filing date of the provisional patent application).

F.   **Is Software or a Business Method Patentable?** Patentability of software-based inventions and business methods is in a state of flux. Historically, the PTO has issued "business method patents" as a form of utility payment provided that the underlying software performed an algorithmic function and actually processed data. At the advent of the "dot com" era in the late 1990s, the PTO was inundated with business method patent applications, many of which did nothing more than arrange information. As a result, the courts have struggled to define the line of patentability. The courts have said, for example, that patent law protects "functional and palpable applications in the field of computer technology, but a "method that can be performed by human thought alone is merely an abstract idea and is not patent eligible" subject matter. As a result, business method patents are vulnerable and have lost value.

G.   **What If I Show My Invention to Others?** United States patent laws do not allow a patent to be granted, or issued, for an invention that has been on sale, in public use, or described in a publication for more than one year prior to the filing date of a patent application for the invention. Also, you will lose international patent rights from the moment of the first public disclosure. Therefore, maximum protection of rights requires that you must disclose what will ultimately become part of a patent application only if there is a confidential relationship.

H.   **Who Can Claim Patent Rights?** Patent rights arise in individual inventors, and not in organized entities or enterprises such as corporations and limited liability companies. Therefore, an employer does not automatically own the patent rights to inventions created by an employee, even within the scope of employment, in the absence of a written employment agreement that assigns patent rights to the employer. This is in direct contrast to the "works made for hire" doctrine under copyright law described below.

I.   **How Do I Start the Patent Application Process?** The patent process begins with a search of the "prior art." The purposes of the search include: (1) to ascertain whether the invention has been patented or disclosed previously (remember that if your invention is not new, it cannot receive patent protection); (2) to avoid filing a patent application and having it summarily rejected by the PTO because of an identical or substantially similar invention which would render your invention not new or not non-obvious; and (3) to allow the drafting of a better patent application by emphasizing those features of the invention not discovered in the search. The patent application is kept confidential for 18 months, which gives an applicant the ability to file a patent application and then abandon it if trade secret protection is preferred.

J.   **How Is a Patent Application Prepared?** Unlike a copyright application, a patent application is not a simple form which can filled in and sent to the PTO. Instead, each patent application is a carefully-crafted original document, much like a research paper, which must follow certain organizational rules and contain specific types of information required by the PTO. In order to prepare a patent application, the drafter of the patent application must be supplied with a complete explanation of the invention, including, if possible and appropriate, drawings or sketches of the invention. It is also beneficial for the drafter and inventor to sit down and discuss the invention to enable drafting of a more coherent and precise application. In most cases, a working model or prototype of the invention is not required, although it can be helpful as an aid to the drafter.

1.   **Utility Patent Applications.** A utility patent application includes a description of a problem, or problems, to be solved by the invention, a brief summary of the invention, a detailed description of the best mode of practicing the invention, a set of legal "claims" which define the metes and bounds of the protection sought by the inventor, and, if appropriate, a set of drawings which illustrate the invention.

2.   **Design Patent Applications.** Unlike a utility patent application, a design patent application includes a relatively brief written description of the invention. On the other hand, a design patent application can require a larger number of drawings than a utility patent application.

K.   **Duty of Candor and Disclosure.** While preparing a patent application and during the entire period of prosecution of the application, you have a legal duty of candor and disclosure with respect to the application in several respects. First, as noted above, there is a duty to disclose, in your patent application, the "best mode" of practicing the invention which is known at the time of filing your application. Second, you have a duty to disclose all "prior art" which is materially relevant to the prosecution of your patent application. The PTO requires that all materially relevant prior art known to the inventor and the inventor's attorney be submitted to the patent examiner in charge of the application. Such prior art includes all types of publications and other documents and things that disclose information which is pertinent to the invention. Third, the inventor and the inventor's attorney have a duty to disclose any known evidence or information showing any offers for sale or public use of the invention more than one year prior to the filing date of the patent application. Should the inventor or the inventor's attorney fail to make such disclosures to the PTO and should a patent issue from your patent application, a court may find your issued patent invalid in subsequent future litigation related to the issued patent.

L. **What Can I Do After the Patent Application is Filed?** Once your patent application is filed in the PTO, you can mark the invention (or its packaging if it is not possible to mark the invention itself) with the words, "Patent Pending" or "Patent Applied For." It is unlawful to use these words prior to filing of your patent application.

M. **What Happens If There Are Competing Applications?** For the entire history of United States patent law until passage of the Leahy-Smith America Invents Acts in 2011, the United States, unlike virtually all other industrialized nations, followed the rule that the "first to invent" had priority. The America Invents Act reversed that policy and, effective as of March 16, 2013, priority goes to the "first inventor to file," putting the United States in line with other industrialized nations.

N. **How Is a Patent Application Processed by the PTO?** Each examiner at the PTO is responsible for handling patent applications in a particular field of invention. The claims of most patent applications are "rejected" in the first substantive action (known as an "Office Action" or "Examiner's Action") by the PTO. To continue the process of trying to get an issued patent for your invention (i.e., the entire process being known as "prosecution"), a response must be submitted to the Office Action. The response can take the form of arguments as to why the claims are allowable, amendments to the claims which attempt to make the claims allowable, or both.

O. **How Long Does the Application Process Take?** Unless the application qualifies for prioritized examination, many months will likely pass before any substantive action regarding the application is received from the PTO. A number of factors contribute to this delay. First, unless special circumstances are present, patent applications are examined in chronological order based upon the date that they are received at the PTO. Second, a patent application, when received by the PTO, is assigned to an examiner responsible for the field of its invention, and, because more inventions are being made in some fields than in others (for instance, a plethora of inventions are being made every day in the fields of telecommunications, computer hardware, and computer software), some examiners have very large backlogs of applications to examine, whereas other examiners have smaller backlogs. The America Invents Act permits applicants to pay for expedited application processing, reducing the wait time for examination to months rather than years, but the program is limited to 10,000 applications per year.

P. **What Happens When a Patent is Issued?** When the PTO determines that the claims of your application are allowable and patentable, the PTO will issue a "Notice of Allowability," after which you have approximately three months from the date of mailing of the Notice of Allowability in which to pay the "issue fee" for your patent.

Q. **What Is the Duration of a Patent?** The length of time for patent protection is different for different types of patents. For "utility" patents, which protect the physical structure of the invention (i.e., the "apparatus") or the function of the invention (i.e., the "process" or "method"), the limited monopoly lasts for a period of 20 years from the date on which the underlying patent application was filed in the PTO. For "design" patents, which protect the ornamental appearance of an article, the limited monopoly lasts for a period of 14 years from the date of issuance of the patent.

R. **How Does United States Patent Law Relate to Foreign Patent Law?** The one year "grace period" afforded by the United States patent laws in which to file for patent protection after a prior offer for sale, use, or publication of an invention is not recognized in most foreign countries. Instead, the patent laws of most foreign countries have an "absolute novelty" requirement; that is, an invention must not have been on sale, in use, or published at any time prior to the filing of the foreign patent application. This distinction between the United States and foreign patent laws should be considered before offering an invention for sale, using an invention publicly, or publishing articles or advertisements describing an invention.

S. **What Is the Paris Convention Priority Right?** To mitigate the risk of disclosing patentable inventions and timely filing of patent applications, nearly all industrialized nations are parties to the Paris Convention for the Protection of Intellectual Property, which dates back to 1883. The Paris Convention provides the "Paris Convention priority right," which permits a patent applicant to use the patent applicant's filing date from one contracting nation as the effective date in another contracting nation provided that the applicant files subsequent patent applications within twelve months from the date of the first filing. The Paris Convention, with almost 180 members, covers most of the world, but there are some notable non-participants, such as the Republic of China (Taiwan) and Myanmar (formerly Burma).

IV. WHAT ARE THE FUNDAMENTALS OF COPYRIGHT LAW?

A. **What Is a Copyright?** Copyright is a form of protection grounded in the United States Constitution and granted by law for original works of authorship fixed in a tangible medium of expression. Copyright is an intangible personal property right that covers both published and unpublished works. Basically, copyright protects expressions. Copyright does not protect the medium in which the work is embodied. In other words, you can own a book, but you do not own the copyright in the book, or you can own a musical CD, but you do not own the copyright in the underlying musical work.

B. **What Body of Law Governs Copyrights?** Copyrights were formerly governed by both the states under the common law and federal law after the work was published. However, the federal Copyright Act of 1976 preempted all state laws, and, today, the Copyright Act of 1976, as amended, governs all copyright law.

C. **What Rights Comprise a Copyright?** Copyright is not an single intangible property. Under the Copyright Act, a "copyright" is actually a bundle of rights that protects "original works of authorship fixed in any tangible medium of expression." There are five exclusive rights that comprise a copyright, each of which is individually conveyable by time, territory, or other manner, such as a specific medium, described as follows:

1. **Reproduction.** The right to make copies of a work.

2. **Distribution.** The right to distribute copies of a work.

3. **Derivative Works.** The right to create derivative works based on an underlying work.

4. **Performance.** The right to perform a copyrightable work.

5. **Display.** The right to display a copyrightable work.

D. **What Works Are Copyrightable?** The Copyright Act covers the following original works of authorship:

1. **Literary Works.** Works expressed in words, numbers, or symbols regardless of the material objects, including, for example, books, tapes, and disks, in which they are embodied. Computer programs and source code on which they are based are literary works.

2. **Musical Works.** Musical works, including any accompanying words.

3. **Dramatic Works.** Dramatic works, including any accompanying music.

4. **Pantomimes and Choreographic Works.** While not specially defined in the Copyright Act, it is generally understood that this category includes dance routines, ballet, and gymnastic routines, but the expression must be "fixed" (filmed or written down).

5. **Pictorial, Graphic, and Sculptural Works.** All two-dimensional and three-dimensional works of art (fine art, graphic art, and applied art), photographs, prints, reproductions, maps, globes, charts, diagrams, models, and technical drawings (including architectural plans).

6. **Motion Pictures and Other Audiovisual Works.** "Audiovisual work" is broadly defined as a series of related images that are capable of being shown by some device along with sounds that accompany the visual portion of the work. "Motion picture" is a specific type of audiovisual work in which the images, when displayed, give the impression of motion. Examples: movies; slide shows; video games.

7.   **Sound Recordings.** A fixation of music, spoken information, or other sounds but not including sounds that accompany a motion picture or other audiovisual work.

E.   **What Works Are Not Copyrightable?** Under no circumstance will copyright protect the following:

1.   **Titles and Slogans.** Titles, names, short phrases, and slogans; familiar symbols or designs; mere variations of typographic ornamentation, lettering, or coloring; all of which are generally protected as trademarks.

2.   **Ideas.** Ideas, procedures, methods, systems, processes, concepts, principles, discoveries, or devices, all of which are generally protected by patents.

3.   **Commonly Known Information.** Works consisting entirely of information that is common property and containing no original authorship. For example: standard calendars, height and weight charts, tape measures and rulers.

4.   **Business Forms.** Mere forms, without expression, are not protectable.

5.   **Information That Can Be Expressed in Only One Way.** You cannot assert exclusive rights in information that can be stated in only one way, such as a mathematical algorithm.

6.   **Domain Names.** Domain names are not copyrightable.

F.   **How Is a Copyright Obtained?** Copyright arises in the author of the work upon the moment of creation.

G.   **Who Can Claim a Copyright?** Only the author or parties that obtain rights through or from the author through a transfer of ownership can rightfully claim a copyright. However, under copyright law, the person who creates the copyrightable work may not be the "author" of the work.

1.   **Works Made for Hire Doctrine.** When the "works made for hire" doctrine applies, the employer or other person for whom the work was prepared is deemed to be the "author" of the work. The works made for hire doctrine operates as follows:

a.   **Employment.** Materials created by employees within the scope of their employment are "works made for hire," and the employer is considered the "author" of the work, even in the absence of a written employment agreement. This rule applies only to W-2 employees: it does not typically apply to independent contractors.

b.   **Independent Contractors.** There are only limited circumstances under which the entity that engages an independent contractor to create a copyrightable work is considered to be the "author" of the work. In the usual situation, the works made for hire doctrine does not apply to an independent contractor arrangement. Therefore, it is necessary to provide in a written agreement that the independent contractor transfers the independent contractor's copyright in the work to the entity that engages the independent contractor. This material difference is frequently missed by entrepreneurs and can create major missing links in the chain of title to an enterprise's intellectual property. For example, many business plans require the creation of computer software, a copyrightable work. Even if an enterprise pays for the computer programming, the programmer is considered the "author" of the software under copyright law unless the parties enter into a written agreement that transfers copyright ownership. These flaws are often discovered only when the enterprise reaches the point where it is necessary to raise private equity or in the event of a merger or acquisition. For example, before seeking private equity, it is necessary to disclose all "risk factors" to potential investors (because the misrepresentation or concealment of a material fact can lead to allegations of "securities fraud"). Consequently, an enterprise might need to disclose that a computer programmer may assert rights in software that is necessary for the business plan, which naturally devalues the enterprise and may make it impossible to obtain financing.

2.   **Joint Works**. Whenever two or more persons contribute to a copyrightable work, it is a "joint work of authorship" which assumes that the contributions are intended to be merged into a single work. Unless there is a written agreement to the contrary, each "author" of a joint work has an undivided, equal interest in copyright ownership, and each co-author has the right to commercially exploit the work with only an obligation to account to all of the other co-authors for their percentage interest in profits derived from distribution of the work. Consequently, it is extremely important for any enterprise to enter into a written agreement with any person or entity that makes even an arguable contribution to a copyrightable work.

H.   **Is a Copyright Notice Required to Preserve My Copyright?** No. A copyright notice or symbol was required on protected works prior to March 1, 1989. At this point, major changes in law occurred to make the laws of the United States consistent with the law of much of the rest of the world. The notice requirement was eliminated for all works after that date. However, displaying the copyright notice or symbol still remains an important incentive to a copyright owner wanting to maximize protection of an original work. The absence of a copyright notice does *not* mean a work can be copied freely. Generally, protected works display the following notice: (1) the word "copyright," or the abbreviation "Copr.," or the symbol © (except for recordings, which use a circled "P"); (2) the name of the copyright owner; and (3) the year the work was first published.

I. **What Benefits Can Be Derived From Copyright Registration?** Registration of a copyright with the Copyright Office is not required to protect or preserve a copyright, but registration has value and, therefore, increases the value of a business enterprise. The Copyright Office does not examine materials submitted with a copyright registration; it merely examines whether the material is a copyrightable work. Therefore, issuance of a copyright registration is only *prima facie* evidence of the validity of a copyright, and the validity of a copyright is challengeable. Advantages of registering a copyright include the following:

1. **Ability to File a Lawsuit for Infringement.** Registration is a prerequisite for filing a suit for infringement.

2. **Statutory Damages and Attorneys' Fees.** Registration will allow a copyright owner to recover damages regardless of the amount of actual damages as well as attorneys' fees.

J. **How Is a Copyright Registration Obtained?** Copyright applications are relatively easy to complete: with minimal training, a business enterprise can complete and file their own copyright applications. To register a work, the copyright claimant must send a properly completed simple application form (there are different forms for different works; Form TX for books, magazines, computer software; Form VA for videos, movies, etc.), and a filing fee of $35 to $55 per application if the work is registered online and $85 if mailed in hard copy, each of which requires a deposit copy or copies of the work. Completed applications are sent and reviewed by the Copyright Office, and if eligible, a federal registration will issue. The Copyright Office does not examine materials submitted with a copyright registration; it merely examines whether the material is a copyrightable work.

K. **How Long Does a Copyright Stay in Effect?** Generally, for 70 years after the death of the author, or in the case of a joint work, the death of the last surviving author. For works made for hire, the term is either 95 years from the date of first publication or 120 years from the date of creation, whichever expires first.

L. **Do I Always Have to Get the Permission of a Copyright Owner Before Using a Work?** Generally, yes. However, under the "fair use" doctrine, there are certain conditions when copyright law permits the use of copyrighted work without the permission of the copyright owner. You can generally use portions of copyrighted material for such purposes as criticism, comment, news, teaching (including multiple copies for classroom use), scholarship, or research and it is generally not an infringement of copyright. However, some restrictions apply to these cases as well. Anyone using a photocopy or reproduction for purposes in excess of "fair use" may be liable for copyright infringement. The following factors are used by courts to determine if a particular use is a "fair use:"

1.   "The purpose and character of use," including whether such use is of commercial nature or is for nonprofit educational purposes.

2.   The nature of the copyrighted work.

3.   The amount and substantiality of the portion used in relation to the copyrighted work as a whole.

4.   The effect of the use upon the potential market for or value of the copyrighted work.

There are also specific laws regarding use of computer software.

M.   **Is My Copyright Valid in Other Countries?** The United States has copyright relations and treaties with most countries throughout the world, and, as a result of these agreements, we honor each other's citizens' copyrights. However, the United States does not have such copyright relationships with every country.

V. WHAT ARE THE FUNDAMENTALS OF TRADEMARK LAW?

A.   **What Is a Trademark?**

1.   **Identification of a Unique Source of Goods or Services.** Trademarks are marks or symbols that designate a source of goods or services and are recognized in almost every legal system. From the medieval ages, when guilds affixed their marks to silverware and glassware, to modern times, when companies spend millions of dollars to increase worldwide recognition of their business, trademarks have served a core role in our commercial society.

2.   **Trademarks Represent "Good Will," and "Good Will" Represents Value.** "Good will" can be defined as an intangible asset valued according to the advantage or reputation a business has acquired (over and above its tangible assets) or an asset of a business based upon the business's established relationships with its customers. Although "good will" is intangible, standard accounting practices can be used to develop a monetary value of the asset.

B.   **What Are the Functions of Trademarks?** In general, trademarks embody a business enterprise's reputation and perform four interrelated functions:

1.   **Source of Goods or Services.** Trademarks identify one seller's goods or services and distinguish them from goods and services sold by others.

2.   **Single Source of Goods and Services.** Trademarks signify that all goods or services bearing the trademark come from or are controlled by a single source.

3.   **Quality.** Trademarks signify that all goods or services that are identified by the trademarks are of equal quality.

4.   **Enhance Sales.** Trademarks help to sell goods or services. These functions are extremely valuable to the owners of such marks as GUCCI®, POLO®, and CHANEL®. However, these functions are also valuable even to companies that are not in the consumer brand business.

C.   **What Are Trademark Formats?** Trademarks can assume almost any format that performs the four functions listed above. Most commonly, trademarks consist of letters, numbers, words, designs, or combinations of any of these. MICROSOFT®, ROLEX®, 7 UP®, GOOGLE®, iPAD®, the AT&T® Globe, and the NIKE® Swoosh are all familiar trademarks to world-wide consumers and serve to identify and distinguish their owner's goods or services. Likewise, slogans, such as JUST DO IT®, A DIAMOND IS FOREVER®, INTEL INSIDE®, and WHAT CAN BROWN DO FOR YOU?®, also function as valuable trademarks for their owners. Alternatively, trademarks can assume the form of color (OWENS-CORNING® "pink" insulation), music (the NBC chimes), product packaging (the COCA-COLA® bottle), or architecture (the McDONALD's® golden arches).

D.   **What Distinguishes a Strong Trademark From a Weak Trademark?** Although trademarks can take different formats, they are not created equal. For purposes of trademark protection, this is known as the "spectrum of distinctiveness."

1.   **Arbitrary Marks.** Arbitrary marks are strong marks. An arbitrary trademark has a common meaning, but the meaning is unrelated to the goods or services for which it is used. Examples of arbitrary marks are APPLE® for computers and electronic devices and MUSTANG® for automobiles.

2.   **Fanciful Marks.** Fanciful marks are also strong marks. Absent marketing or sales to promote the connection, "fanciful" marks, such as EXXON®, KODAK®, and XEROX®, have no relation to the goods or services they identify or are coined specifically for the purpose of functioning as a trademark, and they, together with arbitrary marks, are generally afforded the greatest protection against other trademarks.

3.   **Descriptive and Geographic Marks.** Descriptive marks are the weakest marks. At the other end of the spectrum are descriptive marks which immediately convey the nature or a characteristic of the goods or services they identify, such as AFTER TAN sunning lotion, BEER

NUTS salted nuts, or INTERNET banking services. Also, marks that describe a business enterprise by geographic location are weak (for example, CHICAGO STYLE PIZZA). In general, descriptive marks are not registrable unless they acquire "secondary meaning" as described below. This trips up many entrepreneurs. There is a tendency to want to describe the good or service by its function, but that is the least valuable mark and generally cannot be protected for exclusive use.

4. **Suggestive Marks.** Between these two ends of the spectrum lie "suggestive" marks which bear a relation to the identified goods or services, but which require a degree of imagination or "multi-step reasoning" between the product and mark to identify these descriptive qualities. Suggestive marks include 7-ELEVEN® convenience stores, SPRAY 'N VAC® rug cleaner, and CITIBANK® financial services.

5. **Generic Marks.** A generic mark cannot be protected as a trademark because it describes a specific category of product or service. Sometimes a previously strong mark becomes so associated with a product or service it comes to define it. For example, the term ESCALATOR to describe a moving stairway or ASPIRIN to describe a pain medication were once protectable trademarks but are now generic. Some marks require substantial monitoring and aggressive protection to keep a mark from becoming generic. Examples are XEROX® to describe paper copying and KLEENEX® to describe tissues.

6. **Secondary Meaning.** Classifying marks on this spectrum of distinctiveness is not without considerable difficulty and is often the subject of significant disagreements, the outcome which can be critical in trademark registration and litigation because courts will protect, and the United States Patent and Trademark Office ("PTO") will register, arbitrary, fanciful, or suggestive marks upon use in commerce as "inherently distinctive." However, descriptive marks are not eligible for registration or protection absent a showing of "secondary meaning;" namely, that the mark has become distinctive of the goods or services identified thereby through advertising, promotion, or sales. AMERICAN® airlines, PAYLESS® drug stores, and KENTUCKY FRIED CHICKEN® are examples of marks that would have been labeled as "descriptive," and therefore not initially protectable, but which have acquired "secondary meaning" reflecting that the public recognizes these trademarks as indicators of source, and not just descriptive words. In general, a mark must be in continuous use for five years to acquire secondary meaning.

E. **How Are Trademark Rights Created?** In general, you obtain trademark rights by using the trademark in commerce. The general rule is that the first to use an inherently distinctive mark in commerce is recognized as the party possessing superior rights in the geographic area where the party has used the mark.

F.   What Law Governs Trademarks? There are separate bodies of state and federal trademark law, but federal law is dominant in practice.

1.   State Trademark Law.

    a.   Common Law Protection. Use of the mark without a federal registration gives an enterprise common law rights under state law. But as with much of trademark law, there are several exceptions and conditions to this maxim, which is particularly complicated by the presumptions and rights afforded federal "use" and "intent-to-use" applications and registrations.

        i.   What Trademark Protection Do I Get Under Common Law Rights? Without a federal trademark registration, your trademark rights may only cover the geographic area in which the trademark is being used.

        ii.   What Problems Arise From Relying Only on Common Law Rights? A problem may occur when the territories of two common law trademark owners with similar trademarks on similar goods or services overlap. Most often, the owner that first used the trademark in the contested market will prevail and the other owner will be prevented from expanding into the overlapping territory. However, it is important to note that these situations are not categorical - the facts for each circumstance need to be examined to determine the outcome.

        iii.   How Do I Put the World on Notice That I Claim Common Law Trademark Rights? You can use the designations "TM" or "SM" without any kind of registration.

    b.   State Trademark Registration. For minimal fees, a business can register its trademark with the state in which the mark is used, usually with the Secretary of State. This is a simple and relatively quick process, and, after registration, it will appear in data bases used for trademark searches. However, state registrations do not require evidence of priority rights, and a state trademark registration is not very valuable in and of itself.

2.   Federal Trademark Law. If a mark is used in interstate commerce, it can be registered with the PTO. Federal registration of a mark in the PTO conveys several important practical and procedural benefits, but no federal registration is required for creation of trademark rights. Marks are registered in different classes of goods and services. A relatively recent development in federal trademark law allows a party to file an "intent to use" application if it has a *bona fide* intent to use the mark in commerce, which effectively reserves the mark in the PTO and, if registered, gives it a priority date back to the date of filing, but again, trademark rights do not arise until the mark is actually used in commerce.

a. **How Do I Start the Federal Trademark Registration Process?** You begin by determining whether there are any prior users of the mark by searching publicly available data bases. You must take reasonable efforts to determine your rights in the mark before proceeding with the registration process.

b. **How Much Does Federal Trademark Registration Cost?** PTO charges range from $225 to $400 per mark per class of goods or services, but there are additional costs related to the trademark search and the preparation of the trademark registration application.

c. **What Trademark Rights Do I Get With Federal Trademark Registration?** The primary benefit of obtaining a federal trademark registration is that it establishes nationwide protection to registered marks, regardless of the geographic areas in which the mark is actually being used.

d. **What Are Some Additional Advantages of Obtaining Federal Trademark Registration?** Trademark registration provides many legal and practical advantages, examples of which are as follows:

    i.   An application or registration acts as a deterrent. By placing the mark on the register, you alert others who may want to use your trademark that it is already being used, and it shows the world you are serious about protecting your trademarks.

    ii. Enables you to use the registration notice "®" and notifies others of your trademark rights.

    iii. Safeguards future opportunities for nationwide expansion.

    iv. Provides access to federal courts to enforce trademark infringement rights and allows for the possibility of greater recovery of damages for infringement.

    v.   Gives the registrant the ability to stop importation of goods that utilize infringing marks by depositing a copy of the registration certificate (and subsequent renewal certificates) with United States Customs.

      vi. Your registration will show up in trademark searches, which may deter entities from even adopting a confusingly similar mark.

      vii. The PTO will not permit registration of marks that are confusingly similar to your mark, and it will help police your mark from infringers for free.

      viii. It creates value in your enterprise to the capital markets.

  e. **What Is the Principal Register of the PTO?** The Principal Register is the register in which marks are provided with the fullest extent of trademark law protection. If you create an arbitrary or fanciful mark that is not confusingly similar to an existing mark, it will be registered on the Principal Register.

  f. **What Can Be Done to Protect Descriptive Marks or Other Marks That Are Not Eligible for Registration on the Principal Register?** Marks that do not meet all of the requirements for registration on the Principal Register can be registered on the PTO's Supplemental Register. While this puts the world on notice of a claim of rights, registration on the Supplemental Register does not provide any rights greater than common law rights.

G. **What Is the Difference Between a Trade Name and a Trademark?** A trade name is merely the name of your business, and availability of a trade name does not give a business any trademark rights. In other words, just because the Secretary of State says a corporate name is available, and just because the business is incorporated under that name, does not mean that the business has the right to use that name in commerce as a trademark.

H. **Likelihood of Confusion: Cornerstone of Trademark Infringement and Unfair Competition.** For use of a mark to constitute trademark infringement of another mark, it is not necessary for the marks to be identical, and, even if the marks are identical, there may be no trademark infringement. Rather, likelihood of confusion, or, for federally-registered marks, whether a defendant's mark is "likely to cause confusion, or to cause mistake, or to deceive," are the tests for trademark infringement and its cousin, unfair competition. The following are samples of likelihood of confusion:

1. Resemblance between the sight, sound, and meaning of the conflicting marks.

2. Similarity of the goods or services identified by the conflicting marks.

3. Similarity of marketing methods and channels of trade.

4. Characteristics of purchasers or intended purchasers of the goods or services and the degree of care used in the purchasing decision.

5. The distinctiveness of the senior user's mark.

6. The junior user's intent in adopting the mark.

7. Actual confusion.

I. **What Is "Trade Dress" and How Is It Different from Trademarks?** Trade dress is the distinctive and non-functional physical detail and design of a product or its packaging, which indicates or identifies the product's source and distinguishes it from the products of others. In other words, it is the product's "total image" or "overall appearance." Trade dress includes color schemes, textures, sizes, designs, shapes, and placements of words, graphics, and decorations on a product or its packaging. A trade dress is non-functional if, taken as a whole, the collection of trade dress elements is not essential to the product's use or does not affect the cost or quality of the product, even though certain particular elements of the trade dress may be functional. Examples includes the "brown" theme for UPS® and the "orange" theme for HOME DEPOT®.

1. **Federal "Unfair Competition" Law.** In the usual situation, use of a symbol in commerce without federal registration would be subject only to state common law protection. However, there is a federal law that covers unfair use of "trade dress" under Section 43(a) of the Lanham Act, which provides protection for "any word, term, name, symbol, or device, or any combination thereof" used "on or in connection with any goods or services, or any container for goods."

2. **Federal Trademark Registration.** A product's trade dress can be registered on either the Principal or Supplemental Register of the PTO. The requirements for registration of a trade dress are the same as those for traditional word or logo marks. Also, like standard trademarks, the standard for determining trade dress infringement is "likelihood of confusion." To prevail on a trade dress infringement claim under Section 43(a) of the Lanham Act, the plaintiff must prove three elements: (a) its trade dress is inherently distinctive or has acquired secondary meaning; (b) its trade dress is primarily nonfunctional; and (c) the defendant's trade dress is confusingly similar.

3. **Trade Dress Rights and Other Forms of Protection.** Trade dress protection may also be available in connection with products, packaging, or business forms and stationery which are worthy of design patent, utility patent, or copyright protection. If these other forms of protection have expired or were never obtained, trade dress rights may nonetheless remain

available. Like protecting configurations, this area of the law, especially with respect to patents, is constantly evolving and varies from circuit to circuit.

J.   How Are Protection of Domain Names and Trademarks Related? Reserving a domain name alone does not provide any trademark or service mark rights. Trademark law prohibits commercial websites from using a domain name that would cause a likelihood of confusion to consumers with respect to the parties' goods or services.

1.   How Are Domain Names Regulated? The Internet Corporation for Assigned Names and Numbers (ICANN) is responsible for managing and coordinating the Domain Name System to ensure that every address is unique and that all users of the Internet can find all valid addresses. It does this by overseeing the distribution of unique IP addresses and domain names, and it also ensures that each domain name maps to the correct IP address. As a private-public partnership, ICANN is dedicated to preserving the operational stability of the Internet; to promoting competition; to achieving broad representation of global Internet communities; and to developing policy appropriate to its mission through bottom-up, consensus-based processes.

2.   What Are Typical Domain Name Issues? Issues that commonly arise include the following:

   a.   Domain Name Already Registered. Company attempts to register a domain name and discovers that it is registered by someone else.

   b.   Lapse of Domain Name Registration. Company allows the domain name registration to lapse, and the domain name is registered by someone else.

   c.   Another Company Has Registered a Domain Name Incorporating Your Trademark. Company discovers that someone else has registered a domain name that incorporates its trademarks.

3.   How Are Domain Name Issues Resolved?

   a.   Cease and Desist Letter. This is an informal way to put a party on notice of a domain name issue, but it has no legal significance.

   b.   ICANN Complaint. There are three essential elements of an ICANN Complaint: (i) the domain name is identical or confusingly similar to your trademark; (ii) the infringing party has no rights or legitimate interests in the domain name; and (iii) the infringing party has registered and is using the domain name in bad faith (A) to try to sell it "for profit"; (B) if a competitor, to divert customers; (C) the mark is well known, so bad faith may be inferred; or (D) the party is not using domain name, so bad faith may be inferred. The ICANN decision is appealable for *de novo* review by a United States court.

c. **Federal Complaint Under the Anticybersquatting Consumer Protection Act.** You can file a complaint under the federal Anticybersquatting Consumer Protection Act, which requires essentially the same elements as an ICANN complaint.

K. **What Are the Dangers in Not Protecting My Trademarks?** As discussed earlier, trademarks = reputation = goodwill = value. If you allow others to use your trademark, or a mark similar to your mark, you run the risk of hurting your reputation and diminishing the value of the business enterprise. Does this other trademark user care about quality, service, or reputation? Do you want to trust your valuable name to others? Are you willing to risk lost sales from dissatisfied customers or from customers who have been diverted to a trademark infringer? Are you willing to risk lawsuits mistakenly filed against your company which should have been filed against another company? Are you willing to allow a diminution of value of your business enterprise to the capital markets? If the answer to any of these questions is "no," then you need to protect your trademark.

L. **What Should I Do Before I Use a Mark in Commerce?** Every business enterprise should access trademark and trade name data bases before commencing doing business. Failure to do so could lead to unforeseen expenses. A simple internet search engine inquiry is a good start, but there are other suitable data bases. Some are inexpensive and are suitable for "knock out" searches. Some are more comprehensive and should be accessed before filing an application for trademark registration with the PTO.

CHAPTER 9

CORPORATE GOVERNANCE AND FIDUCIARY DUTY

I. FUNDAMENTALS OF CORPORATE GOVERNANCE

A. **Election of Officers and Directors.** A corporation is managed by its directors and officers. In a "for profit" corporation, shareholders elect directors, and directors elect officers. In a "non-profit" corporation, the Board of Directors can be either elected by "members" or appointed through a "self-nominating Board."

B. **Responsibility of Officers and Directors.** Generally, the Board of Directors is responsible for making major business and policy decisions, and the officers are responsible for carrying out the Board's policies and for making daily business decisions. While some corporations may involve their directors in day-to-day activities, the Board of Directors is not usually expected to participate in the daily business affairs of the corporation. Rather, most Boards generally delegate management functions for daily business affairs to the officers or to executive committees of the Board.

C. **Power and Authority of Directors.** The Board of Directors is statutorily vested with ultimate responsibility for control of all of the business affairs of the corporation and has the authority to exercise all of the corporation's powers. Specific duties of the Board of Directors typically include the following:

    1. **Appointment of Officers.** Election, removal, and supervision of officers.

    2. **By-Laws.** Adoption, amendment, and repeal of by-laws.

    3. **Compensation Issues.** Fixing management compensation, pension, retirement, and other compensation plans.

4. **Financial Management.** Overseeing audits of the corporation's finances.

5. **Extraordinary Corporate Acts.** Initiating extraordinary corporate action (for example, amendments to articles of incorporation, mergers, asset sales, and dissolution) which may require shareholder approval.

D. **Actions of the Board of Directors.** Action by the Board of Directors must be taken in accordance with the applicable Business Corporation Code and usually involves a resolution, properly adopted at a meeting of the Board of Directors, setting forth the appropriate action to establish the corporate policy.

II. DUTIES OF OFFICERS AND DIRECTORS TO SHAREHOLDERS

A. **Fiduciary Duty.** Directors and officers are fiduciaries of the corporation and its shareholders, and as such owe them duties of loyalty and care. The duty of loyalty is a duty to act loyally, honestly, and in good faith for the sole interest of the corporation and its stockholders. The duty of due care is a duty to act prudently with the same amount of care which ordinarily careful men and women would use in similar circumstances. This is as true for deciding how to respond to an acquisition overture as it is for making routine decisions.

B. **Duty of Loyalty.** The duty of loyalty encompasses two core areas—conflicts of interest and corporate opportunities. These duties are intended to ensure that directors and officers will place the best interests of the corporation ahead of their personal interests.

1. **Conflicts of Interest.** On occasion, a corporation will enter into a transaction in which a director or officer has a direct or indirect interest. This type of transaction is considered a conflict of interest because it puts a director or officer in a position that may cause him or her to put his or her individual interests ahead of the interests of the corporation.

   a. **Common Law Principles.** Under common law principles, it is essential that these types of transactions and conflicts are considered carefully by the Board to ensure that the transaction is fair to the corporation and disclosed to, and authorized, approved, or ratified by, disinterested directors or the shareholders.

   b. **Fairness of the Transaction.** Disinterested directors reviewing the fairness of a transaction having self-dealing elements are essentially seeking to determine whether the proposed transaction is on terms that are at least as favorable to the corporation as might be available from other persons or entities and, if minority shareholders could be adversely affected, the directors should be especially concerned that the minority shareholders receive fair treatment.

    c.   **Pursuit of Other Business Ventures.** In general, officers and directors of a corporation are allowed to pursue business ventures and employment with other corporations as long as they uphold their fiduciary duties to both corporations.

    d.   **Federal Law Prohibition.** Under certain circumstances, federal law forbids officers or directors from serving on two companies that are competitors. Section 8 of the Clayton Act provides that no person shall, at the same time, serve as a director or officer in any two corporations that are engaged in whole or in part in commerce and are competitors. The reasoning behind this is simple: to eliminate the opportunity or temptation of interlocking officers from violating antitrust laws. The Clayton Act only applies when a person is simultaneously engaged with at least two corporations that are competitors, each of which has capital surplus and undivided profits of at least $10,000,000 (as periodically adjusted for inflation).

2.   **Corporate Opportunity Doctrine.** In general, the duty of loyalty requires that a director or officer make a business opportunity available to the corporation before the director may pursue the opportunity for the director's or officer's own or another party's benefit. Under the common law, whether a corporate opportunity must first be offered to the corporation depends on the following factors:

    a.   **Awareness.** The circumstances under which the director or officer became aware of the opportunity.

    b.   **Significance.** The significance of the opportunity to the corporation and the degree of interest of the corporation in the opportunity.

    c.   **Relationship to Existing Business.** Whether the opportunity relates to the corporation's existing or contemplated business.

    d.   **Reasonableness.** Whether there is a reasonable basis to expect that the director or officer should make the opportunity available to the corporation.

C.   **Duty of Care.** As a general rule, in the corporate context, the duty of care focuses on the exercise of diligence by directors in the execution of their respective official duties. Generally, this duty requires directors to attend meetings and to investigate matters presented to them prior to making decisions. However, when acting in good faith, a director is allowed to rely on information, opinions, reports, or statements, including financial statements and other financial data that is given to them by:

1. **Officers.** An officer that is reasonably believed to be reliable.

2. **Experts.** Lawyers, accountants, or other persons reasonably believed to be within their professional or expert competence.

3. **Board Committees.** A committee of the Board upon which the director or officer does not serve which is duly designated, acting within the committee's authority, and which the director reasonably believes to merit confidence.

D. **Business Judgment Rule.** If a director adheres to the above-referenced standards for the "duty of care," the "business judgment rule" generally will shield the director from liability arising from his or her business judgments that prove to be erroneous so long as the director in question deliberated the matter in good faith at the time it was decided. For most actions by a Board of Directors, or a committee thereof, the business judgment rule is applicable. The rule is a presumption that in making a business decision the directors of a corporation acted on an informed basis, in good faith, and in the honest belief that the action taken was in the best interests of the company (in other words, in accordance with their fiduciary duty). When the business judgment rule is applicable, the burden is on the party challenging a Board's decision to establish facts rebutting the presumption created by the rule, thereby making it more difficult for a challenger to be successful and making it easier to dispose of challenges at an early stage in litigation or to discourage challenges altogether.

    1. **Applicability of the Business Judgment Rule.** For the rule to be available, various conditions must be satisfied. Each condition must be met, and failure to meet even one will prevent the rule from being available. While each court case has a slightly different formulation of these conditions, the conditions generally require that:

        a. a decision be made;

        b. the decision be by a group of directors who are disinterested; and

        c. those directors use due care.

    2. **Process and Procedure May Be More Important Than Substance.** As illogical as it may seem, making the correct decision may not protect you as well as following the procedures necessary for the business judgment rule to be available. The best example of this is the Delaware case

of *Smith v. Van Gorkom.* In that case, the Delaware Supreme Court reversed a lower court's holding in favor of directors and found directors personally liable for a breach of due care in approving a cash-out merger which had been negotiated by the corporation's management. The court found several factors significant to its finding that the directors were grossly negligent: (a) the failure of the directors to make meaningful inquiries into the circumstances that led to the negotiated transaction; (b) the failure of the directors to question senior management regarding the value of the company; (c) the Board's approval of the transaction after only limited consideration "without . . . the exigency of a crisis or emergency;" (d) the absence at the time of the Board's approval of written documents regarding the proposed transaction; and (e) the Board's failure to seek a fairness opinion from an independent financial adviser (although the court made it clear that there was no absolute obligation to obtain a fairness opinion). The merger under consideration could very well have been in the best interest of the corporation's stockholders, and the outside directors were all respected businessmen who were eminently well qualified to make that determination, but the directors did not satisfy the requirement of due care in the process that they followed to reach that conclusion and could not rely on the business judgment rule to dispose of the complaint. Instead, they had to defend their actions for the next several years and ultimately settled the claims.

3. **Evolution of "Bad Faith" Theory of Director Liability.** After the *Van Gorkom* case, the Delaware legislature eliminated the concept of "gross negligence" for outside director liability for violation of the duty of care. However, in its place, the Delaware Chancery Court has implicated that an outside director may be liable for proceeding in "bad faith," which is part of the duty of loyalty, not the duty of care, under certain circumstances when the director might rely on the business judgment rule.

4. **Meaning of "Disinterested".** Whether a director is "disinterested" has been interpreted as requiring not just that the directors who make a decision have no personal financial interest in the outcome of the decision (other than as a typical stockholder), but also that the directors not have a competing interest and possibly that directors not have a significant business or personal relationship with an interested person. A director needs to consider carefully the impact of a potential transaction on the director, the director's investments, and any businesses with which the director may be affiliated to ensure that the director does not have a personal or competing interest.

E. **Advisors.** Directors and officers should liberally seek out the advice of experts. Many states provide directors and officers who act on the advice of experts with substantial protections. In any event, reliance is favored, and the courts have recognized it as one aspect of exercising the "due care" required by the business judgment rule. An important aspect of relying on advisors is selecting them with "due care" as well.

F.　**D&O Liability Insurance.** Many companies obtain directors' and officers' liability insurance. The coverage usually has various exclusions, including liability attributable to gaining "personal profit or advantage" or committing a "dishonest, fraudulent, or criminal act or omission."

G.　**Indemnification.** Most states allow a corporation's articles of incorporation and by-laws to provide for indemnification of directors. The range of losses that are covered is broad and may include attorneys' fees, although there is no obligation to advance attorneys' fees and other expenses.

　　1.　**No Indemnification If Director Does Not Act in Good Faith.** However, there is no indemnification for a claim if the director did not act in good faith and in a manner reasonably believed to be in or not opposed to the best interests of the corporation or, in the case of a criminal action, unless the director had no reasonable cause to believe the conduct was unlawful.

　　2.　**Shareholders' Derivative Actions.** With respect to shareholders' derivative actions, there is also no indemnification with respect to claims when the director is adjudged to be liable for negligence or misconduct in the performance of his or her duty to the corporation unless and only to the extent that the court determines upon application that, despite the adjudication of liability but in view of all circumstances in the case, the person is fairly and reasonably entitled to indemnity.

　　3.　**Other Restrictions on Indemnification.** In addition, there may be statutory and public policy restrictions on a director's ability to be indemnified.

III. DIRECTORS' AND OFFICERS' FIDUCIARY DUTIES TO CREDITORS

A.　**Directors' and Officers' Fiduciary Duty to Creditors.** Under the law of most states, both officers and directors of insolvent corporations are charged with the duty of conserving and managing the remaining assets in trust for the creditors. For example, officers and directors of corporations may be held personally liable for corporate indebtedness if they make preferential transfers of corporate assets to themselves while the corporation is insolvent.

B.　**When Is a Corporation Insolvent?**

　　1.　**Insolvency Standards.** There are two primary standards applied by courts in determining whether a corporation is insolvent: (a) equitable insolvency; and (b) balance sheet insolvency. Equitable insolvency simply refers to a person's or corporation's inability to pay its debts as they become due, while balance sheet insolvency focuses on whether an entity's total liabilities exceed its total assets.

2. **Application of Insolvency Standards.** Most state corporation codes follow both equitable insolvency and balance sheet insolvency in setting the standard as to when a corporation may make distributions to its shareholders. In order for a corporation to make a distribution to its shareholders, it must (a) be able to pay its debts as they become due (equitable insolvency) and (b) have total assets in excess of its total liabilities (balance sheet insolvency).

C. **Delaware Law Governing Directors' Fiduciary Duties to Creditors and Other Constituencies.**

1. **Directors' Fiduciary Duties to a Corporation's Community of Interests.** Under Delaware law, once a corporation becomes insolvent or enters into the "vicinity of insolvency," a director's fiduciary duties run not only to the corporation but also to the corporation's "community of interests," including its creditors. This expansion in a director's fiduciary duties does not require a Board of Directors to place creditors' interests above any other corporate constituency. Moreover, Delaware law does not permit or require directors to conduct the affairs of an insolvent corporation "in a manner that is inconsistent with principles of fairness or in breach of duties owed to the stockholders." However, creditors have a right "to expect that directors will not divert, dissipate or unduly risk assets necessary to satisfy their claims." The director's duty to creditors has been characterized as a duty to "protect the contractual and priority rights of creditors."

2. **When Is a Corporation Insolvent or in the Vicinity of Insolvency Under Delaware Law?** Delaware courts, like most state courts, typically apply the equitable insolvency standard in determining whether a corporation is insolvent. Thus, under Delaware law, a corporation that is unable to pay its debts as they fall due in the usual course of business is insolvent. In making this determination, Delaware courts consider the amount of cash or cash equivalents the corporation has on hand, the size of a corporation's accounts payable, and various other factors indicating that a corporation is unable to pay its debts as they become due.

3. **What Does "Vicinity of Insolvency" Mean?** Delaware courts and courts in other jurisdictions interpreting Delaware law have applied different standards for determining when a corporation is in the "vicinity of insolvency." In one case, the court reasoned that the vicinity of insolvency "seems to refer to the extent of the risk that creditors will not be paid, rather than balance sheet insolvency." Other courts have looked precisely at corporations' balance sheets in order to determine whether the corporation was in the "vicinity of insolvency." At least one court interpreting Delaware law has held that if a director is aware that a certain event or decision will render the corporation insolvent, the corporation is in the "vicinity" of insolvency even if the corporation is solvent at the time the decision is made. Because there is an absence of clear guidance as to when a corporation enters the "vicinity of insolvency,"

directors should be mindful of their potential fiduciary duties to creditors and other constituencies at the outset of financial trouble.

IV. DOES A SHAREHOLDER EVER HAVE FIDUCIARY DUTY TO THE CORPORATION?

A. **Delaware Law.** There is some authority under Delaware law for the proposition that a controlling stockholder may owe some fiduciary-type duty to other stockholders.

B. **Domination and Control by Less Than Majority Shareholders.** In the absence of majority stock ownership, a stockholder must dominate the affairs of the corporation through actual control of corporate conduct for a fiduciary duty to arise.

V. FIDUCIARY DUTIES IN PARTNERSHIPS AND JOINT VENTURES

A. **Presumption of Confidential Relationship.** In general, the common law presumes that a confidential relationship exists in partnerships. Confidential relationships do not necessarily arise, however, from contractual relationships between businessmen, even if the parties repose trust and confidence in one another. If a confidential relationship does exist, then the parties have a duty of utmost good faith, including the disclosure of material facts. Similarly, if a confidential relationship exists, then the suppression of a material fact may constitute fraud.

B. **Confidential Relationships Arise from Obligations Involving Good Faith.** Under the law of most states, a confidential relationship arises when, from a situation of mutual confidence between the parties, such as in a partnership, the law requires the utmost good faith. The relationship can arise from a contract, statutory provisions, or the circumstances of the business arrangement, and typically, a partnership does create a confidential relationship. A confidential relationship is never presumed, however, and the burden of proof is upon the party asserting the existence of the relationship.

C. **Duty to Disclose.** If a confidential relationship is found to exist, however, then the ordinary diligence required in a business transaction, such as the reading of the contract or the independent investigation of industry facts, does not generally apply. A duty to disclose may also arise when a confidential relationship exists, or if the particular circumstances of the case warrant disclosure. That same duty to disclose can give rise to a fraud claim as well.

D. **Self-Dealing in Partnerships.** In the case law in most states regarding partnerships, the courts have found a breach of the fiduciary duty of disclosure if one party engages in self-dealing that specifically harms the other party, withholds information about profits, or under-invests in the joint venture.

VI. INDIVIDUAL RESPONSIBILITY FOR CORPORATE OR ORGANIZATIONAL ACTS

A. **Evolution of the Law.** The law has evolved to make responsible officers, directors, and managers individually liable, both criminally and civilly, for organizational acts, even if the responsible officers, directors, and managers were not directly involved in the questionable conduct.

B. **Responsible Officer Doctrine.** In the context of submission of claims for payment to a division of the United States government that come within enforcement under the federal False Claims Act, courts have held certain managers and officers liable for criminal acts of an organization related to government contracts under the "responsible officer" doctrine.

   1. **Managers Are Responsible for Corporate or Organizational Acts.** The doctrine may be applied to those who by virtue of their managerial positions could be deemed responsible for commission of an illegal offense. United States v. Park, 421 United States 658, 672 (1975).

   2. **Knowledge Not Required.** No direct knowledge of the facts revealing the offense or active participation is required. United States v. Dotterweich, 320 United States 277 (1943).

   3. **Willfulness Arising From Responsibility.** The willfulness or negligence of the actor will be imputed to him or her by virtue of his or her position of responsibility. United States v. Britain, 931 F. 2d 1413, 1419 (10th Cir 1991).

C. **Individual Director Liability for Corporate Acts Under** *In re: Caremark International, Inc.* **Derivative Litigation.**

   1. **Standard of Conduct Applicable to Corporate Directors.** The Delaware Chancery Court has considered the legal standard that governs a Board of Directors' obligation to supervise or monitor corporate performance in the case of *In re: Caremark International, Inc.* The Delaware Chancery Court posed the question as follows: what is the Board's responsibility with respect to the organization and monitoring of the enterprise to assure that the corporation functions within the law to achieve its purposes? The court stated that this question is given special importance by an increasing tendency, especially under federal law, to employ the criminal law to assure corporate compliance with external legal requirements, including environmental, financial, employee, and product safety law as well as assorted health and safety regulations.

   2. **The Role of the Federal Sentencing Guidelines in Determining the Standard of Care.** The court recognized that, in 1991, pursuant to the Sentencing Reform Act of 1984, the United States Sentencing Commission adopted Organizational Sentencing Guidelines

(the "Federal Sentencing Guidelines"). As stated by the Delaware Chancery Court, the Guidelines offer powerful incentives for corporations to have in place compliance programs to detect violations of law, promptly to report violations to appropriate public officials when discovered, and to take prompt, voluntary remedial efforts. Ironically, the Federal Sentencing Guidelines provide corporations with the only proactive alternative to engage in action that may be potentially exculpatory for the corporation and its responsible officers and directors: implementing a Corporate Compliance Plan that conforms with certain elements set forth in the Guidelines. When the *Caremark* case was decided, application of the Federal Sentencing Guidelines to federal criminal proceedings was mandatory. Since the *Caremark* case was decided, the federal courts have ruled that the Federal Sentencing Guidelines are advisory only and that strict application of the Guidelines is unconstitutional. However, as discussed below, the Federal Sentencing Guidelines for organizational defendants continue to provide the platform for the structure of compliance programs.

3.   **The Duty Under Delaware Law.** Accordingly, under Delaware law, corporate directors have a duty to assure that a corporate information gathering and reporting system exists which represents a good faith attempt to provide senior management and the Board with information regarding material acts, events, or conditions within the corporation, including compliance with applicable statutes and regulations. The court specifically notes the potential impact of the Federal Sentencing Guidelines on any business organization:

Any rational person attempting in good faith to meet an organizational governance responsibility would be bound to take into account this development and the enhanced penalties and the opportunities for reduced sanctions that it offers.

4.   **The Danger of Misplaced Reliance on Prior Standards.** No longer may corporate Boards believe that their obligations are satisfied if they are reasonably informed concerning the corporation's operations without assuring themselves that information and reporting systems exist in the organization that are reasonably designed to provide the senior management and the Board itself with timely, accurate information sufficient to allow management and the Board, each within its scope, to reach informed judgments concerning both the corporation's compliance with law and its business performance.

5.   **Expansion of *Caremark* Duties to Officers.** In the case of *In re: World Health Alternatives, Inc.*, a federal bankruptcy judge applying Delaware law ruled that a corporate officer is subject to the same minimum standards of supervision and monitoring applied to the corporate directors under the *Caremark* Delaware Chancery Court decision. Therefore, at least under Delaware law, corporate officers are now subject to the new standard of conduct.

D.   Federal False Claims Act.

1.   **Qui Tam Actions.** Under the False Claims Amendments Act of 1986, private parties, known as "relators" may bring a "qui tam" action, which is a civil lawsuit in the name of the United State Government against those who submit false claims to the government. Private citizens may prosecute such actions either with or without the Department of Justice, dependent on whether the Department of Justice exercises its right to intervene.

2.   **Damages.** Damages can be as high as approximately $11,000 to $22,000 per claim (which increases annually based on a cost of living index) plus three times the amount claimed. The private parties whose qui tam actions are successful can recover from 10% to 30% of the judgment or settlement of the lawsuit, plus awards for attorneys' fees and expenses, with the balance of the recovery going to the United States Treasury.

3.   **Whistleblowers.** Employees who bring a qui tam action are entitled to reinstatement, two times the amount of back pay, and other special damages, including litigation costs.

4.   **Individual Liability.** Responsible officers can be held individually liable for False Claims Act damages.

E.   Intermediate Sanctions Against Tax Exempt Organizations. Officers, directors, and managers of tax exempt organizations are also exposed to potential individual liability for organizational acts. For many years, the only sanction available to the Internal Revenue Service for acts that violate the laws governing tax exemption was losing exempt status. Recognizing that this "death penalty" may not serve the interests of the public or the organization, the IRS is now authorized to administer "intermediate sanctions" against tax exempt organizations and their managers.

1.   **Purpose.** The "intermediate sanctions" legislation was enacted to discourage certain transactions that do not reflect fair market value between tax exempt entities and non-tax exempt entities called "excess benefit transactions." In general, this is defined as any transaction in which an economic benefit is provided by an applicable tax-exempt organization directly or indirectly or for the use of any disqualified person, and the value of the economic benefit provided exceeds the value of the consideration received for providing the benefit. To prevent organizations from converting to taxable status to avoid penalties, the "intermediate sanctions" also apply to organizations that are not tax-exempt at the time of the excess benefit transaction.

2.   **Individual Liability.** Under the "intermediate sanctions" regulations, officers and directors who authorize arrangements that violate the statutes and regulations governing tax-exempt organizations may be exposed to individual excise taxes.

3. **Disqualified Person.** A for-profit company will only be subject to penalty taxes if it is a "disqualified person." Generally, a "disqualified person" is any person who was in a position to exercise substantial influence over the affairs of an applicable tax-exempt organization at any time during the five-year period ending on the date of the transaction.

4. **Penalties.** Penalty taxes are imposed on the difference between the actual consideration paid and the fair market value (the spread).

    a. A tax is imposed on the tax-exempt organization's management, equal to the lessor of 10% of the spread to a maximum of $10,000.

    b. An initial 25% tax is imposed on the spread against the for-profit organization.

    c. The for-profit has a specified period to remedy the transaction if it transfers enough cash or property to the tax-exempt party to make up for the less-than-FMV consideration it originally paid.

    d. If the transaction is not remedied, then a second tax equal to 200% is imposed.

    e. Common law applies if the tax liability cannot be satisfied by the organization. The IRS will come after the shareholder.

F. **Piercing of the Corporate Veil.**

1. **General Rule.** The corporate (or LLC or LLP) shell protects investors, officers, and directors from individual liability for corporate acts unless (a) an individual personally guarantees in writing to assume responsibility for a corporate debt, (b) the obligee can "pierce the corporate veil," or (c) the corporate trust doctrine applies.

2. **When the Corporate Veil May Be Pierced.** Under a broad principle of federal law, a corporate entity may be disregarded in the interests of public convenience, fairness, and equity. Each situation must be evaluated on its own facts and circumstances. Factors to be considered are as follows:

    a. Failure to observe corporate formalities.

    b. Nonpayment of dividends.

    c. Siphoning of funds by the dominant shareholder.

    d.   Non-functioning of other officers and directors.

    e.   Absence of corporate records.

    f.   Commingling of corporate and personal assets.

    g.   Distribution to the shareholders, directors, or officers when the corporation is insolvent.

3. **Corporate Trust Doctrine.** Analogous to a traditional piercing of the corporate veil, this doctrine holds that a corporation's assets are, by law, held in trust for the payment of creditors, and a breach of that trust could lead to individual shareholder, officer, or director liability.

4. **Key Element to Liability.** In the cases in which the Medicare program has successfully pierced the corporate veil or invoked the corporate trust doctrine, there is one core, critical fact: the dominant shareholder or officer repaid loans from the dominant shareholder or officer to the corporation and then the corporation ceased business with a debt to the Medicare program.

G. **Sarbanes-Oxley Act of 2002.** The Sarbanes-Oxley Act of 2002 imposes potential individual liability for corporate acts on an entity's responsible officers when the organization's stock is publicly traded.

1. **Rationale of Act.** The Sarbanes-Oxley Act of 2002 was enacted in the wake of the corporate scandals that reduced confidence in public company accounting procedures and financial information.

2. **CEO and CFO Certification of Financial Statements and Periodic Reports.** CEOs and CFOs, in their individual capacities, are required to certify the accuracy of each quarterly and annual report filed with the SEC, including financial statements filed therewith. This certification requirement applies to all public companies.

3. **Certification Requirements.** To meet the requirements, the CEOs and CFOs must certify that: (a) the signing officer has reviewed the report and, to the officer's best knowledge, it is accurate and does not contain any materially untrue or misleading statements; (b) to the officer's best knowledge, the financial statements and related information fairly present the financial condition and results of operations of the issuer; and (c) the company's internal controls are effective.

4. **The Role of Independent Directors.** Sarbanes-Oxley effectively ends the era of the "professional director" and requires publicly traded corporations to involve independent directors in critical committees of the Board, such as the Audit Committee and the Compensation Committee.

5.   **Penalties.** A knowing violation by the CEO or CFO of the Act's financial statements certification requirement is punishable by a $1,000,000 fine and up to 10 years in prison. A willful violation is punishable by a $5,000,000 fine and up to 20 years in prison. If the issuer is required to prepare an accounting restatement as a result of a material noncompliance with the reporting requirements due to misconduct, the CEO and CFO will be required to return to the company any bonuses, other incentive-based compensations, and profits from the sale of issuer's stock for the 12-month period following each improper financial report. Persons who destroy property or falsify corporate records in an attempt to impede or obstruct an investigation shall be subject to fines and imprisonment up to 20 years. Persons who commit securities fraud shall be subject to fines or imprisonment of up to 25 years.

H.   **Inadequate Management; Failure to Supervise Corporate Affairs.** The law in many states has evolved to make individual officers and directors liable for damages suffered by non-shareholder third parties for alleged inadequate management and failure to supervise corporate affairs. Examples include the following: failing to detect misconduct by employees; negligently managing underwriting risks; and gunshot wounds to a mall patron after management reduced mall security to maximize profits.

I.   **DOJ Directive to Pursue Individuals for Corporate Fraud.** The United States Department of Justice ("DOJ") erased all doubt that individuals are being targeted for acts of both civil and criminal corporate fraud when, on September 9, 2015, Sally Quillian Yates, then the DOJ Deputy Attorney General, issued a directive to DOJ division leaders and United States Attorneys to combat corporate fraud by seeking individual accountability for corporate wrongdoing in what is referred to as the "Yates Memo." According to the Yates Memo, which remains in effect, the DOJ intends to fully leverage its resources to identify culpable individuals at all levels in corporate cases. The directive identifies six key steps to strengthen the government's pursuit of individual corporate wrongdoing as follows:

- to qualify for any cooperation credit, corporations or other organizations accused of wrongdoing must provide to DOJ all relevant facts relating to the individuals responsible for the misconduct;

- criminal and civil corporate investigations should focus on individuals from the inception of the investigation;

- criminal and civil attorneys handling corporate investigations should be in routine communication with one another;

- absent extraordinary circumstances or approved DOJ policy, DOJ will not release culpable individuals from civil or criminal liability when resolving a matter with a company;

- DOJ attorneys should not resolve matters with a company without a clear plan to resolve related individual cases and should memorialize any declinations as to individuals in such cases; and

- DOJ civil attorneys should consistently focus on individuals as well as the company and evaluate whether to bring suit against an individual based on considerations beyond that individual's ability to pay.

VII. FEDERAL SENTENCING GUIDELINES: THE BIRTHPLACE OF CORPORATE COMPLIANCE.

A.   **Creation of the Sentencing Guidelines.** As cited in the *Caremark* case, the Sentencing Reform Act of 1984 required federal judges to impose upon defendants convicted of violations of federal criminal statutes a sentence called for by sentencing Guidelines, unless there is a factor present for which the Guidelines do not adequately account. The initial set of Guidelines drafted by the United States Sentencing Commission took effect on November 1, 1987, and has been amended several times. Effective November 1, 1991, the Sentencing Commission made the Guidelines applicable to business organizations. The Guidelines were revised in 2004, and an explanation of the revisions is attached as **Attachment 9-A**. Although initially application of the Guidelines was mandatory, it is now discretionary. However, as a practical matter, judges are required to consider the Guidelines when imposing sentences.

B.   **Application of the Guidelines to Organizational Defendants.** Buried deep in the Guidelines are Guidelines for Organizational Defendants. Like the individual guidelines, the organizational Guidelines provide a scoring system for assessing fines, restitution, forfeiture, costs to prosecute, and even imposing a period of probation on an organization convicted of a federal criminal offense. There are four general principles underlying the Federal Sentencing Guidelines.

1.   **Curing the Harm.** First, the court must, whenever practicable, order the organization to remedy any harm caused by the offense.

2.   **Divestiture of Assets.** Second, if the organization operated primarily for a criminal purpose or primarily by a criminal means, the fines should be set sufficiently high to divest the organization of all its assets.

3.   **Effect of Corporate Acts on Fines.** Third, the fine range for any other organization should be based on the seriousness of the offense and the capability of the organization, which will

be determined by the steps taken by the organization prior to the offense to prevent and to detect criminal conduct, the level and extent of involvement in or tolerance of the offense by certain personnel, and the organization's action after an offense has been committed.

4. **Possibility of Probation.** Fourth, probation is the appropriate sentence for an organizational defendant when needed to insure that the company will fully carry out a sanction imposed by the court, or to insure that the business will take steps to reduce the likelihood of future criminal conduct.

C. **Mitigation of Sentencing Through Implementation of a Corporate Compliance Plan.** Under the Guidelines, sentences are imposed by assessing numerical points related to each charge or violation. However, points may be reduced based upon corporate acts, such as cooperation and effective implementation of a Corporate Compliance Plan. The Guidelines provide specific criteria for implementation of an effective Corporate Compliance Plan. Consequently, it is somewhat ironic that the entire compliance industry sprang from criminal sentencing guidelines.

VIII. CHARACTERISTICS OF CORPORATE COMPLIANCE PLANS

A. **Corporate Compliance Plans Are Necessary.** Corporate Compliance Plans, at a minimum, mitigate sentencing under the Federal Sentencing Guidelines. If the organization has a system to prevent and detect improper conduct by its employees and agents, commonly referred to as a "compliance program," and the court deems that program to have effectively deterred and ferreted out misconduct, the Guidelines call for a decrease in the business's culpability score. If even for this reason alone, every organization that is involved in commerce should implement a Corporate Compliance Plan in accordance with the Federal Sentencing Guidelines.

B. **Self-Assessment and Detection of Fraud.** Compliance Plans establish rigorous self-assessment systems intended to detect fraud within an organization and prevent the occurrence of additional incidents of fraud and abuse. In other words, it permits an organization to engage in meaningful self-assessment to detect and avoid compliance issues rather than having regulatory agencies impose a self-assessment system.

C. **Culture of Compliance.** Compliance Plans instill a culture of compliance within an organization. This is critically important to effective implementation of a Corporate Compliance Plan. The Plan must be more than a document that is filed in a drawer or placed on a shelf: it must be a living, breathing part of every organization.

D. **Protection and Avoidance of Sanctions.** Compliance Plans may insulate an organization from activities of fraud and abuse by a rogue employee who fails to follow the procedures stated in the

Plan. If allegations of fraud and abuse arise, then the existence of a compliance program may help an organization, and its responsible officers and directors, avoid sanctions. It may also reduce a long, drawn out inquiry to a short investigation.

IX. STARTING THE COMPLIANCE PROCESS: THE REGULATORY ASSESSMENT

A. **Assessment.** A Compliance Plan regulatory assessment is, at minimum, a review of the legal duties imposed on an organization, violation of which subjects the organization to federal criminal prosecution or violation of federal civil laws such as the False Claims Act. Regulatory assessments should identify conduct, reports, and the like which may put the organization at risk of violation of federal criminal or civil law and identify all material federal criminal or civil statutes which reasonably apply to the business. It is not, however, an "audit" to find all material loss contingencies.

B. **Employee Interviews.** Employee interviews should be aimed at gaining an understanding of the organization's operational logistics and ferreting out any unethical or illegal conduct.

C. **Documents and Records Review.** The assessment includes thorough review of an organization's records and documents, especially the organization's contracts and business arrangements with third parties, including referral sources.

D. **Attorney-Client Privilege.**

1. **Protection of Attorney-Client Communications.** Communications from clients to attorneys are usually privileged, including communications to consultants engaged by the attorneys.

2. **Protection of Attorney Work Product.** The attorney's work product is generally protected.

3. **Limitations on Attorney-Client Privileges, Including the "Crime-Fraud" Exception.** Arguably, work product is not protected unless there is a dispute or threat of litigation or some other proceeding. Also, it can be argued that the work product was part of commission of a crime. Last, the DOJ and other prosecutors frequently require waiver of the attorney-client communication and attorney work product privileges when negotiating possible settlement.

X. REQUIRED ELEMENTS OF A CORPORATE COMPLIANCE PLAN

A. **Seven Requirements.** The Guidelines for Organizational Defendants set forth seven specific elements that must be set forth in every Corporate Compliance Plan.

1.   **Standards of Conduct.** The organization must establish compliance standards and procedures to be followed by its employees and other agents that are reasonably capable of reducing the prospect of criminal conduct.

    a.   Should contain specific ethical standards and policies.

    b.   Should clearly advise employees of standards they are expected to follow and of the consequences for failure to do so.

    c.   Should include all applicable laws and regulations.

    d.   Should be distributed to all officers, directors, and employees.

2.   **Governing Body Oversight.** Specific individuals within high-level personnel of the organization must be assigned overall responsibility to oversee compliance with such standards and procedures.

3.   **Delegation of Authority.** The organization must use due care not to delegate substantial discretionary authority to individuals whom the organization knew, or should have known through the exercise of due diligence, had a propensity to engage in illegal activities.

4.   **Communication.** The organization must take steps to communicate effectively its standards and procedures to all employees and other agents by, for example, requiring participation in training programs or by disseminating publications that explain in a practical manner what is required.

5.   **Monitoring and Auditing.** The organization must take reasonable steps to achieve compliance with its standards by, for example, instituting monitoring and assessment systems reasonably designed to detect criminal conduct by its employees and other agents and by having in place and publicizing a reporting system whereby employees and other agents can report criminal conduct by others within the organization without fear of retribution.

6.   **Discipline.** The standards must be consistently enforced through appropriate disciplinary mechanisms, including, as appropriate, discipline of individuals responsible for the failure to detect an offense (adequate discipline of individuals responsible for an offense is a necessary component of enforcement; however, the form of discipline that will be appropriate will be case specific).

7.   **Prevention.** After an offense has been detected, the organization must take all reasonable steps to respond appropriately to the offense and to prevent future similar offenses, including any necessary modifications to its compliance program to prevent and detect violations of law.

B. **Formality of Compliance Plan Will Vary.** The size and complexity of the organization will dictate the formality of the Compliance Plan.

XI. IMPLEMENTATION OF A CORPORATE COMPLIANCE PROGRAM

A. **Implementation Challenges.** Once an organization has completed the self-assessment and created the Compliance Plan document, it will confront the challenge of implementing the Plan. This can be a painstaking and difficult process, so it should be carefully planned.

B. **All Compliance Programs Shall Include Written "Codes of Conduct".**

   1. **Ethical Standards.** The Plan contain specific ethical standards and policies. A Code of Ethics was not a specific requirement of the original Guidelines, but, with the 2004 revisions, it is clear that ethics plays an important role in an effective Compliance Plan.

   2. **Employee Notification.** The Plan should clearly advise employees of standards they are expected to follow and of the consequences for failure to do so.

   3. **Description of Laws.** The Guidelines state that the Plan should include a description of all applicable laws and regulations.

   4. **Distribution.** The Plan should be distributed to all officers, directors, employees, and other agents, including, for example, independent contractors. It may not be necessary to distribute the entire Plan to every person in the organization, so the organization may need to engage in specific educational programs as they relate to a person's function within the organization.

C. **Compliance Officers or Committee and Access to Upper Management.** The Compliance Plan should also identify the organization's Compliance Officers and the process for engaging upper level management in the compliance function.

   1. **Description of Duties.** The Plan should identify Compliance Officers and their duties in writing.

   2. **Continuing Assessment.** Compliance Officers should work with general counsel and outside legal counsel to monitor development of the compliance process.

   3. **Access to Management.** The Plan should always provide access to the Chief Executive Officer and the Board of Directors.

4. **Appointment of Compliance Committee.** Depending upon the size and complexity of the organization, it may be appropriate to delegate compliance responsibility to a Compliance Committee.

D. **Government Audits and Investigations.** Although not a requirement under the Guidelines, every effective Compliance Plan requires a system to control an organization's interactions with regulatory and investigatory governmental agencies.

1. **Communications With Government Agents.** The Plan will educate the company's representatives regarding their rights when approached by a government agent and how to report any such contact through the compliance process.

2. **Reporting Outside Inquiries.** The Plan will include mechanisms for reporting outside inquiries received by the company's representatives.

E. **Internal Mechanisms for Reporting Suspected Misconduct.**

1. **Anonymity.** To the extent possible, the Plan will conceal the identity of reporting representative. This may not be entirely possible in small organizations.

2. **Discipline.** Reporting cannot be the sole ground for discipline, but failure to report may be grounds for discipline.

F. **Corporate Document Retention System.** Although not required by the Guidelines, an appropriately administered document retention system promotes the compliance function.

1. **Retention System: Remember Arthur Andersen.** A system for document retention should include their creation, distribution, security in storage, and destruction.

2. **Cornerstone of Compliance.** Document retention is a cornerstone of compliance.

XII. FEDERAL AGENCY COMPLIANCE PLAN IMPLEMENTATION GUIDANCE

A. **Department of Justice Compliance Program Guidance.** With the exception of skilled nursing facilities, there is no absolute legal requirement for enterprises to implement Corporate Compliance and Ethics Plans. However, existence of an effective Compliance Program is definitely a mitigating factor if an organization is exposed to allegations of federal criminal and civil misconduct, and it is an absolute best practice. While federal agencies have published guidelines for structuring Corporate Compliance and Ethics Programs for many years, there has been little guidance on how a Compliance Program is expected to operate. All enterprises now have Compliance Program implementation guidance directly from the main governmental enforcement agency. On April 30, 2019, the Fraud Section of the United States Department of Justice ("DOJ") published comprehensive guidance on "Evaluation of Corporate Compliance Programs" (the "DOJ Compliance Program Guidance") that is accessible on the DOJ web site at the following link: https://www.justice.gov/criminal-fraud/page/file/937501/download.

B. **The DOJ Compliance Program Guidance Complements Other Compliance Guidance.** The DOJ identifies three fundamental lines of inquiry for determining effectiveness of a Compliance Program, each of which is followed by a series of specific questions for focused evaluation. Most of the questions dovetail neatly with the Federal Sentencing Guidelines as well as Compliance Guidelines promulgated by other governmental agencies such as the United States Department of Health and Human Services, Office of the Inspector General ("OIG") and statutory requirements for skilled nursing facility Compliance and Ethics Programs enacted through Section 6102 of the Affordable Care Act of 2010 (which for convenience are collectively described as the "Other Compliance Program Guidelines"). In addition, the DOJ Compliance Program Guidance reflects the growing emphasis on identifying individual persons who are involved in the compliance process as first expressed in the "Yates Memo" issued by former Deputy Attorney General Sally Yates that, in essence, directs DOJ to identify potentially culpable individuals as part of any DOJ investigation of an organization.

C. **Summary of DOJ Compliance Program Guidance In the Context of Other Compliance Program Guidelines.** Putting the DOJ Compliance Program Guidance into perspective, the Other Compliance Program Guidelines are prophylactic in nature and address what an organization should do to prevent allegations of wrongdoing in specifically identified risk areas, while the DOJ Compliance Program Guidance describes how DOJ determines whether the organization has in fact implemented an effective Compliance Program after an allegation of misconduct arises. Overall, the topics and questions that DOJ uses when evaluating the effectiveness of a Compliance Program are much more focused and detailed than the seven core requirements of a Corporate Compliance and Ethics Plan as described in the Federal Sentencing Guidelines and are much more process oriented than the more substantive Other Compliance Program Guidelines.

D. **The DOJ Three Prong Review Process.** The DOJ process involves three separate lines of inquiry:

- Is the Compliance Program **well designed**?

- Has the Compliance Program been **effectively implemented**?

- Does the Compliance Program **work in practice**?

In a nutshell, "design" addresses development of the Compliance Program, "implementation" addresses communicating with and educating all agents of the enterprise regarding the Compliance Program, and whether the Compliance Program "works" asks why, if a Compliance Program is well designed and effectively implemented, it may have failed in detecting the wrongful conduct that is the subject of the DOJ fraud investigation. The following is a summary of some key points on each of the DOJ's three Compliance Program review prongs.

E.   **Is the Compliance Program Well Designed?** Critical factors in evaluating any Compliance Program include whether the Compliance Program is adequately designed for maximum effectiveness in preventing and detecting wrongdoing by employees and other agents and whether corporate management is enforcing the program or is tacitly encouraging or pressuring employees to engage in misconduct. DOJ breaks the design analysis down into the following lines of inquiry:

- Risk Assessment;

- Policies and Procedures;

- Training and Communications;

- Confidential Reporting Structure and Investigation Process;

- Third Party Management; and

- Mergers and Acquisitions.

1.   **Risk Assessment.** Because an effective Compliance Program begins with an organization's assessment of its regulatory risk, DOJ prosecutors are directed to determine whether the Compliance Program is designed to detect the misconduct most likely to occur in an organization's line of business and complex regulatory environment, the effectiveness of the organization's internal risk assessment and the manner in which the organization's Compliance Program has been tailored based on that risk assessment, and whether the risk assessment criteria are periodically updated to address compliance issues that have arisen over time. The questions under this topic relate to the Other Compliance Program Guidelines requiring a baseline assessment of regulatory risk and include inquiries regarding the following:

    – The methodology that the organization used to identify, analyze, and address its particular regulatory risks;

– What information and metrics the organization used to help detect the misconduct in question;

– Whether the organization dedicates sufficient resources to policing high risk areas rather than low risk areas; and

– Whether the risk assessment is current and subject to periodic review.

2. **Policies and Procedures.** DOJ states that any well-designed Compliance Program has policies and procedures that give both content and effect to ethical norms and that address and aim to reduce risks identified in the organization's risk assessment process. As a threshold matter, DOJ prosecutors are instructed to determine whether the organization has a Code of Conduct that is accessible and applicable to all of the organization's employees and other agents and describes the organization's commitment to full compliance with relevant federal laws. DOJ Compliance Program assessment under this topic corresponds to the Other Compliance Program Guidelines requiring standards of conduct and communicating the standards of conduct to the organization's agents and include inquiries regarding the following:

– The process for designing and implementing policies and procedures, including responding to changes in the legal and regulatory environment;

– How the organization manages accountability for supervisory oversight of performance in accordance with the standards of conduct; and

– What guidance and training were provided to the "key gatekeepers in the control process" (likely Compliance Officers) regarding how to detect misconduct and when to escalate an internal investigation with reporting to upper management.

3. **Training and Communications.** Another hallmark of a well-designed Compliance Program is appropriately tailored training and communications. DOJ states that prosecutors should assess the steps taken by the organization to insure that policies and procedures have been integrated into the organization, including through **periodic training and certification for all directors, officers, relevant employees, and, when appropriate, other agents and business partners**. The questions under this topic relate to the Other Compliance Program Guidelines requiring effective communication of the Compliance Program standards and procedures to all employees and other agents and include inquiries regarding the following:

– Whether the organization provided tailored training for high-risk and control employees that address the risk in the area where the misconduct arose;

– Whether supervisory employees have received different or supplementary training;

– How the organization measures effectiveness of the training;

– What senior management has done to let employees know the organization's position on the misconduct;

– What communications are generally made when an employee is terminated for failure to comply with the organization's standards of conduct;

– What resources are available to employees to provide guidance regarding compliance policies; and

– Whether the organization has assessed whether its employees know when to seek advice and whether they are willing to do so.

4. **Confidential Reporting Structure and Investigation Process.** A well-designed Compliance Program is expected to have an efficient and trusted mechanism by which employees can anonymously and confidentially report allegations of a breach of the organization's Code of Conduct, breach of policies and procedures, or suspected or actual misconduct. The questions under this topic relate to the Other Compliance Program Guidelines requiring responding to allegations of misconduct and preventing further similar offenses and include inquiries regarding the following:

– Whether the organization has an anonymous reporting mechanism and, if not, why not;

– How the compliance hotline or other reporting mechanism is communicated to employees;

– Whether the compliance reporting mechanism has been used;

– How the organization collects, analyzes, and uses information from its compliance reporting mechanisms and determined which complaints merit further investigation;

– How the organization insures that investigations are independent, objective, appropriately conducted, and properly documented;

– Whether the organization uses timing metrics to insure responsiveness;

– Whether the organization has a process for monitoring investigation outcomes and insuring accountability for responding to the findings;

– Whether sufficient financial resources are dedicated to the reporting and investigating mechanisms; and

– Whether the organization periodically examines compliance reports for patterns of misconduct or other red flags for compliance weaknesses.

5. **Third Party Management.** In general, regulatory authorities distrust independent contractor arrangements under the theory that they are more susceptible to fraud and abuse. Accordingly, all Compliance Programs are expected to address the risks associated with third party management companies. The questions under this topic relate to the Other Compliance Program Guidelines requiring delegation of authority for implementing the Compliance Program to qualified persons when an organization's operations have an independent, third party management company and include inquiries regarding the following:

– How the organization's third party management process has corresponded to the nature and level of the enterprise risk identified by the organization;

– Whether this process is integrated into the relevant procurement and vendor management process;

– The business rationale for using a third party management company;

– What mechanisms the organization uses to insure that the third party management company contract terms specifically describe the services to be performed and have appropriate payment terms, the described contractual work is actually performed, and that compensation is commensurate with the services rendered;

– How the organization analyzes the third party's incentive model against compliance risks;

– How the organization monitors third party management performance;

– How the organization has trained the relationship managers about what the organization's compliance risks are and how to manage them;

- How the organization has incentivized compliance and ethical behavior by third party management companies;

- Whether red flags were identified from the due diligence of the third parties involved in the misconduct and how they were resolved;

- Whether a similar third party has been suspended, terminated, or audited as a result of compliance issues; and

- How the organization has monitored situations to insure that compliance issues related to vendor relationships do not arise again.

6. **Mergers and Acquisitions.** Compliance issues frequently arise in acquisition due diligence. Consequently, DOJ expects organizations to include a comprehensive compliance risk assessment as part of the organization's due diligence process. The questions under this topic relate to review of the compliance function in a specific setting and do not precisely fall into the requirements identified in the Other Compliance Program Guidelines and include inquiries regarding the following:

- Whether the misconduct or risk of misconduct was identified during due diligence;

- How the risk assessment due diligence was conducted and who individually conducted it;

- How the compliance function has been integrated into the merger, acquisition, or integration process;

- What has been the organization's process for tracking and remediating misconduct identified in due diligence; and

- What has been the organization's process for implementing compliance policies and procedures at new entities.

F. **Is the Compliance Program Effectively Implemented?** DOJ says that even a well-designed Compliance Program may be unsuccessful in practice if implementation is lax or ineffective. Prosecutors are instructed to probe whether a Compliance Program is a "paper program" or one implemented, reviewed, and revised in an effective manner. DOJ breaks the effectiveness of implementation analysis down into the following lines of inquiry:

• Commitment by Senior and Middle Management;

- Autonomy and Resources; and

- Incentives and Disciplinary Measures.

1. **Commitment by Senior and Middle Management.** The DOJ states that, beyond compliance structures, policies, and procedures, it is important for an organization to create and foster a culture of ethics and compliance with the law. The effectiveness of a Compliance Program requires a high-level commitment by organizational leadership to implement a culture of compliance from the top. DOJ emphasizes that the organization's top leaders, specifically the Governing Board and executive officers, set the tone for the entire organization. The Governing Board is responsible for implementation of an effective Compliance Program, and that responsibility cannot be delegated. In fact, the DOJ expects an organization's Governing Board to include a representative with compliance expertise. The questions under this topic relate to the Other Compliance Program Guidelines requiring specific high-level personnel to have overall responsibility for implementing the Compliance Program and include inquiries regarding the following:

   – Whether compliance expertise is been available on the board of directors;

   – Whether senior leaders, through their words and actions, encourage compliance, including the type of misconduct involved in the investigation.

   – Whether senior leaders have demonstrated leadership in the organization's compliance and remediation effort and what specific actions senior leadership has taken in that regard;

   – Whether the board of directors have held executive or private sessions with the compliance and control functions;

   – What types of information the Governing Board and senior management examined in their oversight of the area in which the misconduct occurred;

   – Whether managers tolerated greater compliance risks in pursuit of new business and greater revenue; and

   – Whether managers encouraged employees to act unethically to achieve a business objective or impeded compliance personnel from effectively implementing their duties.

2. **Autonomy and Resources.** As evidence that a Compliance Program is more than a piece of paper kept in a drawer, DOJ instructs prosecutors to inquire into the sufficiency of the

personnel and resources dedicated to the compliance function and in particular whether compliance officers have (a) sufficient authority within the organization, (b) sufficient resources, particularly staff available to undertake the requisite auditing, documentation, and analysis required of an effective Compliance Program, and (c) sufficient autonomy from operating management, such as direct access to the organization's Governing Board or the Board's audit committee. Prosecutors should also evaluate the resources the organization has dedicated to compliance, the authority and independence of the compliance function, and availability of compliance expertise to the Governing Board. The questions under this topic relate to the Other Compliance Program Guidelines requiring communicating compliance standards and procedures to all employees and other agents as well as requiring specific high-level personnel to have overall responsibility for implementing the Compliance Program and include inquiries regarding the following:

– Whether the Governing Board established an information and reporting system that is reasonably designed to provide management and the Governing Board with timely and accurate information sufficient to allow them to reach an informed decision regarding the organization's compliance with applicable law;

– Whether the Compliance Program is an independent function reporting to the CEO or Governing Board (which is preferred under all Guidelines) or whether it reports to the legal department or business department (which is disfavored);

– How the compliance function compares to other departments regarding rank, titles, resources, compensation levels, and access to key decision makers;

– Whether compliance personnel are properly qualified;

– Whether the compliance officers had direct reporting lines to the Governing Board;

– How often do Compliance Officers meet with the Governing Board or the Board's audit committee and are members of senior management present for these meetings;

– How does the organization insure independence of the compliance function;

– Whether the compliance department received proper funding and resources; and

– Whether the organization outsourced the compliance function to an external firm or consultant and if so how that decision was both made and managed.

3.   **Incentives and Disciplinary Measures.** Discipline is an obvious fundamental element of an effective Compliance Program. DOJ instructs prosecutors to assess the extent to which the organization's communications convey to all of its representatives that unethical conduct is not tolerated and will bring swift and consistently applied consequences, regardless of the position or title of the representative who engages in the misconduct (implying that disciplinary measures must apply as much to senior management as to mid or low level employees). As stated above, when confronted with a fraud investigation, the first response from an organization to mitigate potential consequences is frequently to inform the investigators that "we have a Compliance Program." Investigators sometimes attempt to validate the assertion by countering "then let me see your disciplinary records." DOJ also instructs prosecutors to review whether the Compliance Program provides incentives for improving and developing a Compliance Program or demonstrating ethical leadership. Prosecutors are instructed to conduct the following inquiries under this topic:

- Who participates in making disciplinary decisions;

- When and how the reasons for discipline and disciplinary actions in response to the misconduct are communicated to representatives;

- Whether the organization has ever terminated or disciplined any person for similar misconduct;

- Whether disciplinary actions are consistently and fairly applied; and

- Whether the organization incentivizes engaging in compliant and ethical conduct.

G.   **Does the Compliance Program Work in Practice?** Prosecutors are required to assess the adequacy and effectiveness of the Compliance Program at the time of the offense that is under investigation and at the time of the charging decision. DOJ reviews the following in determining whether a Compliance Program works in practice:

- Continuous Improvement, Periodic Testing, and Review;

- Investigation of Misconduct; and

- Analysis and Remediation of Any Underlying Misconduct.

1.   **Continuous Improvement, Periodic Testing, and Review.** DOJ says that one hallmark of an effective Compliance Program is its capacity to improve and evolve because actual

implementation of compliance controls in practice necessarily reveals areas of risk and potential adjustment. Every organization's business changes over time as do the laws that govern its actions, industry standards, and the general competitive environment in which the organization operates. Accordingly, DOJ instructs its prosecutors to consider whether the organization has engaged in meaningful efforts to review its Compliance Program and insure that it is not stale. In evaluating whether a Compliance Program works in practice, prosecutors should consider revisions to the Compliance Program in response to lessons learned. Prosecutors are specifically directed to determine whether an organization has taken reasonable steps to insure that the organization's Compliance Program is followed, including monitoring and auditing to detect potential misconduct and evaluating periodically the organization's Compliance Program. Inquiries under this topic relate to the Other Compliance Program Guidelines requiring monitoring and auditing the effectiveness of the Compliance Program and include inquiries regarding the following:

— The organization's process for determining when and how frequently the organization has undertaken an internal audit of the effectiveness of the Compliance Program;

— What kind of audits would have revealed the misconduct before it occurred, whether those audits conducted, and what were the findings of any such audit;

— Whether relevant audit findings and remediation progress have been reported to senior management and the Governing Board on a regular basis and whether senior management and the Governing Board have followed up;

— How often internal audits are generally conducted in high risk area assessments;

— What control testing the organization has generally undertaken;

— Whether the organization updated its risk assessments and reviewed its compliance policies, procedures, and practices;

— How often and how does the organization measure its culture of compliance; and

— Whether the organization seeks input from all employee levels to determine whether all employees perceive senior and middle management's commitment to the Compliance Program.

2.   **Investigation of Misconduct.** DOJ prosecutors are instructed to determine whether the organization has a properly functioning system for the timely and through investigation of any allegations or suspicions of misconduct by the organization and its employees and other

agents. This line of inquiry relates to the Other Compliance Program Guidelines requiring organizations to "respond" to allegations of misconduct and take action to "prevent" further similar offenses and include inquiries regarding the following:

- Whether the organization insures that investigations are independent, objective, appropriately conducted, and properly documented;

- Whether the organization's investigations are used to identify root causes, system vulnerabilities, and accountability lapses, including among supervisory managers and senior executives;

- The organization's process for responding to investigative findings; and

- How high up in the organization the investigative findings are reported.

3.   **Analysis and Remediation of Any Underlying Misconduct.** Under DOJ's internal rules, to receive full credit for timely and appropriate remediation of misconduct, an organization should demonstrate a "root cause analysis" and, when appropriate, remediation to address the root causes. Accordingly, prosecutors are instructed to consider any remedial actions taken by the organization including appropriate discipline of all employees and other agents involved in the misconduct, either through direct participation or oversight failure, as well as those with supervisory authority over the area in which the misconduct occurred. This is a common theme: DOJ expects effective discipline and accountability for senior management, up to and including the "C-Suite." Inquiries in this area include the following:

- The organization's analysis of the root cause of the misconduct and whether the response revealed "systemic issues" (in contrast to an isolated incident);

- Who was involved in making the analysis;

- If policies and procedures should have prohibited the misconduct, whether they were effectively implemented and whether employees and other agents with responsibility for implementing the policies and procedures have been held accountable;

- Whether there were prior opportunities to detect the misconduct, and, if so why the opportunities were missed;

- What specific remediation has addressed the issues identified in the root cause and missed opportunity analysis;

– Whether the organization took timely disciplinary action in response to the allegation of misconduct;

– Whether the organization considered disciplinary action for failures in supervision; and

– Whether the organization has ever terminated or otherwise disciplined any representative for the misconduct at issue.

H. **Using the DOJ Compliance Program Guidance for Self-Assessment.** Organizations now have a detailed template for understanding how the DOJ assesses existing Compliance Programs when there is an allegation of wrongdoing. It is therefore advisable for all organizations to engage in a self-assessment of the effectiveness of their Compliance Programs using the DOJ Compliance Program Guidance as a baseline for how Compliance Programs are expected to perform. While DOJ attempts to break its Compliance Program analysis into three prongs, each with detailed lines of inquiry, there is substantial overlap between the three prongs. Consequently, it is helpful to take a step back and identify some fundamental elements that can guide any organization regarding assessment of its Compliance Program. Reflecting on the content of this analytical framework, we see the following themes:

1. **Compliance Expertise Must Be Made Available to the Governing Board.** The Governing Board must actively oversee implementation of the organization's Corporate Compliance and Ethics Plan. This is consistent with the standard of conduct for directors of Delaware corporations established in *In re: Caremark International, Inc.*, which, in essence, provides that directors may be exposed to individual liability for breach of the duty of care if the organization fails to implement a Corporate Compliance and Ethics Plan that satisfies the seven elements described in the Federal Sentencing Guidelines for Organizational Defendants.

2. **The Governing Board Should Include a Director with Compliance Expertise.** The DOJ expects an organization's Governing Board to include a representative with compliance expertise.

3. **Senior Management Must Be Actively Involved In Supervision of the Compliance Process.** When an allegation of misconduct arises, DOJ can make senior management accountable, even if senior management is not directly involved in the alleged misconduct. This is consistent with both the "Responsible Office Doctrine" that has long been part of federal False Claims Act law and the "Yates Memo" that focuses on making individuals responsible for corporate acts.

4. **The Compliance Function Must Have the Ability to Report Directly to the Governing Board.** This addresses the concern expressed in the Compliance Program Guidelines that compliance concerns reported to compliance officers through the organization's internal reporting

system might be blocked by senior management (such as the chief financial officer, general counsel, or chief executive officer), whose performance may be implicated in the report.

5. **DOJ Distrusts Independent Contractors.** In general, federal regulatory agencies believe that there is more opportunity for misconduct through independent contractor arrangements than there is through *bona fide* employees, and the DOJ Guidance is consistent with that belief. For example, it is perfectly permissible for an organization to outsource the compliance function to an independent contractor, but, if so, then how and why that decision was made and how it was managed must be explained. This leads back to informed decision making by the Governing Board. Also, the DOJ dedicates an entire topic to Third Party Management, demonstrating that DOJ perceives third party management as a regulatory vulnerability. Although third party management agreements are also perfectly permissible, they are subject to intensified scrutiny when an allegation of misconduct arises. Once again, responsibility for oversight of the third party management agreement and accountability of third party vendors in general falls on the organization's Governing Board.

6. **The Organization Is Expected to Engage in Continuous Self-Critical Analysis and Regulatory Risk Assessment.** A Corporate Compliance and Ethics Plan cannot be a static piece of paper filed in a notebook in the organization's bookcase: it must become a living, breathing part of the organization. Resources must be allocated for active management of the compliance function and periodic assessment to identify potential regulatory risk.

XIII. THE ROLE OF BUSINESS ETHICS IN REGULATORY COMPLIANCE

A. **The Relationship Between Fraud, Compliance, and Ethics.**

1. **Relationship Between Compliance and Fraud.** Compliance and fraud are related only because they are opposites.

2. **Relationship Between Ethical Conduct and Compliance.** Ethics involves distinguishing between good and evil in a moral, not legal, context. Conduct that is unethical or immoral may not be illegal or technically non-compliant.

3. **Avoidance of Allegations.** To avoid punishment, we are compelled to act in accordance with a set of laws, mores, and standards, which involves both legal compliance and ethical behavior. Compliance and proper behavior take practice.

B. **Code of Ethics.** As stated above, development of a Code of Ethics is a critical element of an effective Compliance Plan.

ATTACHMENT 9-A

COMPLIANCE ALERT

UNITED STATES SENTENCING COMMISSION PUBLISHES NEW REQUIREMENTS FOR CORPORATE COMPLIANCE AND ETHICS PROGRAMS

New federal guidelines will require all Compliance Officers to update their Corporate Compliance Plans. In order to receive credit for having a plan in place, and in case a relevant issue ever arises, Compliance Officers must ensure that their company's Corporate Compliance Plans conform with the "Guidelines for Organizational Defendants" set forth in the United States Sentencing Commission's Federal Sentencing Guidelines. The original Guidelines were published in 1991 and, without substantial detail, listed the seven elements of an effective Corporate Compliance Plan. On April 30, 2004, the Commission published its first amendments to the original Guidelines, and they became effective on November 1, 2004. The amendments embellish upon the original seven elements and describe in greater detail what an organization must do to implement a Corporate Compliance Plan that effectively prevents and detects violations of law.

Creating a Culture of Compliance. To be effective, a Corporate Compliance Plan must be a prominent and vital element of an organization's culture. A Corporate Compliance Plan is not just a self-serving document. It must be effectively implemented to encourage ethical conduct and a commitment to compliance with the law. Effectiveness requires commitment and oversight from an organization's governing board and top level management, including an active role in defining the content and operation of the program. At a minimum, the amendment explicitly requires organizations to identify areas of risk where criminal violations may occur, train high level officials as well as employees in relevant legal standards, and give their compliance and ethics officers sufficient authority and resources to carry out their responsibilities.

An Emphasis on Ethics. One recurring theme of the amendments is an emphasis on ethical conduct rather than strict compliance with laws. Ethics involves distinguishing between good and evil in a moral, and not necessarily legal, context. Conduct that is unethical or immoral may not be illegal or technically non-compliant. However, ethical conduct usually results in legal compliance. To avoid punishment, we are compelled to act in accordance with a set of laws, mores, and standards, which requires both legal compliance and ethical behavior. Compliance and proper behavior take practice, and the Commission's amendments require organizations to infuse a culture of ethical conduct through an effectively implemented Corporate Compliance and Ethics Plan.

This emphasis on ethical conduct represents an expansion of the scope of the original Organizational Sentencing Guidelines. The original focus of the Guidelines was the detection and prevention of criminal misconduct. The emphasis on ethical conduct broadens the scope of the Guidelines to encompass not only criminal misconduct but also "violations of law, whether criminal or non-criminal (including a regulation), for which the organization is, or would be, liable." Of course, organizations with effective Compliance Plans have traditionally expanded their scope to non-criminal, regulatory compliance, but the amendments now clearly state that ethical conduct resulting in regulatory compliance is an expected result of an effectively implemented Plan.

Involvement of Senior Management. The amendments also provide new guidance on how a Compliance Officer must fit into an entity's organizational structure. The Guidelines have always required that responsibility for a Compliance Plan must be delegated to specific, high-level individuals within the organization. The amendments create more specific criteria. Senior management must have direct, over-all responsibility for effective implementation, even if day-to-day operational responsibility is delegated to personnel who are not involved in senior management. Compliance Officers should report at least annually directly to the Board of Directors or a Board committee. Furthermore, senior management must provide individuals responsible for day-to-day operations with adequate research and appropriate authority to implement an effective Plan.

The new amendments also emphasize that the governing board and senior management must be directly knowledgeable about the Compliance Plan's content and operation, and the governing board must provide active oversight of the Compliance Plan's implementation and effectiveness. Although new to the Guidelines, most entities with effective Compliance Plans actively engage senior management and the governing board for several reasons. First, under Delaware law, an independent director may be individually liable for an organization's wrongful conduct if the organization does not effectively implement a Compliance Plan that conforms with the Federal Sentencing Guidelines.* Since many publicly traded corporations are organized under Delaware law, this is a strong incentive to have the governing board directly involved in active oversight of an effective compliance program. Second, other governmental agencies have provided industry specific compliance guidance that contemplates involvement of senior management and the governing board in the implementation of an effective Compliance Plan. For example, the Department of Health and Human Services, Office of the Inspector General (the "OIG"), has published compliance guidance for health care providers that requires a direct link between the Compliance Officer and the governing board. The OIG has also stated that it does not prefer delegation of Compliance Officer duties to either in-house legal counsel or the Chief Financial Officer due to fears that filtering compliance through either channel could compromise the free flow of information related to potential non-compliance. Therefore, the OIG's guidance requires direct access to senior management and the governing board.

The amendments also require that all personnel, including directors and senior management, must receive compliance training.

Regulatory Assessments. The amendments also state that regulatory assessments are an essential component of an effective Compliance Plan. An organization needs to create a standard for measuring its compliance efforts through a baseline regulatory assessment. Again, this is commonplace in some

---

* *In re: Caremark Int'l, Inc.,* Del. Ch. 1996)

industries. For example, a baseline regulatory assessment is a featured element of the OIG's health industry guidelines.

Once the Compliance and Ethics Plan is implemented, the Guidelines require periodic assessments to measure adherence to compliance standards.

Monitoring and Auditing the Effectiveness of the Plan. The amendments require that the effectiveness of the Plan must be periodically evaluated through monitoring and auditing, and procedures that facilitate the free flow of compliance related inquiries and complaints must be established. The amendments emphasize that all organizations must take reasonable steps to insure that all personnel can anonymously or confidentially report potential or actual violations of law without fear of retaliation. The Commission expects that Compliance Plans will be internally promoted, with appropriate incentives for engaging in compliant conduct and utilizing the Plan's reporting channels and appropriate discipline when non-compliance is confirmed. In fact, disciplinary logs are frequently used by federal regulators as a test of the effectiveness of a Compliance Plan.

Self Reporting of Non-Compliance. Last, the amendments place substantial emphasis on self reporting. If, through the Plan, an instance of non-compliance in confirmed, then the organization should come forward and report the incident to the appropriate regulatory agency. Again, this is commonplace in the health industry, where both the OIG and the Medicare program have published procedures for self-disclosure of non-compliance.

These amendments provide detailed guidance to all entities regarding how to implement an effective Corporate Compliance and Ethics Plan. Every Compliance Officer should consider these embellishments when assessing the effectiveness of their organization's Plan. Although these detailed instructions may be new to industries in which implementation of formal Corporate Compliance and Ethics Plans is only emerging, some industries, like the health industry, are already in step with these newly stated expectations.

ABOUT THE AUTHOR

Thomas William Baker has almost 40 years of experience as a corporate and business transactions attorney and over 15 years of experience as an Adjunct Professor in the Auburn University Executive MBA Program, for which he wrote this book. He received his A.B. degree in political science from Syracuse University in 1972, his M.B.A. from Georgia State University in 1978, and his J.D. from Vanderbilt University in 1981. Mr. Baker: is the Managing Member of Coronat Services, LLC (www.coronatservices.com), which provides educational, strategic planning, business advisory, and corporate governance services; is the Chairman and Chief Executive Office of Boncrest Resource Group, Inc. (www.boncrest.org), a tax exempt organization dedicated to developing charitable opportunities for the benefit of the public through innovative organizational structures and creative financing; and continues to practice law in the Atlanta, Georgia office of Baker Donelson, a prominent national law firm.

CPSIA information can be obtained
at www.ICGtesting.com
Printed in the USA
BVHW011057140819
555860BV00020B/1428/P